Evaluating Exceptional Children

A Task Analysis Approach

Evaluating Exceptional Children

A Task Analysis Approach

K. W. Howell
Arizona State University

J. S. Kaplan
Portland State University

C. Y. O'Connell
Idaho State University

Charles E. Merrill Publishing Company

A Bell & Howell Company

Columbus   Toronto   London   Sydney

Published by
Charles E. Merrill Publishing Company
A Bell & Howell Company
Columbus, Ohio 43216

This book was set in Optima and Hobo.
The production editor was Linda Hillis Bayma.
The cover was prepared by Will Chenoweth.
Cover photo by Tom Hutchinson.

Library of Congress Catalog Card Number: 77-94238

International Standard Book Number: 0-675-08389-3

1   2   3   4   5   6   7   8   9   10/86   85   84   83   82   81   80   79

Printed in the United States of America

Evaluating Exceptional Children

is
dedicated
to
three
educators—

Richard L. Hughes   Owen R. White   Marilyn Cohen

Preface

We have written this book for use as the basic text in a first course on the evaluation of exceptional children. The idea for the book grew out of our frustration over the lack of straightforward, classroom-oriented texts on assessing handicapped children. True, the literature for practitioners is filled monthly with the business of assessment — journal articles with baseline and intervention data, task analyses, statistical operations of all sorts, critiques and defenses of one or another of the seeming hundreds of tests used to identify, label, place, or program for handicapped children. But nowhere could we find a text that discussed the basic concepts and issues in assessing handicapped children, that offered a teachable format for explaining how to analyze what to teach, and that gave preservice or practicing teachers a useful set of tools for measuring a child's progress from day to day.

Not surprisingly, those three needs have dictated the plan of this book. Part One consists of five chapters on the basic models of evaluation — psychomedical and task analytic — and the corresponding concepts and terminology associated with each. Part Two consists of nine chapters that explain, demonstrate, and encourage practice in the task analytic model. This part concludes with a comparison of several common approaches to formative evaluation (in Chapter 11) and two chapters (Chapter 12 and 13) on precision teaching — one of the most effective approaches to continuous measurement of pupil progress currently in use. Finally, an appendix is included as a source of support for teachers who want a quick (and, we hope, understandable) guide to the statistics they often face in evaluation literature. A second appendix offers an instructional program on the basics of writing good performance objectives for learners. A glossary and reference list complete the book.

No doubt our biases are clear, but we have tried not to force them onto the format of the book. We use the book (or the materials which became this book) in a performance-based, criterion-referenced instructional design. For the instructor who teaches in such a fashion, we have prepared an extensive manual of additional criterion-referenced pretests and posttests, alternative learning exercises, and analyses of the tasks and subtasks we expect our students to master in our course. The manual is free on adoption by writing Merrill. On the other hand, the instructor who prefers a more conventional course design will find that these materials are not part and parcel of the book. We have included only objectives at the start of each unit of material and a corresponding "checkpoint" at the conclusion, in order to allow students to evaluate their own progress on that material. We have also presented some of the material in a programmed format, however, whenever our experience told us that students responded better to the material or procedures when presented in that format.

We would like to thank the reviewers whose comments helped us refine our presentation of the material here. Joseph R. Jenkins, John O. Cooper, Paul F. McGhiey, and John R. Hills reviewed the manuscript and offered many valuable suggestions.

Finally, we are especially grateful to Linda Hillis, Merrill production editor, whose experienced editing, careful attention to detail, and devotion to this project have improved it greatly.

K.W.H.   J.S.K.   C.Y.O.

Contents

Evaluating Exceptional Children

A Task Analysis Approach

Introduction

Educational Diagnosis: Art or Science?

Many classroom teachers consider educational diagnosis something of an art requiring a specific innate ability in order to perform it satisfactorily. If this were true, it would logically follow that conducting an educational diagnosis would require competencies that cannot be learned. After all, how does one learn an innate ability. You either have it or you do without. The authors disagree with the premise that educational diagnosis is an art. We suggest that it is a science and, as such, can be taught. The competencies involved may be acquired and eventually mastered.

At the risk of being irreverent (or irrelevant), we'd like to draw an analogy between educational diagnosis and cooking. Many of us have known at least one person who was a good cook—someone who could take an old shoe, throw it in a pot of boiling water, add just the right amount of seasoning, and come up with a great tasting bowl of soup. Yet whenever pressed for the recipe, the cook would shrug his shoulders and exclaim, "What recipe? I cook by instinct?" He seemed to have that innate ability to make all foods taste good whether they were your favorites or not. But those who cook by instinct are not the only ones who became good cooks. We know that it is possible for people to learn to cook well even if they don't have a knack for it. Of course they would probably have to use the same recipe over and over before they had enough confidence in their cooking to depart from the plan and be as creative as the cook in our example. Still, they could do it. People start out with recipes and add their own touches until the recipes are no longer needed. They have replicated this process over and over with other recipes until they became good cooks. The point is that some of us need recipes while others can start from scratch.

The same may be said for educational diagnosis. Just like our cook, there are people who can accurately diagnose a child's learning problem which has previously baffled others. In the beginning, these experts may have started out without a recipe, or plan, to follow. We may say that they have a knack for diagnosing learning problems much as others have a knack for cooking. Is it possible, then, for others without the knack to do as well? We think so. In this text, we present a cookbook approach to educational diagnosis. We encourage you to use it as a starting point, and as you gain experience, to add your own "seasoning."

Educational diagnosis does not have to be left to the experts. Given the right recipe, the classroom teacher can be just as effective a diagnostician as the specialist. In fact, we might even say that most teachers would probably be more effective since they seem to have a more realistic picture of the child to begin with. Because they see the child every day in a number of different situations, they can probably obtain more reliable test results than a stranger who sees the child alone, out of the classroom, in a small quiet office for one or two brief sessions. Also, educational diagnosis is an ongoing process that is technically not finished until the teacher finds something that works for the child. If the teacher is also the diagnostician, he is in a better position to continuously assess the performance of the student and make the necessary educational decisions when they need to be made without waiting for a third party. Given the above, it is imperative that teachers become more involved in the diagnostic evaluations of their students. The overwhelming ratio of children to psychologists as well as the current trend of mainstreaming makes this involvement mandatory. We predict that, in the months to come, special education and regular classroom teachers will have to develop a greater degree of competence in educational diagnosis. This text is designed to promote this higher degree of competency. The text is divided into two parts. Part One deals with the theoretical considerations of evaluation. Part Two presents the methods by which an evaluation can be carried out.

Part One

Theoretical Considerations in the Evaluation of Exceptional Children

In order to become skilled at evaluation it is necessary to know the assumptions and premises which underlie it. Part One of this text deals with these basic considerations. Chapter 1 contrasts two different models of evaluation—psycho-educational and task analytical. By carefully outlining the basic premises of the task analytical model, Chapter 1 becomes an overview for the rest of the text. Tables in the chapter summarize the philosophy behind the text and should be referred to whenever the reader wants to know the rationale behind recommendations made in the text.

A brief historical perspective is presented in Chapter 2. Special education has long been confused by the need to explain the cause of handicaps while also attempting to cure them. This confusion has been increased by attempts to carry out the precise medical approach with imprecise tools. In some cases educational and psychological measurement instruments have actually changed the definitions of the things they were meant to describe.

Chapters 3, 4, and 5 present current practices in educational evaluation. These chapters build on Chapter 1 by showing how the psycho-educational and task analytical models are reflected in different procedures for planning curriculum, deciding what to teach, and deciding how to teach.

The topics discussed in Part One can be presented in varying depth. We have chosen to discuss some of them thoroughly while only mentioning others. For this reason Part One is heavily referenced to help you find primary sources when additional depth is desired. Another aspect of educational evaluation is its link to measurement, statistics, and testing. Information pertaining to these topics is presented in Part One; however, we have chosen to separate the majority of this content and present it in Appendix A. By placing this information in one place, it will be easier for you to use the text as a reference. We encourage you to pay close attention to topics such as reliability, validity, gain scores, and profile analysis which are presented in Appendix A. This information is not secondary to that included in the text, it has merely been placed in an appendix for your convenience.

3

Models of Evaluation

Some Groundwork

It isn't possible to sum up a person with test scores. Measurement is limited to the characteristics of things. People have physical characteristics and behavioral characteristics which are investigated and measured for various reasons. However, it should never be assumed that even the most thorough evaluation is capable of actually explaining the total person. This point is made at the outset to promote a realistic understanding of the limitations of all evaluation, not necessarily to promote an increased commitment to human individuality. (The same statement applies equally well to trout and car transmissions.)

Thorndike and Hagan (1969) have outlined three steps which are common to all types of measurement.

1. Identify the characteristic to be measured.
2. Devise a procedure to make the characteristic observable.
3. Devise a numerical system for summarizing the observations.

Davis (1973) has suggested another essential step. In order for the results of educational measurement to be of practical use, this fourth step should be included.

4. Ensure that the measurement procedure corresponds to reality.

These four steps can be followed no matter what is being measured. For example, suppose the teacher wants to measure the computational skills of a student. The heading "computation" includes a number of operations, so the teacher must first identify which are to be measured (step 1). If the teacher identifies working multiplication facts as the characteristic to be measured, she must next think of a way to observe the student multiplying. The obvious procedure is to supply the student with a sheet of multiplication problems and a pencil. The student's behavior on the task can be observed by checking the worksheet (step 2). The number of problems completed correctly and incorrectly can be counted in order to numerically summarize the work done (step 3). If the teacher ensures that the problems on the worksheet are similar to classroom multiplication problems, then the results of the measurement may be applied to the classroom (step 4).

It is essential that those who evaluate children

periodically review the assumptive basis for their actions. Testing should never be carried out in a piecemeal fashion. Unfortunately, this is often the case in special education. As Deno (1971) points out, some educators judge the quality of a testing program by the number of tests routinely given. It is not uncommon to find special education programs which subject all referred students to a standard battery of tests regardless of their needs.

Thorndike's first step is to identify the characteristic to be measured. But what can be measured? If a teacher reads test catalogs and notes the various titles, she might conclude that there are a lot of things that can be measured (Lennon, 1962). For example, a teacher can order tests of auditory discrimination, reading, superego forces, IQ, spelling, or self-concept. In reality, of course, the title of a test tells little about its content. Titles reflect the selective interests of past investigators and the current needs of test buyers. In addition, some things are easier to measure than others, and tests to measure them may develop regardless of interest or need. A comparison of nationally established educational goals to available tests revealed that there are many high priority objectives (ranging from handwriting to the free enterprise system) for which there are few or no published measures (Hoephner, 1974).

The second and third steps suggested by Thorndike raise other issues. How can something be measured which cannot be seen? How does a teacher know a high score from a low score? And in the case of Davis' fourth step—is the test score of any real value?

One of the problems with educational evaluation has been a failure to define terms. This text has a glossary but certain terms need to be presented here. It is unlikely that these definitions will set the world straight and get everyone to understand each other. They are, however, necessary for understanding this text. Throughout the text an effort will be made to stick consistently to these definitions. Some are easier to stick to than others.

"Measurement is the assignment of numerals to objects or events according to rules" (Campbell, 1940). Measurement is a tool which facilitates evaluation.

Evaluation is the process by which investigators come to understand things, and by which they attach relative values to things. Comparison is an essential component of evaluation.

Educational diagnosis is a form of evaluation which collects data on the current performance of a student. This data must be causally related to the future performance of the student on a specific task. Educational diagnosis guides instruction.

Assessment is used synonymously with diagnosis by some educators. However, assessment implies direct and frequent observations of the student's behavior.

Classification is the evaluative process of labeling or naming things. Its purpose is to facilitate communication, and therefore understanding.

Labeling in this text is synonymous with classification but does not mean diagnosis. In other words, a label alone doesn't supply the information needed to guide instruction.

Testing is a process by which educators try to learn about how a kid functions in the classroom by having the kid do things which correspond to classwork.

The most important term is *educational diagnosis*. *Diagnosis* is a medical term which describes the physical status of the individual. Educators have adopted the term for their own use and as a result have changed its meaning. The confusion of terminology is one of the biggest problems of special education. It is also one of the biggest problems facing the authors of this text. Probably the best way to clarify the term *diagnosis* would be to give it back to the medical profession. Since that wouldn't be a practical solution, we have placed the modifier *educational* before it. When the term *diagnosis* is used in the text, we are referring to *educational diagnosis*. Diagnosis in this context is something done to guide instruction. If tests are used to make diagnostic statements then their scores must have the power to relate the characteristics they summarize to the future behavior of the student. If an educator is to make treatment decisions from test scores, then she has to assume a direct relationship between the test behaviors and the educational program. For example, students who score low on achievement tests are often placed into a small class. This is a common example of an educational intervention based upon the use of general measures of achievement. If broken down, the rationale

1. The achievement test reveals that the student has a low level of prior learning.
2. Many educators believe that students with low achievement need increased instructional support.
3. Many educators believe that the smaller the instructional group the greater the instructional support available to the child.

for this grouping follows a cause and effect line of reasoning.

Therefore, low scores on achievement tests are used diagnostically to select the size of the class into which a student is placed. This particular conclusion may or may not be a good one depending on how often it works. But it does represent the typical reasoning by which test scores influence treatments.

Evaluative Models

There are many different models of evaluation. As will be discussed later, the psycho-medical model (otherwise known as the medical, psycho-educational, traditional, or diagnostic-prescriptive model) has been used extensively in special education. This text will present a different, but not new, model of evaluation. That model is the task analytical model (otherwise known as the behavioral or behavior analysis model). Considerable debate has gone on between proponents of these two models.

It is important to be familiar with both the psycho-medical and task analytical models because each has its particular limitations and strengths. Efforts have been made to take the two models and blend them together, but they are legitimately at odds with each other in several respects and therefore cannot be easily compromised. Also it should be remembered that when two philosophies are in fact combined, a third and different model is produced. Rather than expend time trying to reconcile two different points of view, it is sometimes better to switch from one to the other according to need. An efficient evaluator must be able to pick and choose between models, as well as procedures, according to need. Some models are better for one purpose than for another.

The two models are briefly contrasted in Table 1.1. The characteristics which are not easily compromised revolve around the source of failure, variables measured, and direction of treatment.

Table 1.1

A Comparison of Two Models of Evaluation

	Psycho-medical Model (Psycho-educational)	Task Analytical Model (Behavioral)
1. The basic assumption is . . .	if a student fails at a task it is because the student has something wrong with his cognitive or perceptual abilities.	if a student fails at a task it is because he has not mastered an essential subtask of that task.
2. The source of failure . . .	resides within the student.	resides within the environment.
3. Evaluation begins with . . .	the student.	the task on which the student is failing.
4. The tests used . . .	try to measure cognitive or perceptual abilities.	try to measure student behavior.
5. The most frequently used tests are . . .	norm-referenced tests based on logically developed theories of learning.	criterion-referenced tests based on empirically validated sequences of tasks.

Table 1.1 *(cont.)*

6. The conclusions drawn include . . .

| the student's cognitive or perceptual strengths and weaknesses. | what the student can or cannot do. |

7. Treatment is directed at . . .

| changing the student's cognitive or perceptual abilities. | changing the student's task-related behavior. |

8. Instruction involves . . .

| presentations which allow for weaknesses while taking advantage of strengths. | presentations which are directly related to a sequence of tasks. |

9. Instructional treatments are identified by . . .

| making predictions from tests of student ability. | monitoring the student's progress in several treatments. |

The Task Analytical Model

Table 1.2 elaborates on the task analytical model. Some of the premises on which this model is based may seem either ridiculously obvious or hopelessly obscure at this point. However, the model is presented now in order to get you to think along the lines the text will follow. The model in Table 1.2 is a preview of the text. Everything which follows will be an attempt to speak to the issues or train the skills outlined.

Table 1.2

The Task Analytical Model

PREMISES

---

1. The student is behaving improperly.
2. Instruction can change improper behavior.
3. The reason the student has failed to change already is that he has received inappropriate instruction.
4. Instruction is inappropriate when:
   a. It teaches the wrong thing.   b. It teaches the right thing poorly.
5. Diagnosis answers the questions:
   a. What to teach?   b. How to teach it?
6. Diagnosis cannot take place in the absence of information about tasks (what is taught) and treatments (how it is taught).
7. Diagnosis is not complete until the student has been placed in a treatment and his progress has been monitored.
8. The model of educational evaluation which is most useful is the model which evaluates variables teachers can control.

PRODUCTS OF DIAGNOSIS

A. What to teach?	B. How to teach it?
A1. Teach the content that the student needs to learn.	B1. Use only direct instruction.
A2. Teach only those tasks which are related to the content.	B2. Use instruction which is well designed.
A3. Teach only the essential subtasks of a task.	B3. Select instruction which is appropriate to the student's characteristics.

Table 1.2 *(cont.)*

SKILLS NEEDED FOR DIAGNOSIS

1. <u>TASK ANALYSIS</u>	2. <u>TREATMENT ANALYSIS</u>
a. able to specify tasks.	a. able to review relevant research.
b. able to identify essential sub-tasks.	b. able to specify instructional variables.
c. able to test essential subtasks.	c. able to monitor the effectiveness of a treatment.

3. <u>LEARNER ANALYSIS</u>
   a. able to assess students' needs.
   b. able to identify physiological limitations.
   c. sensitivity to individual differences.

Premises 1, 2, and 3

The first three premises are of great importance because they shift the "blame" for student failure off the student and onto the teacher. The reasoning goes like this.

PREMISE 1. The student is behaving improperly. If the student isn't behaving improperly (sometimes called inappropriately, or deviantly, or just badly) then he would not have been sent to special education in the first place. It is important to remember that special education functions on a deficit model; that is, it does not function at all unless something has gone wrong. The usual conclusion reached is that what went wrong went wrong with the kid. Premises 2 and 3 put that conclusion in doubt.

PREMISE 2. Instruction can change improper behavior. This premise is basic to the entire teaching profession. What it means can be seen in Figure 1.1a and 1.1b. In Figure 1.1a the student is moving across time but is functioning at a low level (improperly). Then the student is placed into special education. As a result of the placement, the student ends up functioning at a high (proper) level.

Even if the situation in Figure 1.1a does not always work out quite that well it is imperative that educators think it will. This is the most basic premise of all formal education: *that instruction matters.*

The solution in Figure 1.1b is only slightly different. In this case the student has received appropriate instruction all along. As a result the kid has never fallen behind. The illustration is not intended to build a case for early intervention. Instead, it is intended to make the point

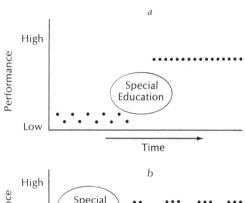

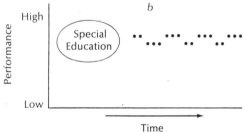

Figure 1.1

The premise that instruction matters.

that if a student can be caught up by special instruction then the lack of it can make the student fall behind. In short, if the pupil has not learned, the teacher has not taught.

PREMISE 3. The reason the student has failed to change already is that he has received inappropriate instruction. It is interesting to note that talking about inappropriate instruction tends to alienate some teachers much faster than talking about improper student behavior. Of course, neither the teacher or the pupil is "bad" in the permanent sense of the word. Both get to be inappropriate in the context of their surroundings. But it is true that while a teacher may reassure parents that the substandard performance of their child isn't anything to feel angry or guilty about, the same teacher won't accept it too well if the source of the substandard performance is traced to her.

"Inappropriate instruction," as the term is used in Premise 3, is not synonymous with bad teaching. "Improper behavior," as used in Premise 1, is not synonymous with bad children. What inappropriate instruction means is that it didn't work. It means that, for some reason, the variables which influence learning were not arranged for the student's benefit. The teacher, of course, has the primary responsibility for arranging these variables.

Premises 4, 5, 6, and 7

The next four premises, while equally important,

are more obvious than the first three. They will be expanded upon later in the text.

Premise 8

The model of educational evaluation which is most useful is the model that evaluates variables teachers can control. In order for an evaluative system to have high instructional utility, it must deal with instructional variables. It must test in areas which instruction can influence. If that is done then the results of the evaluation can be used in the classroom. If the evaluation tests variables which are beyond the ability (or duty) of teachers to change, then the test results cannot be used in the classroom and teachers should not be held accountable for them.

2

Evaluating Exceptional Children

A Brief History

Evaluation is an educational necessity which no competent teacher would ignore. Yet no one format and/or method for evaluation is accepted by a majority of educators. In the field of special education, evidence of fragmentary evaluative practice is everywhere. Special education, as a field, has been scattered across psychology, sociology, medicine, education, and law—retaining bits of each. It has at times reflected an almost contradictory interest in the separate purposes of explaining and serving its clients. The two questions which immediately come to every professional's mind are, (1) How did that kid get to be that way? and (2) What can I do to straighten the kid out? Professionals have often confused the two questions. Today the confusion of cause and treatment has reached a stage at which many educators don't know when they are just classifying and when they are diagnosing. This confusion is the result of a failure to understand the origins of current evaluative practices, as well as a confusion of the various purposes for which evaluation takes place.

The products of the educational complex in this country seem to fall into four areas. These are (1) promotion of knowledge, (2) promotion of skill, (3) custodial service, and (4) certification (Boulding, 1972).

Originally, skill and knowledge were probably the most important of these four areas. However, the last two areas, custodial service and certification, have gradually begun to outweigh the first two in the public's expectation of educational service. Evidence is plentiful to indicate that certification, in the form of degrees and diplomas, is valued well above the knowledge and skill which they supposedly represent. Likewise, the services which schools perform in the custodial area are economical and social factors of great consequence (Glass, 1974b). For example, while four-year high schools keep teen-agers off the work force, kindergartens allow a larger percentage of parents on the work force. There are indications that many labor groups supported raising the age of compulsory education in the early seventies to offset the employment effect of ending the military draft.

Since its inception, special education has tended to reflect the community's interest in custodial service and certification (classification), more so perhaps than has education as a whole. One explanation for this preoccupation has been parental pressure.

Originally, many parents were content to settle

for only custodial service. In their defense, it should be noted that during the early part of this century, parents were functioning in a framework which viewed orphans as retarded, and the physically handicapped as mad. These early special education students were severely handicapped, and their admission to schools even on the custodial level was a landmark victory. Their admission into the educational setting did not, however, mean admission to *all* the services education can supply. Later, when the courts handed down many decisions supporting the handicapped child's right to have equal access to the public schools, there were fewer decisions regarding equal educational opportunity and programming (Prehm & Goldschmidt, 1975). Not until the early seventies did parents and some educators begin to lobby for the handicapped student's right to participate in the areas of skill and knowledge.

Litigation and Legislation

The field of special education has changed dramatically over the last decade. Many forces have combined to bring about these changes. One of these forces has been litigation. Court decisions have had a massive impact on the evaluative practices of special education. Combined with legislation such as Public Law 94-142 (the Education for All Handicapped Children Act), court decisions have spelled out procedures for the evaluation, placement, and treatment of exceptional children.

There are many reasons why the special education field has come to the attention of the courts. Originally, parents sought remedies from the courts when their children were not given educational services because of handicapping conditions. Some of these decisions found that handicapped students were being denied property (an education represents future earning power) without due process of law. Other courts found that students who were mislabeled as special had been deprived of liberty (as a result of being stigmatized) without due process. In these cases the courts commented not on education itself but on the process by which education was being administered. Judges are often reluctant to decide if students are receiving an appropriate education because they do not con-

sider themselves competent in the area of education. These same judges do, however, feel competent to consider the equitable distribution of funds or the procedural safeguards associated with classification and/or transportation of children. There have been few court decisions which have actually specified the type of treatment a student should receive. Instead, the courts have outlined steps which must be followed before a student is denied treatment. One such decision involved the Pennsylvania Association for Retarded Children. In this decision the judge spelled out due process guidelines for the treatment of exceptional children which later appeared almost intact within the procedural safeguards section of P.L. 94-142.

The overrepresentation of students from racial and cultural minorities in special classes led to other cases. The two classic cases of this type were *Diana* v. *State Board of Education* in California and *Hobsen* v. *Hansen* in the District of Columbia. Both of these cases found the use of standardized tests to be inappropriate because of their tendency to separate out minority students. These decisions have had a direct effect on educational testing. Essentially they have increased the risk of using standardized IQ and achievement tests for placement purposes. Some districts have found the risk to be so high that the tests have been abandoned.

Under the pressure of parent groups and following the lead set by the courts, new legislation has been written regarding the handicapped. P.L. 94-142 is designed to provide districts with support so that they can make court-mandated changes. One important aspect of the public law is the Individualized Educational Program (IEP):

> (19) The term 'individualized education program' means a written statement for each handicapped child developed in a meeting by a representative of the local educational agency or an intermediate educational unit who shall be qualified to provide, or supervise the provision of, specially designed instruction to meet the unique needs of handicapped children, the teacher, the parents or guardian of such child, and, whenever appropriate, such child, which statement shall include (A) a statement of the present levels of educational performance of such child, (B) a statement of annual goals, including short-term instructional objectives, (C) a statement of the specific educational services to be provided to such child, and the extent to which such child will be able to

participate in regular educational programs, (D) the projected date for initiation and anticipated duration of such services, and appropriate objective criteria and evaluation procedures and schedules for determining, on at least an annual basis, whether instructional objectives are being achieved. (Section 4, Definitions)

The IEP clause has the effect of formalizing what has been preferred educational practice for years. Essentially it says teachers must state where their students are, where they are going, and how they will get there. In order to do so, teachers should be able to engage in task-specific, objective-based evaluation and monitoring. One disadvantage of the IEP clause is that the procedure for writing plans has become an area of controversy. Just as the early seventies saw a rash of workshops on how to write behavioral objectives, the late seventies and early eighties will probably see countless IEP workshops.

Federal rules and regulations for administering P.L. 94-142 will require the existence of child evaluation teams. These teams will most often include the student's regular classroom teacher, a special education teacher, an administrator, and a licensed diagnostician such as a school psychologist. Membership on the child evaluation team will bring teachers into direct contact with psychologists and administrators. One evaluative ramification of this clause is that teachers will now be called upon to interpret test data for placement purposes.

It is difficult to assess the effects of legislation and litigation on educational evaluation. This is primarily because the process of change is on-going. Some believe that the first rule of helping is to avoid hurting. Educational evaluation has frequently violated this basic tenet by causing handicapped children to be excluded from regular classrooms. It is difficult to decide if evaluation has enabled students to get the help they need, or stigmatized them by fragmenting them into categories.

Changing Technology

The initial inclusion of severely handicapped children into the public schools was handled in the most efficient means available to the institution, which usually included the grouping of students for segregated services. Homogeneous grouping has long been touted by educators as a means of dealing with students efficiently and is displayed in forms ranging from special class placement to leveling by reading ability. All grouping practices require some type of evaluative procedure for sorting individuals. These procedures may be as arbitrary as a birth date (for grade level) or as subjective as a teacher's first-day impression. The evaluative practices used in a grouping program are often related more to the purpose of the grouping than to the characteristics of the group members. To use an extreme example, if the purpose of a grouping program is physical control (custodial service), then it can be argued that it is easier to physically control a group of similar things than it is to physically control a group of dissimilar things. The control of ten dogs may be less of a bother than the control of five dogs and five cats. The initial evaluative procedures evolved for grouping handicapped students were often only sensitive enough to tell the dogs from the cats, or the ambulatory from the bedridden.

As educational technology improves, the handicapped are being taught to do more and more things. When instruction is designed to teach the handicapped person skills, new models of evaluation are needed. In the past there has been a preoccupation with locating the "cause" of various disabilities. When this cause was found to be a permanent or incurable condition, the evaluation may have halted. In fact, the evaluative procedures used may not have been able to go further. New procedures are needed which go beyond the explanation of a disability and toward the treatment of a handicap. The disability may exist within the biochemical or physical makeup of the child. The disability may even be permanently housed in chromosomes within each cell of the child's body. But a handicap exists somewhere between that cause and the expectation of "normal" behavior held by society (Doll, 1953). At a recent hearing on architectural barriers, a wheelchair-bound witness made the frequently heard observation that her cerebral palsy was her disability, but she was handicapped by the ignorance and prejudice of others.

There is an interaction which takes place between the disability of a person, the expectations of society, and the requirements of tasks. This complex interaction is what makes up a handicap. In order to treat the handicap, it is necessary to go well beyond the causative disability. For example, suppose that the lenses of a child's eyes have been clouded by a cataract condition. As a result of being blind at a young age, the child may develop characteristic rocking and/or self-stimulation behaviors which appear abnormal in comparison to other children. In addition, the child's knowledge of the world may be severely limited. The traditional evaluative practices which center upon the cause of the disability may result in the student being placed into a classroom for the blind. But then suppose the child receives surgery, and her vision is raised to a normal level. Even in this situation, where there is a clear relationship between the cause of the disability and the nature of the handicap, it should be obvious that once the disability has been removed, the handicap is not automatically gone. Other types of evaluation are needed to guide the education of the child whether the child remains severely disabled or not. The instrumentation used to explore the student's eyes will not direct treatment to reduce the student's rocking behavior after the operation. Regardless of whether or not the operation takes place, very different types of technology will be needed to offset the knowledge deficit associated with childhood blindness.

The past decade has seen a growing preoccupation with mildly handicapped students (learning disabled, educable mentally retarded, behavior disordered). These children frequently are not considered deviant until they have experienced failure in the school setting. Unlike the severely handicapped, the mildly handicapped student is not initially denied access, but is excluded due to some conflict which arises after entering the school setting. This conflict is often directly related to the student's acquisition of skill and knowledge—that is, the kid doesn't learn. The mildly handicapped student does not need custodial service. Failure to learn implies the need for instructional control, not physical control. Instructional control cannot be obtained by evaluating students on the gross (dog versus cat type) variables associated with custodial service. The grouping practices and evaluative formats once associated with the purpose of cus-

todial service have therefore come to be viewed as inappropriate for both the mildly and severely handicapped.

Labeling vs. Diagnosis

The question How did the kid get to be that way? has led to a search for causes, and causes are found in the past. The tendency in classification has been to look at the kid in terms of how she got to be that way. This is done by recognizing individuals who are symptomatically the same and who may have had similar histories. If enough similar individuals are found, or if their symptoms are sufficiently extreme, a syndrome or condition may be described. Once described, the condition is labeled and a classification is formed.

The problem with classifications and labels is that they may lack meaning, or worse yet, that they have more meaning than they should. Lack of specific meaning is not limited to labels but is a characteristic of all words. Korzybski (1948) describes a kind of word game in which the players attempt to supply the meaning for words by first giving a definition and then defining the words in the definition. In a short time the players find their vocabularies exhausted as they reach a level at which they "know" but can't "tell" the definition without reusing certain key words. Korzybski says the game takes from 10 to 15 minutes. If the game is played by special educators who use labels such as mentally retarded, learning disabled, or behavior disordered, it takes about 5.

At the other extreme (and ironically at the same time) a label may have too much meaning. This is referred to as *surplus meaning* (Cromwell, Blashfield, & Strauss, 1975), and it comes about when a term is used to describe things which cannot be directly or accurately measured. Once a term is used in a vague manner it can be applied to many situations. A person who hears the term may not know which situation it is referring to because the term has too many meanings. Surplus meaning can obscure understanding.

The term *mental retardation* (or even retardation) is the classic example of a term which has too little *and* too much meaning. The term has various definitions but most include the key words *permanent, limitation, intelligence* (intellectual capacity), *central nervous system,* and *incompetence.* Based on *Webster's Dictionary* (1971), the lack of meaning in the definition can be summarized as follows: the term *mental* relates to the term *intelligence,* and *intelligence* relates to the term *ability.* The term *retardation* relates to the term *limitation* which relates to a lack of *capacity. Capacity* is a term which refers to *potential mental ability,* which leads back again to *mental.*

The surplus meaning of a term like *retarded* is also obvious. It means *slow to develop,* but it carries with it the image of incurable incompetence. It is not uncommon for a school psychologist to note that a child is "retarded in the area of reading." A parent seeing such a comment might never get beyond the word *retarded* and react to such a statement as if his child had been labeled mentally deficient.

An interesting pattern in many special education texts has been to attempt clarification of terms through the presentation of synonyms for the term. This technique increases the surplus meaning. In order for a term to be used specifically, it is best to reduce the use of synonyms, not to promote their use.

Classification, when properly used, is a process which aids the development of theory by promoting understanding between interested parties. Researchers are able to classify according to any number or combination of variables. In special education, students are routinely classified according to source variables (Reynolds & Balow, 1972). Source variables rephrase the What made the kid that way? question to What is the source of the kid's problem? Traditional source variables correspond to the current specific disability categories used in special education such as emotional disturbance, mental retardation, learning disabilities, visually handicapped, crippled and other health impaired, gifted, sensory handicapped, maladjusted, and so forth. These classifications are thought of as the sources of educational problems.

While any number or combination of variables can be used to classify individuals, they do not all have equal utility. For this reason, systems of classification have been proposed which outline the relative importance of different vari-

ables. Cromwell et al. (1975) have proposed criteria for the classification of children. These criteria would first require that labels be agreed upon by the individuals working with them (teachers, psychologists, and parents). In addition, Cromwell et al. (1975) would require labels which are descriptive of a specific group of children, and that would apply equally to all members of the group. They demand that a classification system be logically consistent, have clinical utility, and be simple enough to deal with so that it will be used.

Some of the variables used to classify kids are (1) historical-etiological characteristics, (2) currently assessable characteristics, (3) the interventions in which the individual is placed, and (4) their level of prognosis (Cromwell et al., 1975). Certain of these variables are more applicable to answering a What went wrong? question than a What do I do? question.

These variables and criteria (Cromwell et al., 1975) can be arranged into a rational system for classifying children, but unfortunately, even the best systems are seldom actually put into practice (Haring & Schiefelbusch, 1976). One explanation for this failure may be that searching for causes is not the primary goal of many special educators. For those who consider themselves practitioners, the goal is not to understand but to serve the handicapped. Although these two goals are logically related, limitations in time and resources will cause one to be chosen over the other. Classification (asking What happened?) is a legitimate stage of theory development, but it has limited value in the area of behavioral intervention (Hunt & Lansman, 1975). To those who would try to aid the handicapped, diagnosis is more important than simple classification. However, a brief review of the field of special education will reveal an overwhelming preoccupation with classification as well as a pervasive confusion of classification and diagnosis.

There are several explanations for the confusion of diagnosis and classification, the first being that with certain severe conditions, classification and diagnosis are nearly synonymous. Because the field of special education grew out of treating severely handicapped individuals, the confusion may have been with us from the start (Quay, 1973). Classification may lead to accurate treatment statements when the individual being classified is biologically handicapped. For example, phenylketonuria (PKU) is a pathological condition which usually results in intellectual retardation due to the accumulation of phenylalanine within the bloodstream of the child. The implications of accurately classifying an individual as having PKU are straightforward—don't feed the child things that contain phenylalanine. Even in this case the classification still doesn't have clearcut implications for treatment, as the presence of too much phenylalanine doesn't always result in retardation (Baumeister & Muma, 1975). When the problem is academic deficiency, the variables for classification are less specific. There is no one variable that explains reading failure. In fact, there is no one definition of reading. Yet educators have tended to treat students who fail academically as if they have enzyme deficiencies. That is, they have sought to label students and then make treatment statements from the label. This practice can only succeed when the label is precise and contains no surplus meaning. Of course, our educational labels are far from precise in that a "gifted child" in one school district may be a "slow learner" in another. Bateman (1972) points out the sometimes humorous surplus meaning in the label "minimal brain dysfunction" when she notes that many authors say the syndrome is indicated by either hyperactivity or hypoactivity. In other words, you know an MBD kid when you see one because she is either running around a lot or sitting very still.

One explanation for a preoccupation with classification is that in some severe cases, it works as diagnosis. Another explanation is that it enables school districts to obtain funds. Current evaluative practices are often justified by the reasoning that without the classification of students, school districts would be unable to fund programs for the handicapped. Categorical funding has been the rule in special education for some time. However, there is a growing trend away from specific disability categories and toward general categories such as children with special problems, mildly handicapped, and extreme learning problems. Whichever funding path is taken, the essential point to be remembered is that testing for funding and testing for teaching are different activities which may have

no direct relationship to each other at all. The labels LD, MR, ED, MBD, and so forth, have no instructional utility. They cannot be used as indicators of what a child needs to learn, how she should be taught, or what she can or cannot do.

Classification has a legitimate place in the study of learning, but it is not the final goal (Hunt & Lansman, 1975). The final goal is to develop procedures and theories which can explain and be used to influence learning. These procedures are diagnostic. Classification and diagnosis are not identical. Diagnosis is a process in which information is gathered which directly affects the child's treatment. If a diagnosis is sufficiently powerful, it predicts how the student will behave in the future once the diagnostic recommendations are carried out. Classification may be a part of the diagnostic process, but the terms *diagnosis* and *classification* are not synonymous.

Educational diagnosis hinges upon an assumption of educational utility which can be stated as follows: *In order to diagnose and make instructional recommendations from test data, (1) the testing information must be directly related to instruction and (2) the information must remain directly related long enough for the instruction to be completed.* This is a two-part assumption, the first part of which requires a dependent relationship between test behavior and learning (validity). The second requires the evaluative power necessary to identify stable characteristics over time and across settings (reliability). The power necessary to bring about a true diagnostic relationship between the known test score and the unknown future behavior of the student depends on a number of considerations. The confidence that can be placed in a diagnostic statement depends on the statement's ability to summarize the interactions of the student, the task, and the instruction across time. If the diagnostic statement is sufficiently powerful (and if it's followed by the teacher) the effect should be to advance the student toward an objective (Figure 2.1).

Diagnostic systems can be evolved by making use of the same information used to develop classification systems. These dimensions of information are (1) historical-etiological characteristics, (2) currently assessable characteristics,

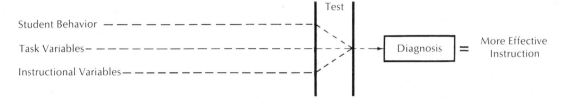

Figure 2.1

The effect of diagnosis.

(3) treatment or intervention, and (4) prognosis (Cromwell et al., 1975). These sources of information are used differently in diagnosis than in classification.

Zubin (1967) suggests the purposes of diagnosis are to (1) make a prognosis and (2) select an intervention. He also suggests that these purposes in the nonschool setting can be advanced through the search for etiology. In the school setting, however, etiology and prognosis are not always valid pursuits. A diagnostic relationship between etiological and educational decisions does not exist (Bateman, 1972). Educators are not employed to merely predict behavior, but to influence it. Past failure is the best predictor of future failure. The special educator deals with a population to which this predictor of future failure applies. The job of the special educator is to discredit that prediction. If the reason a special educator is employed is to alter the behavior of students, then purely predictive instruments such as the IQ test are of less importance (Baumeister & Muma, 1975; Reynolds & Balow, 1972). A professional teacher will keep trying to instruct even when all indications predict the child will not learn. A teacher is paid to instruct.

The most useful diagnostic system is one which accurately identifies behaviors which need changing and matches them to corrective interventions. Such a system answers two questions: (1) Which behaviors should be changed? and (2) Which interventions are most effective? These two questions can be rephrased as: those which ask (1) What does the child need to be taught and (2) How does the child need to be taught? These two questions, while similar in meaning, are resolved by using different techniques to be discussed later.

Evaluation and Definition

In any field, evaluation is closely associated with definition. Sometimes this association can become circular. A circular association is one in which the tool evolved to match a particular definition ends up changing the definition.

Evolution of the IQ Test

Mental retardation is a good example of the circular association which can take place between the definition of a thing and the tools designed to measure it. Our ability to work with and understand a thing is related to our ability to observe and manipulate it. When a label is attached to something, our attention is drawn away from the thing and toward the label. The result is a perceptual block known as stereotyping (Adams, 1974). This has been the case with mental retardation.

Early investigators could easily identify individuals with abnormal physical attributes such as epilepsy and Down's syndrome. These pathological attributes were studied until there resulted a sizable body of information pertaining to the etiological correlates of mental retardation. This led to a biological definition of retardation which had a distinctly medical orientation (Blanton, 1975). The biological definition raised retardation to the status of a label. The label "MR" came to describe a condition which (1) resided within the individual and not the environment and (2) was stable and not subject to treatment. The biological definition has apparently functioned as a perceptual block discouraging investigators from studying the environmental causes of retardation. This definition has also supported the pervasive belief that the retarded person cannot be taught because retardation is permanent (Dunn, 1968). Many educators came to view a retarded person as a person who could not acquire knowledge and skill. At the same time the economic and social realities of supporting them did spark interest in their custodial care. Educators soon were expressing interest in tools which would easily identify students who might be expending instructional resources with no hope of becoming educated. Once identified, the educational alternatives available to these students could be limited according to their intellectual potential. The thrust of this new activity was educational, not medical. The result was an educational definition of retardation which became operational in a typically educational fashion—testing.

When the intelligence quotient (IQ) test was originally designed, its purpose was to predict future performance in school. Because students who perform well in school were said to behave intelligently, it seemed reasonable to conclude that the IQ test was a measure of intelligent behavior. Note that in this case, the word *intelligent* is a modifier used to describe behavior—it isn't necessarily a tangible thing. But it wasn't long before the student who behaved intelligently was being referred to as intelligent. This jump between modifier and noun was aided by the development of the IQ test. The operational definition of intelligence became a test score.

Because intelligence was ill-defined (as it still is), the tests designed to measure it ended up defining it. Intelligence became the thing intelligence tests measure. The evaluation and definition of intelligence are therefore associated in a circular fashion something like this: "I know intelligence is real; there is a test to measure it."

General ability, or intelligence, is a multifaceted construct which can only be indicated. Student behavior on published tests has been used to indicate intelligence while many other indicators have been ignored. Because the original IQ tests, and most of their descendants, were tied to the prediction of survival in school, they sampled school behaviors. An IQ test evolved to predict success in another context (say survival on a desert island) might result in quite a different definition of intelligence.

Today a student with no medical indications

of abnormality may be classified as retarded through the use of the IQ test. The irony is that while the evaluation of retardation has completely escaped the need for medical evidence, the label "retarded" retains its biological connotations. Many educators view the student who is labeled retarded as one who can't be educated due to some internal and permanent deficiency. The score on the IQ test has come to have drastic implications as to what kind of educational service the student receives.

Earlier, an attempt was made to distinguish classification from diagnosis; however, in practice, this is seldom done. For example, a student who is given the Wechsler Intelligence Scale for Children–Revised (WISC–R) and who scores two standard deviations below the mean (–70) may be classified as retarded. In addition, the same test score may be used to justify placement into a certain type of classroom or treatment. In this case the test score is used in a diagnostic manner. The purpose of the IQ test was originally prognostic, not diagnostic (Mercer, 1973). Yet the use of the IQ test as both a classifying and diagnostic instrument is widespread.

There is a high frequency of physiological symptoms among the population of students who score extremely low on IQ tests. These gross physical and sensory defects lent support to the idea that the IQ test could identify permanently handicapped people. However, as the use of the test expanded, the conclusions which were once applied to scores of 25 or 40 began to be applied to scores of 65 or 80. The current definition of mental retardation used by the American Association on Mental Deficiency includes a provision for significantly subaverage intelligence as measured by an IQ test. This should include about 2.3% of the total population. Of this subpopulation, as many as 80% may exhibit no gross pathology (Heber, Garber, Harrington, Hoffman & Falender, 1972). That is, they may have no physiological evidence of abnormality. Of the remaining 20% or 30% of the intellectually subnormal (those who do exhibit pathology), the majority fall into only a few principal syndromes such as Down's syndrome. In view of this, it is remarkable that the image of mental retardation projected in many courses and texts on the subject is centered around pathological symptoms such as chromosome aberrations.

Many students obtaining scores of 60 and 70

have little, if anything, in common with the severely retarded. Unfortunately, the low IQ score is still firmly tied to the idea of gross and irreparable subnormality. People expect less from someone who "fails" an IQ test. This lowering of expectation, plus negative stigma, must be weighed against the instructional advantages gained when a child is tested.

Other Examples

The IQ test is not the only evaluative instrument used by special educators. It is, however, a good example of the developmental sequence which has typified psychological testing. In order to illustrate the idea that the IQ test is not unique, here is another brief example.

Even before formal models of intellectual potential were being developed, researchers had noticed a correlation between brain injury and certain language disorders. Once again, these observations were initially made by medical personnel. These observations formally entered the field of special education in the forties through the work of Goldstein (1942), who investigated the behavior of injured war veterans. These brain-injured adults would often reverse or confuse letters in much the same way as nonreading children. The resulting correlation quickly escalated into a cause and effect assumption; that is, that nonreading students who exhibit certain behaviors, such as symbol confusion, may be brain damaged. Since few nonreading students exhibit any evidence of gross head injury, the assumption had to be modified to include the idea of minimal brain damage. In other words, evidence obtained from the severely handicapped was once again generalized to the mildly handicapped. Soon, the pathological evidence was de-emphasized entirely as educators turned to the test form for information on brain damage. This provided an opportunity for the classification of "brain damaged" to be applied to individuals with no gross pathology.

The category of learning disabilities was originally aligned with evidence of brain damage or minimal brain dysfunction. Minimal brain dysfunction in turn was often linked to abnormal electroencephalogram (EEG) patterns. However, the ability of the EEG to identify patterns related to educational failure was eventually questioned. As a result, the use of EEGs decreased, and the label "minimal brain damage" was modified to "minimal brain dysfunction." Minimal brain dysfunction lingered on to become learning disabilities, a syndrome which can now be defined without any medical evidence of neurological impairment. Just as in the case of mental retardation, the definition of learning disabilities evolved through a gradual shift away from biological criteria and toward testing criteria. The result of this shift has also been an increase in the number of students matching the modified definition.

Minimal brain dysfunction is aligned with the concept of processing dysfunctions if only on the grounds that processing takes place in the brain. It is through this alignment that the classification of learning disabilities derives its diagnostic implications. Investigators eventually began to apply theories of language acquisition and cognitive functioning as possible explanations for why an individual who has no gross biological damage might be educationally handicapped. One explanation which evolved from this line of inquiry was the idea that while the brain may not be physically damaged, it still may not be processing information correctly. This failure to process was explained by Kirk, Wepman, and others through the use of a model of language acquisition developed by Osgood (Paraskevopoulos & Kirk, 1969; Wepman, 1958; Osgood, 1957).

By removing the syndrome from the realm of brain damage to the realm of cognitive processing, investigators raised the possibility that if the behavioral symptoms could be explained by processing dysfunctions, then by training processes it might be possible to change behavior. The next step in the evolution of the learning disability category was, of course, to educationally define it through the development of tests. Tests were developed such as the Illinois Test of Psycholinguistic Ability (ITPA) and the Wepman Auditory Discrimination Test which were then used to both classify students as deviant and make diagnostic statements about how this deviancy might be corrected. Although the developers of the tests had not intended to create classification instruments, the evolutionary process from biological evidence to the test score was again complete, as was the confusion of classification and diagnosis. Psychometric tests may provide a basis for classification but as Hunt and Lansman (1975) point out, they are of little use in describing individual cognition or in selecting treatments.

There are two explanations for special education absorbing an ever increasing percentage of the total student population. The first of these is an inexplicable "plague" of minimal brain dysfunction or some other ill-defined syndrome. The second, and more likely, explanation is that the changing criteria for special services have defined students as "special" who were never special before.

If the normal distribution is used to describe the total student population, then special education is represented by the extremes. In Figure 2.2, the variable illustrated is IQ score. Students who score very high or very low on IQ tests are sorted out for special education. These populations are thought of as retarded or gifted. However, IQ score is not the only variable upon which a student may be considered special. Gifted, for example, has come to include the talented student who may have a normal IQ score. When emotional disturbance is defined as social maladjustment, it can be identified in students of all intelligence levels.

As the variables increase so does the proportion of special education students. The category of learning disabilities (LD) has become the largest category because it is defined by the most variables. In some states a student need only be behind in one academic area to be considered for admission to an LD program. If all students were screened on all of the variables associated with learning disabilities, few would survive the process unlabeled. Popular indicators of learning disabilities include low academic achievement, processing dysfunctions, hyperactivity, neurological impairment, poor coordination, visual and auditory discrimination deficits, hypoactivity, and more. These indicators do not correlate with each other, meaning that students may have one but not the rest. The result is an increased proportion of students identified as special (Figure 2.3). Of course, many of these variables could be expected to overlap, such as emotional disturbance and low academic achievement. But others are mutually exclusive, such as hyperactivity and hypoactivity.

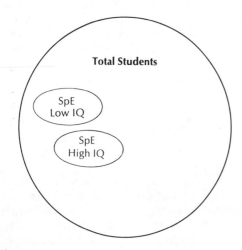

Figure 2.2

The proportion of special education students (SpE) to total students when only one variable is used in the definition.

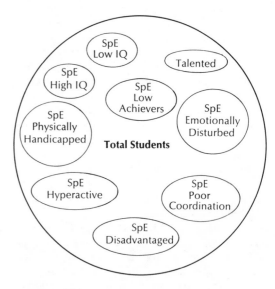

Figure 2.3

The proportion of special education students (SpE) to total students when several variables are used in the definition.

Some states list migrant and/or disadvantaged children as needing special education. Sometimes the same is true for non-English-speaking children.

It appears, then, that the best explanation for why special education has become flooded with mildly handicapped students is not a plague. There has been no real increase in the proportion of such students. Rather, the apparent increase is the result of a gradual change in the definition of "special." In the absence of severe sensory or physical damage, the popular way to define and explain a child's deviant behavior is often through testing. The result has been the proliferation of psychometrically defined categories such as specific learning disabilities, emotionally handicapped, and educable mentally retarded. In addition, the traditional categories of mental retardation, emotionally disturbed, and brain damaged have become less dependent upon medical or behavioral observation and more dependent upon the paper and pencil test.

Throughout the history of special education, there has been one pervasive assumption, medically oriented, which states that the deviant behavior has as its source some form of pathology *within the child*. This assumption has supported a circular association between the definitions of handicapping conditions and the evaluative practices used to describe them.

Students who in the past may have been considered remedial, lazy, or disadvantaged have been dealt with by special educators as if they were severely handicapped. This misapplication is clearest in the area of evaluation. The limitations of testing will be discussed later, but it should be understood that having a disability is not the only reason a child may flunk a test. And lack of intelligence is not the only reason a child may fail to learn.

Changing Evaluative Practice

Using test data for the purpose of classification may have been initially advantageous because this method was quick and easy. In the late sixties and early seventies, however, the use of test scores for classification became expensive. Standardized tests came under fire from parent groups and the courts. In the resulting cases, the arguments most frequently used were that (1) the tests themselves were inappropriate for certain populations and (2) the testers frequently misused the tests to the disadvantage of students.

The primary target in this conflict was the IQ test. Mercer (1973) found that the IQ test was the main tool used to label individuals and to make a diagnosis. She stated that in one community 99% of the public school children labeled

retarded had been given an individual IQ test, while only 13% had been given a medical examination. This movement away from a biological definition of retardation brought with it the liability of test bias. There are many types of test bias, but the most controversial type results from the practice of obtaining normative data from middle-class Anglo populations.

The use of normative tests to define deviance involves basic normative assumptions. In operation, these assumptions dictate that any subgroup of the population is deviant. That is to say, the more unique a small group is the more deviant they are in the normative sense. This situation was initially acceptable because of the widely held beliefs that the schools are the tool by which the American culture is maintained and that American society is a cultural melting pot. Mercer speaks to this issue when she observes that "clinical assessment has reinforced the 'melting pot' process by defining persons who have not 'melted' as subnormal" (p. 9). Normative comparison tends to isolate and stigmatize any subgroup which is truly different from the norm. Two ways in which kids may differ from the norm are by race and wealth. With the increased social awareness of the 1960s, commonplace discriminatory practices of all kinds, which had been accepted before, came under attack. Both race and wealth have been viewed by the Supreme Court as suspect classifications, and court cases have held that the use of middle-class norms is inappropriate for making educational placement decisions (*Diana v. State Board of Education*, 1970, 1973; *Hobson v. Hanson*, 1967). In response, some districts have dropped general ability testing because the practice is legally too risky (Deno, 1971).

Another line of attack against ability testing followed the argument of Rosenthal and Jacobson (1968). These authors cited the self-fulfilling prophecy as one danger of reporting low test scores to teachers. The self-fulfilling prophecy idea suggests that negative information about a student may cause teachers to develop a mechanism of selective perception which makes them notice only student failure (Brophy & Good, 1974). The result may be that the information originally intended to help the student hurts the student by causing the teacher to always view the student in a negative context. The actual research findings presented by Rosenthal and Jacobson have been widely disputed. However, their conclusions have such a popular appeal that they have been generally accepted.

A final objection to many traditional psychoeducational tests is that they necessitate the involvement of the school psychologist. This is of particular interest to the authors as two of them are certified school psychologists. To many teachers, the psychologist has become the evaluative headhunter whose purpose is only to find and classify kids rather than to provide instructional guidance. Often the teacher is denied the opportunity to even meet with a student until a formal evaluation has been completed by the psychologist. As it turns out, many psychologists are not sufficiently knowledgeable in classroom practice to write a useful instructional prescription (Deno, 1971). The ability to evaluate and/or instruct in any particular area must ultimately depend upon knowledge in that area. For example, knowledge of evaluation is essential to diagnosis in an area such as reading, but so is knowledge of reading and reading instruction. Many school psychologists lack sufficient background in instruction to write an instructional diagnosis. Perhaps the ultimate school psychologist joke is an unfortunately true one reported by Sullivan (1977). He tells of a psychologist who, after years of testing and labeling students as retarded, finally went to visit an MR classroom. In the classroom, the psychologist spotted two Down's syndrome children and, turning to the teacher, inquired, "Are those two kids related? They look so much alike."

Experience has taught many teachers to simply disregard the almost exclusively prognostic and interpretive data supplied by some psychologists. Other teachers have grown to resent the expense associated with psychologist-based evaluation because the product has such limited educational impact. When two of the authors asked over 100 special education teachers to list their greatest complaints about current evaluative practices, 92% of them listed the school psychologist in the top five.

Many psychologists find themselves trapped into endlessly administering IQ tests for the purpose of classification, which causes them to disappoint teachers who are interested in diagnosis. As long as the confusion of classification and diagnosis persists, the disappointment can be expected to persist. Filler, Robinson, Smith,

Vincent-Smith, Bricker, and Bricker (1975) reviewed current practices in the evaluation of mental retardation. In their conclusions they observed that "psychologists must be trained to assume responsibility not only for evaluation but also for educational programming" (p. 228). They go on to call for the retraining of psychometricians who believe that retarded children suffer from an irreversible inability to learn which necessitates their protection from the regular classroom.

The legal, social, and educational price being paid for the use of traditional normative testing for the purpose of classification will almost certainly continue to rise. As it does, it will be interesting to see at what point this use is simply discontinued because of the confusion and misunderstanding this practice breeds.

The following paragraph reports some of the main points raised at a conference on minority testing and evaluation. Those in attendance at the conference were primarily school psychologists, with some state department personnel, school district personnel, and parents. Almost all participants agreed that it was advisable to immediately establish local minority norms for intelligence tests. The result, they concluded, would be to decrease the bias of the tests. What they apparently forgot was that the purpose of the IQ test was to predict success in the average school setting. Developing culturally or racially specific norms would destroy the predictive validity of the tests. The irony, of course, was that the workshop participants were so dedicated to the IQ test that they would cling to its use even after changing it to the point that its purpose was destroyed.

When it was suggested to the conference that labels derived from normative testing were not necessary for all remediation, a psychologist complained that the districts would lose categorical funding. It was then pointed out that about one-third of the local special education students were supported strictly by the districts; because the districts did not receive any categorical reimbursement, the students needed no labels. In response, a district representative proclaimed that the districts were trying not to exceed the state and federal funding sources and were working to get rid of these surplus students (no one asked where). Taking up the issue, a state department spokesperson pointed out that some districts were exceeding the maximum state funding with just the category of learning disabilities, leaving no money for other areas of exceptionalty. Someone then suggested a limit on the percentage of LD students allowed to receive state funds. At this point, the local LD parent group became enraged, and to help them along, a superintendent stated that such a limitation would force the districts to relabel the surplus LD students MR (apparently under the assumption that mislabeling is better than no labeling at all). The conference degenerated from that point.

Similar discussions take place daily in state department and school district meetings throughout the country. Special education has come a long way from its basic interest in the severely handicapped. As the field has taken in more and more mildly handicapped students, the emphasis has shifted from medical evidence to psychometric evidence of abnormality. Yet the medical orientation has lingered on in the form of specific disability categories which, in reality, have lost all their specificity. Certification has become a major preoccupation in special education. The evolution of public policy toward the handicapped has had a major impact on the choices of evaluative instrumentation and practices used by the field. As a result the confusion between classification and diagnosis has steadily increased.

It can be argued that any field or discipline must evolve. The trouble is that special education isn't really as independent a field as some would like it to be. It is a conglomerate of education, psychology, medicine, and more recently, sociology and law. Special education's evolution has been redundant in that it is recycling controversies already resolved by its related fields. When special education dealt exclusively with the severely handicapped, "emergency" decisions were made which were simple and clear-cut. By moving into the area of the mildly handicapped, special education has been forced to come to grips with subtle issues which hopefully will have refined its thinking. In the long run, special education may come out ahead. Having dealt with both basic and subtle issues, it will be in a better position to decide which way it wants to go as a field (May, 1975). The trouble is that kids grow up faster than academic disciplines. Today's clients will not receive any benefits from what happens in the long run.

3

Deciding
What to Teach

When a teacher evaluates a student diagnostically, she is trying to decide what the student needs to be taught and how the student needs to be taught. Of the two decisions, what to teach would seem to be the easiest. You should teach the kid what he doesn't know. The trouble is that there are a lot of things we all don't know. A teacher has to select tests which are appropriate for the kid and for the instructional objectives. The question of what to teach gets clouded when rephrased to: (1) What tests are appropriate for special students? and (2) What are the instructional objectives for special students?

What's Appropriate for the Child?

The ability of the terms *special, exceptional, retarded,* and so forth, to confuse an issue is directly related to lack of specificity. As has already been discussed, these terms have surplus meaning. The truth is that special students in general, or any of the specific disability categories of students (MR, LD, BD), are not a homogeneous population. Because all LD students do not behave in the same way, there can't be any such thing as an LD test. For example, let's go back to Bateman's observation that many authors

say LD is indicated by *both* hyperactivity and hypoactivity (Bateman, 1972). If this is true, then a test which is supposed to be appropriate for all LD students must take into account two contradictory factors. Maybe what is really needed is a separate test for hyperactive children and for hypoactive children. Of course no one really knows what *hyperactive* means either, and in fact, some authors have split that population into two subgroups—hyperactivity and hyperreactivity. The hyperactive student is supposed to exhibit fluctuations in attention and activity level regardless of what situation he's in, whereas the hyperreactive student exhibits these same fluctuations only in relation to certain situations. If that's true, then there could not be any one test appropriate for *all* hyperactive students. And of course, if one wants to look closely at the idea of hyperreactivity, one must conclude that different kids will react differently in different situations. Therefore, it is extremely unlikely that any group of hyperreactive children would all be the same either. In summation, there may be tests which are appropriate to behaviors but not to labels (Figure 3.1).

The alternative to labels is to look at the characteristics of each student. If the student can't write well, then you shouldn't give a written

24

Label	Behaviors Described
Exceptional	All Kinds
Learning Disabled	Hyperactive and Hypoactive
Hyperactive	Hyperactive and Hyperreactive
Hyperreactive	Situational Behavior

Figure 3.1

The descriptive power of labels.

spelling test. If the student can't attend to written work for longer than 10 minutes, then you shouldn't give a 15-minute written test. This means that a teacher must be able to analyze the requirements of the test and compare them to the kid's characteristics. Figure 3.2 is a simplified example of comparing a child to a test. In the example, the test's purpose is to find out what the student does and does not know about history. Ideally the child will only fail those test items with historical information he doesn't know. But the analysis indicates that the student may actually fail an item because of a decoding problem, not a history problem. In other words, an academic characteristic of the child has changed the test from a history test to a reading test. It may seem overwhelming to compare all students to all tests (especially since student characteristics will not remain stable), but the alternative is to risk not evaluating what you think you're evaluating. The decision as to which tests are appropriate to which students can be made only by looking at the characteristics of both the students and the tests. The label "MR" does not describe a functional set of kid characteristics. The label "History Test" does not describe a functional set of test characteristics.

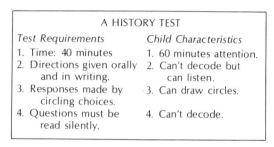

A HISTORY TEST	
Test Requirements	*Child Characteristics*
1. Time: 40 minutes	1. 60 minutes attention.
2. Directions given orally and in writing.	2. Can't decode but can listen.
3. Responses made by circling choices.	3. Can draw circles.
4. Questions must be read silently.	4. Can't decode.

Figure 3.2

Comparing a student to a test.

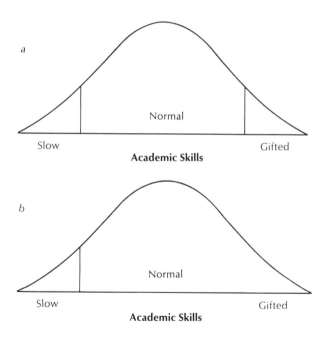

Figure 3.3

The relationship of handicapped to normal students on the variable of academic achievement.

What is Appropriate for the Task?

Teachers must also select or develop tests which are appropriate to task objectives. A test of motor ability is not appropriate to a reading class. In terms of appropriateness, difficulty arises at the time when the objectives are selected. The history test described in Figure 3.2 was inappropriate because it sampled behaviors other than history. It might also be inappropriate if it sampled things about history which the student had no need to know. When a teacher asks the question, What should I teach? she is also asking, What does the kid need to know?

The extent to which instructional objectives are different for special children than for normal children is hard to determine. In fact, it's given surprisingly little thought by special educators. This is particularly unfortunate when you consider that the majority of special education students are mildly handicapped and most of them are only considered deviant because of their failure to meet certain academic objectives. A mentally retarded student who can read, write, spell, do math, and socialize normally would never be identified in the first place. Most states list academic deficits as basis for the identification of learning disabilities (Mercer, Forgnone,

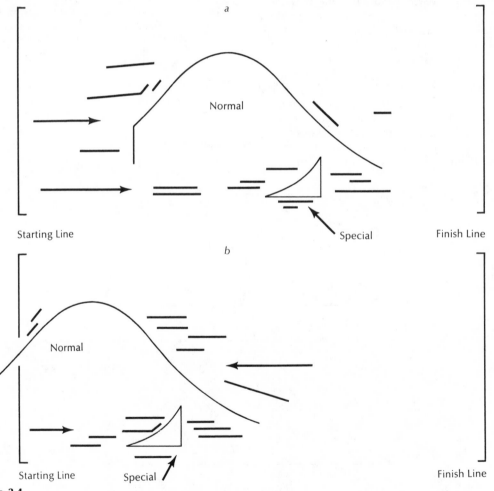

Figure 3.4

Two ways of helping special children catch up.

& Wolking, 1976). It may therefore be possible to "cure" learning disabilities by remediating academics. If the purpose of special education is to "cure," then implied within that purpose is the idea that handicapped kids must be taught to do what normal kids do as well as normal kids do it.

numerous efficient means of instruction but these methods were quickly adopted by regular education. So rather than just accelerating the slow students, new technology has advanced the entire curve (Figure 3.5). Today's handicapped students are doing more things than they did a decade ago, but they are still at the left of

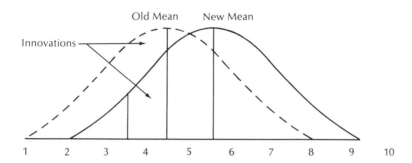

Figure 3.5

The effect of improved education on the normal curve.

In the distribution of academic skills (Figure 3.3a), special education students are at the extremes. The handicapped student is well below the n. m and the gifted student is well above it. For the purpose of this example, we can disregard the gifted child because he can already do what normal children can do, if we consider gifted to be high on the distribution of academic skills. (There are, of course, gifted students who score low on distributions of academic skills. These students would be considered gifted according to some other criterion such as adaptive behavior, IQ scores, or measures of talent.) So for the handicapped, the distribution in Figure 3.3b is most descriptive. Special students are behind—we must help them catch up.

There are only two ways to help someone catch up if he is behind. One is to make him go faster (Figure 3.4a). The other is to make the kid who is ahead go slower (Figure 3.4b). Both systems would work, but the second doesn't seem likely to obtain wide acceptance. Most educators would rather make the slower kids speed up, but that is hard to do as long as the model for academic achievement is a normal curve. The normal distribution *requires* a lower half. In the past, special education has developed

the distribution. As long as the mean of a normal distribution is considered to be the desired level of academic ability, there will always be handicapped students.

An alternative model would involve setting minimal objectives which all students should meet. Figure 3.6a shows a hypothetical distribution of decoding skill with a mean of 5. But suppose it was found that in order to survive in society, a child must actually be able to decode at the 6 level. (In other words, an average score on the test doesn't guarantee a child can read.) The goal would then be to raise all students to competency and, in the process, to destroy the normal curve (Figure 3.6b). In Figure 3.6b, even the student who scores lowest is not considered handicapped because all students have scored above the competency level. An efficient learning situation is one in which the distribution on important objectives is *not* normal (Davis, 1973). The goal of instruction should be to destroy the normal curve by trying to get *all* students to score high on the posttest. Many special educators do exactly the opposite. These special educators guarantee a normal distribution by engaging in activities which inhibit their students from reaching competency.

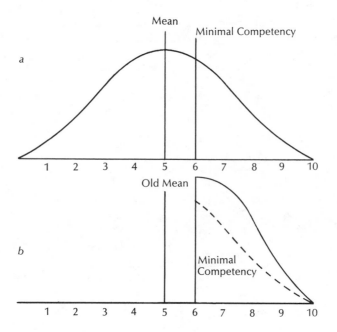

Figure 3.6

Efficient instruction destroys the normal curve.

Limiting Curriculum

If special education implies special instruction, then the curriculum of the special classroom must vary from that in the regular classroom. Logically, this means the curriculum for the handicapped student should be limited with the goal of helping the student learn faster (because he is behind and considered special because of it). There are at least five models for limiting curriculum which are currently popular, some of which actually guarantee that the special education student will remain behind.

Model A: One Small Step at a Time

In this model, the goal is to teach the same objectives as those in the regular class, but slower. The idea is that if special students can't learn as fast, teachers should teach them slowly. The result is that the special student doesn't get exposed to parts of the curriculum as early as the normal student. In the case of EMR students, the time lag is several years. So if a regular student is exposed to multiplication facts in the fourth grade, the EMR student may not confront them until the ninth grade. Of course, EMR students don't live five years longer than the rest of us, or go to school five years longer, so they emerge from the system behind, which is the way they went in. On the surface, this is a ridiculous model for helping academically deficient students. However, it isn't uncommon to hear teachers say that academically handicapped students need to "move slowly, one step at a time." Actually, they need to go like mad to catch up.

Using Model A, a teacher will decide what to teach by comparing her special children to objectives which are appropriate for younger, normally achieving children.

Model B: The Parallel Curriculum

One day, two of the authors were out looking at schools for the retarded and they came across a high-school program. The program's director announced with great pride that his was the first high school for the retarded in Arizona to have a total parallel curriculum. The term *parallel curriculum* probably has many different meanings, but in this case it meant that for each curricular area covered in the regular high-school program there was a corresponding area in the special high school. If the regular students have music, the special students have music. The catch is that the two groups have different music objectives. In the area of industrial arts, for example, the regular high-school students were learning mechanical drawing; the special students were learning to run a drill press. "How did you set your objectives?" Dr. Kaplan asked. "Easy," the director replied, "I've checked and that's what my retarded people do when they graduate." And he was probably right, because that is what he prepares them to do.

The parallel curriculum gives the special student skills, but different ones than those held by the so-called normal student. One result of the parallel curriculum is that there are fewer employment alternatives for the special student. This results in the data which support the whole process through a classic example of circular reasoning.

Using Model B, a teacher decides what to teach by comparing the students to a list of objectives which represent the traditional areas of content, but which are totally different from those taught to regular students.

Model C: But You Can't Expect As Much

This is a lowering of criteria model. In the "you can't expect as much" model, special students are given the same objectives as the regular students but are not expected to perform them

as well. For example, many spelling books have weekly word lists which are divided into two parts, basic words and supplemental words. Using the same spelling book, a teacher might require a regular student to master both lists, but require the special education student to master only the basic words. In this case, both students meet the objective of finishing the book, but one will have finished 100% of it while the other will have finished only 50% of it. Other examples frequently come up when establishing criteria for criterion-referenced tests. A teacher may find that successful readers can read consonant–vowel–consonant nonsense trigrams at a rate of 80 per minute, but then she sets the goal for special students at 64 per minute because they have IQs of 80. The result is that the students never completely master a task because they are exposed to a "short fat" curriculum (Figure 3.7).

Using Model C, the teacher decides what to teach the special child by comparing him to objectives which have reduced levels of criteria. Frequently this means a child will never completely master a task because the teacher has decided he is already doing the best that can be expected for a handicapped child.

Model D: They Don't Need It

Another sure way to limit curriculum is to cut out parts of it. This can be done in two ways. In the "they don't need it" model, a whole area

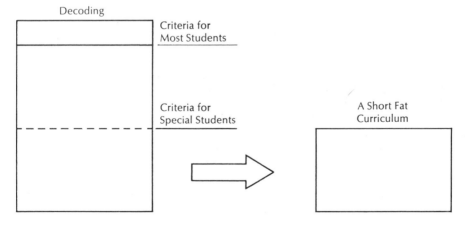

Figure 3.7
Short fat curriculum.

of content may be dropped from a special student's education. Dropping the so-called frills from a student's program has come to be known as a resource room phenomenon because in order to schedule students into resource rooms, it is often necessary to cut out some other part of his daily routine. A cross between this model and Model C is sometimes found in which special children are taught only low level basic skills and then spend the rest of their academic careers in shop, chorus, and physical education. In either case, this method of limiting the curriculum hinges upon a value judgment which is made in favor of one curricular area and against another.

Using Model D, a teacher decides what to teach the student by making a value judgment and deciding what should or shouldn't be taught. Once an area has been selected for instruction, the other models may be applied to it.

Model E: Cutting the Clutter

This model is something like Model D but it is more task oriented. In the "cutting the clutter" model, the teacher first recognizes all of the subtasks of a particular skill or content area. The teacher then determines (through researching, asking, or reading) which of the subtasks are not essential. By dropping nonessential subtasks, time is saved for teaching the essential ones to *full* criteria. This is the task analytical approach, and it is intended to slim down the total task while keeping the essential subtasks intact. Figure 3.8 shows the task of decoding broken into six subtasks (there are many more). Of the six, two are not essential, and the curriculum can be limited by getting rid of them so that the student needn't waste time working on them. The problem with this model is that there is a lot of disagreement over what is and what is not an essential subtask. Nearly every standardized reading test has a subtest in which the kids divide words into syllables as they are divided in the dictionary. (For example: *but/ter*). Many reading teachers don't think that dividing words has anything to do with reading and don't teach it to their students (Waugh & Howell, 1975). Their students score lower on the reading tests which have syllabication subtests because

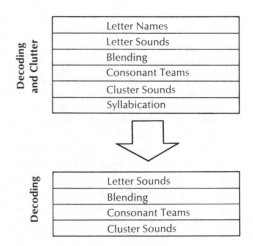

Figure 3.8

A tall skinny curriculum.

they don't teach that subskill.

Using Model E, the teacher decides what to teach the child by analyzing the content and selecting only those subtasks which are essential. Of the five models, we believe this model is the best, because the student is not deprived of any essential content and is given the extra time needed to master (reach the same criteria as everyone else) all essential content. Time is saved by excluding nonessentials. Model E is based on the idea that some things do not need to be taught. The other models are based upon the idea that only special students need not master certain tasks. While that attitude might be expected from members of the general public, it's hard to accept from those who should be advocates of the handicapped—special educators. Still, each of the five models can be found in operation even with students who are only considered exceptional because of academic deficiencies. The task analytical model is advantageous because (1) it allows the special student to master everything which is essential for competition with other students, (2) it is based on the analysis and judgment of the tasks, not the kids, and (3) by raising special students to the criteria of regular students, there is no built-in guarantee of future failure—many students considered special because of academic or behavioral problems would be "cured."

Criterion-Referenced Tests

Once a content area has been selected and objectives written, the teacher can then decide what to teach by comparing the student to the objectives. The most direct means of comparison is the criterion-referenced test as will be discussed in Chapter 8. The resulting data can give a precise picture of exactly what additional things the student needs to learn to master a task.

Norm-referenced tests (NRTs) compare a student's performance to the performance of other students. An example of a normative statement might be, "Ralph is in the eighth grade but he must only be reading at the fourth level, because his test scores show him to be at the thirtieth percentile for his age." Criterion-referenced tests (CRTs) compare a student's performance to a specific task. An example of a criterion statement might be, "Although Ralph can read vowel sounds accurately, his rate is only 20 correct per minute; he must read vowel sounds correctly at a rate of 60 per minute in order to use them efficiently in decoding."

If a teacher is interested in teaching a student tasks, then CRTs are of the most value. In planning instruction, the teacher should try to get information which can actually be of use in instruction. Normative information is of little value, as it relates the student only to other students. Of course CRTs are only of value if they are well designed.

Designing CRTs involves two steps. First, a behavioral objective is written containing a statement of what behavior the student will exhibit and to what criteria. Second, the materials necessary for the student to exhibit the behavior are assembled. If the objective is not important or not precisely stated, the CRT loses validity. Similarly, validity is lost if the student must engage in behaviors to pass the test which are not the same as those required by the original task. For example, many published spelling tests ask the student to identify words which are misspelled. In reality, that's a proofreading skill which isn't the same kind of spelling which people do most of the time. The recognition-of-errors format is adopted in order to allow teachers to give the test to large numbers of students at the same time.

It is not possible to make the blanket statement that for diagnostic purposes all CRTs are better than all NRTs. Instead it must be said that good CRTs are better than NRTs or bad CRTs. It would be easy to develop (and no doubt someone will) a criterion-referenced perceptual-motor test which is intended to diagnose reading problems. The resulting instrument may have content validity as a perceptual-motor test but not construct validity as a reading test, because the relationship of perceptual-motor training to academics is not established in spite of the many existing testing instruments in the area. (See Appendix A, Unit 4.) The ability of educators to get off-task and test the unnecessary hasn't done much damage to the NRT sales, and it probably won't hurt CRT sales. Still, the diagnostic superiority of criterion-referenced measurement over norm-referenced will remain theoretically sound even if test developers fail to keep it operationally sound.

In terms of deciding what to teach, the obvious solution is to teach what isn't known and not waste time on what is known. The best CRTs test only relevant behaviors. These behaviors are subtasks of a terminal educational objective. Consequently, the development of CRTs is dependent on task analysis. The ability to accurately isolate and sequence essential subtasks is basic to developing diagnostically useful CRTs. Once a task has been broken down and its essential subtasks listed, a CRT can be developed by writing a performance objective for each subtask. Students can then be asked to take the CRT in order to decide what they need to be taught and what they already know.

The movement toward using CRTs for diagnosis in special education has been rapid. The field of special education has been frustrated with normative comparison for a number of reasons, not the least of which is that when normative comparisons are made, there *has* to be a population of low scores. Occasionally students who score low on NRTs are placed in special classes when they are competent in life but get low scores on tests. This has been disproportionately true of children from racial, ethnic, linguistic, or financial subgroups. In view of these discrepancies, it now appears that the tests upon which constructs such as intelligence are based may need revision.

New tests of intelligence have evolved which sample the adaptive behavior (social behavior, self-care behavior, home behavior, etc.) of students. These adaptive behavior scales measure behavioral areas which are very similar to the content areas of curriculum plans for the retarded. In other words, the psychologist and teacher both look at the same behavior (for example, the ability to dress oneself), but for different reasons. The psychologist is trying to find a stable and permanent deficiency, and the teacher is trying to find something to change.

If the definition of intelligence is based on trainable behaviors, then the idea that intelligence is a permanent condition must be reviewed. There is a possibility that criterion-referenced adaptive behavior scales could be used to redefine mental deficiency (Baumeister & Muma, 1975). Eventually, these criterion-referenced scales could be used to remediate socio-cultural retardation in much the same way criterion-referenced reading tests can be used to change reading instruction. The prospect of "curing" or "preventing" sociocultural retardation has already received support through studies by Heber et al. (1972), and Becker and Engelmann (1974).

4

Deciding
How to Teach

Evaluating Ability

Deciding how to teach a child is difficult. It involves evaluating the interaction of the student and the task. How a student should be taught raises the time-honored prospect of recognizing the strengths and weaknesses within the child and adjusting instruction to complement or compensate for them.

In trying to evaluate how a student should be taught, the field of special education has generated for itself a major philosophical controversy revolving around the ability or inability of evaluators to recognize and cash in on patterns of human learning and perception.

The first question some evaluators try to answer through testing is What type of kid is this? These evaluators are engaging in diagnosis for the purpose of identifying "types" of students who will do best in "types" of programs. Standard statements heard today in special classrooms are "He's an auditory learner," "They both need kinesthetic feedback," "She needs a quiet setting with no distractions." And following close behind these evaluative statements are intervention statements such as "We must strenghten his visual sequential memory," "We

must remove them from a purely auditory program," "We must train her ability to sort out relevant stimuli."

One of the assumptions underlying these statements is that learning processes (or abilities) can be measured. Another is that they can be trained. Whether to try to test and train abilities or to test and train skills has been viewed as the most important concern facing special education (Hammill, 1976). It is a concern about which many special educators are finding it necessary to take sides. The positions taken by both sides have been contrasted briefly in Chapter 1. But it may be valuable to take a closer look at some of the assumptions underpinning the evaluation of abilities.

To clarify matters, let us state that the authors are not supporters of ability training as it is currently applied in special education. It is our belief that special educators have gone well beyond the boundaries of effectiveness in their speculation about peculiarities in student thinking. We are reminded of a somewhat infamous student teacher who, after many lectures on the importance of individual thinking processes and learning, accounted for the off-task behavior of a child with this statement: "When working, he frustrates easily, and he sometimes is distracted by his own thoughts" (Nelson, 1976). It seems more likely that distinctions reside in the environment.

Mann (1975) has referred to the differential assessment of processing functions (abilities) as psycho-educational evaluation. Because it depends upon many typically medical assumptions, the system is also known as the psycho-medical model of evaluation. Those who distinguish between the psycho-medical and psycho-educational models say the psycho-medical model is a deficit model which assumes pathology—a sick brain. The psycho-educational system, on the other hand, uses an individualistic model—a different brain, but not necessarily a sick one. Both assume the cause and cure of student failure reside within the child. Basically the two are synonymous in that both models hinge on the assumption that cognitive and perceptual abilities can be isolated, measured, and/or trained.

The isolation and training of abilities were popular topics in psychology in the eighteenth century. At that time mental entities such as passion, courage, and intelligence were proposed as recognizable discrete human characteristics (Heidbreder, 1961). The idea behind ability training is that the brain can be exercised and developed something like a muscle; this came to be referred to as faculty psychology (Mann, 1975). In the field of education, faculty psychology accounted for practices such as memorizing verse in order to develop a disciplined mind.

There are three factors on which ability training depends. They are (1) the quality of the model's assumptive basis, (2) the tools the model relies upon, and (3) the model's educational utility. The second and third factors are easy to analyze if one is fairly knowledgeable about the research on current evaluative instrumentation and educational interventions. The problem is that instrumentation and interventions change. This means that an analysis of ability training from only the second and third points might become quickly dated. For example, Hammill and Wiederholt (1972) make the statement that "most of the subtests of the Wechsler Intelligence Scale for children or the Developmental Test of Visual Perception have reliabilities too low to permit confident interpretation (r's less than .80),

thus making profile analysis untenable" (p. 7). This statement is true, but it could quickly change if an improved Frostig test suddenly came on the market. Therefore, teachers need to prepare themselves to evaluate the new tests which are constantly appearing on the scene. You are advised to read the criticisms of current evaluative practices by authors such as Mann (1975), Waugh (1975), Bateman (1972), and Hammill and Larsen (1974b). You are also encouraged to develop the skills needed to judge new instrumentation. An entire generation of students went from first to eighth grade before criticism of the ITPA became widespread.

Aptitude Treatment Interactions

While tools and outcomes may vary, the basic assumptions of a model can't change too much without redefining the model. The ability training model is dependent on several assumptions, one of which is the existence of predictable aptitude by treatment interactions (ATI) (Cronbach, 1967; Glaser, 1972). ATI is the idea that individuals with certain abilities (aptitudes) will behave differently in certain programs (treatments) than in others. The idea is widely accepted because it is logical, but using the idea is harder than accepting it.

Educators have acknowledged the individualistic nature of learning for a long time. For example:

> The best method for one cannot be the best for all. There is not one mind reproduced in millions of copies, for all of which one rule will suffice; there are many differing minds, each of which needs, for its adequate education, to be considered to some extent by itself. (Thorndike, 1917, p. 67)

This quotation is representative of the modern thoughts and statements of special educators even though it was written in 1917. The age of the statement and the frequency with which it's paraphrased today point out the failure which the educational community has experienced in reaching one of its most cherished goals—individualization. Calls for the individualization of instruction, the tailoring of programming to student characteristics, and the meaningful matching of students to methods have filled the journals and teacher lounges of every generation;

they have become the hallmark of special education. Unfortunately, attempts to answer these calls have usually fallen flat.

Obviously all students do not respond to instruction in the same way. While many causes for these differences have been identified for severely handicapped children, there remains a sizable population of students who are slow to learn but illustrate no gross characteristics which obviously cause their failure. The blame for inconsistencies between expected performance and actual performance has often been laid on the influence of one or more personological variables (variables within the person). These variables are referred to as *aptitudes*. Some educators have made the claim that instruction can be adjusted to account for the influence of these aptitudes. The principal thrust of these claims is that certain types of students will learn more efficiently if they are treated in certain ways. ATI is not to be confused with selection of different goals for different students (such as placing some individuals in college prepatory programs and others in industrial arts). And it should not be confused with the selection of treatments under the assumption that those treatments will be more efficient than will other treatments. When special educators test for an individual's strengths and weaknesses, they are attempting to make use of ATIs. For example, "auditory learner" is an aptitude statement; "phonetic program" is a treatment statement; "auditory learners need phonetic programs" is an ATI statement.

The idea of ATI is that a certain trait of a student will cause that student to react to a specific type of instructional treatment dif-

ferently than would a student who did not have the trait. This reasoning underlies such common educational practices as homogeneous grouping, tracking, and special class placement. Cronbach (1957) first used the term *aptitude treatment interaction* (ATI) to describe a process by which certain aptitudes might tend to consistently predict the achievement of a student in a given instructional setting. He states that

> an aptitude, in this context, is a complex of personal characteristics that accounts for an individual's end state after a particular educational treatment, i. e., that determines what he learns, how much he learns, or how rapidly he learns" (1967, p. 23).

Although belief in ATI may be widespread, the empirical evidence of its existence is not so abundant. Two reviews of ATI research in the late 1960s indicated that attempts by teachers to make use of ATIs in their classrooms were premature (Cronbach & Snow, 1969; Bracht, 1969). In their exhaustive work on the nature of ATI, Cronbach and Snow arrived at the following conclusion: "There are no solidly established ATI relations even on a laboratory scale, and no real sign of any hypothesis ready for application and development" (p. 193). They went on to forecast another decade of research before truly functional developments would be made in the ATI field.

Those ATIs which have been found are usually of a basic nature; that is, they reflect the need for stringent laboratory control (Berliner & Cahen, 1973; Bracht, 1970). In addition, many ATI studies have contained faults such as inadequate analysis, poorly stated hypotheses, and a tendency toward trial and error investigation. Cron-

Program Variables

A (Phonics)	B (Whole Word)
Total Students 1,000	Total Students 1,000
Average Pretest = 2 Grade	Average Pretest = 2 Grade
Average Posttest = 3.5 Grade	Average Posttest = 3 Grade
Average Gain = 1.5 Years	Average Gain = 1 Year
BEST	WORST

Figure 4.1

A typical method comparison study.

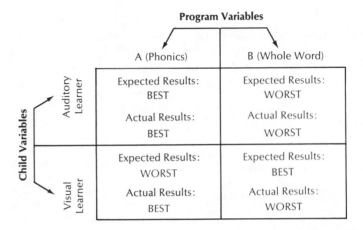

Figure 4.2

An ATI study.

bach and Snow advised, "These faults are the mark of a field where investigators are just learning to crawl" (p. 179). Salomon (1972) adds that in many studies "two treatments are designed, and a large number of aptitude measures tossed in with the hope that some may lead to an ATI" (p. 374).

Prior to the widespread interest in ATI, most educational research was of the horse race variety. That is, groups of students were placed in different methods and then observed to see which method was best. Figure 4.1 shows a typical study comparing phonic reading program A with whole-word program B. The phonic program wins as usual (Chall, 1967).

One problem with this kind of study is that even though phonic programs are best for most students, there are always a few students who will not do well in phonics. So a different type of study has evolved which looks at both program variables and child variables. Figure 4.2 illustrates a typical ATI study, the results of which *do not* indicate an ATI taking place between auditory/visual learners and phonic/whole-word programs. Two explanations why the study may not have been successful are (1) the aptitudes weren't accurately measured and/or (2) the treatments weren't really different.

The choice of the variables which are investigated has a direct influence on the results of the studies. As Shulman (1970) notes, "ATIs are likely to remain an empty phase as long as apti-

tudes are measured by micrometers and environments by divining rod" (p. 374). This has been particularly obvious in the development of tests to be used as measures of specific ability. During the 1960s, a large number of evaluative tools were developed with the intention of measuring modality preferences as aptitudes. The most frequently mentioned sensory modalities were the visual, auditory, and kinesthetic. While the idea of modality preference is not new (Galton, 1883), it experienced a revival with the widespread interest in learning disabilities. Out of the area of learning disabilities has come a preoccupation with testing instruments such as the Marianne Frostig Developmental Test of Visual Perception and the Illinois Test of Psycholinguistic Abilities (ITPA). These instruments are intended to measure aptitudes which relate to instruction. Underlying each is the assumption that psychological processes and/or perceptual characteristics relevant to instruction can be measured in students (Mann, 1975). Many people who believe in these instruments also feel that instruction can be tailored to students on the basis of the test scores. The resulting instructional programs can be lumped loosely under the headings of ability training.

Several authors have suggested that children with certain perceptual characteristics are less able to make use of code emphasis (sometimes called auditory) reading programs (Dolch & Bloomster, 1937; Dunn & Dunn, 1974; Myers & Hammill, 1969; Wepman, 1960). In spite of the general lack of proof, statements similar to the following have been repeated for at least the last 50 years. "Matt has good auditory skills and needs a phonics program" or "Joe is low in auditory ability but high in the visual areas; he should be placed in a whole word program."

The existence of either auditory or visual aptitude treatment interactions has enjoyed almost no empirical support. Yet numerous reading methods, materials, and teacher training courses are based on belief in this particular ATI.

There is little evidence available to indicate that students placed into treatments on the basis of their scores on specific modality measures benefit academically from the experience. Studies investigating the use of the ITPA are representative of this conclusion. A few ITPA studies are reviewed here because, as Mann (1975) points out, the ITPA is the best of the process tests, and therefore of most interest.

Hammill and Larsen (1974a) reviewed 38 studies of the ITPA. They concluded that training programs based on ITPA scores remain nonvalidated. This lack of validation has been particularly evident in studies seeking to establish ATIs through the use of the ITPA. For example, Bateman (1971a) compared the learning of students who scored 9 months higher on auditory subtests than on visual subtests of the ITPA to students who scored higher on visual subtests than on auditory subtests. The subjects classified as auditory learners were placed into an auditory reading method (Lippincott); those classified as visual learners into a visual reading method (Scott Foresman). Half of each modality group was placed in each reading treatment. Bateman found the auditory reading treatment to be superior to the visual treatment with all students regardless of their modality preference (the same results as our hypothetical study in Figure 4.2). These findings were later supported by Waugh (1971) who selected 9 subjects from a population of 166 elementary school students. On the auditory subtests of the ITPA, the 9 subjects each scored 12 or more standard score points (2 standard deviations) above the mean of their performance on the visual subtests of the ITPA. In spite of their extreme scores on the auditory subtests, the subjects did not perform any better on auditory tasks than they did on visual tasks.

It may be unfortunate that the ATI field has become associated to some degree with measures of modality preference. The association is apt to be degrading for the ATI field given the conclusion reached by Waugh (1971):

> The premise that specific abilities can be identified and remediated has not been supported by research evidence. Another example has been added to the long history of failure to find practical uses for measures of specific abilities. (p. 208)

The ATI issue is intriguing and the promise which it holds for instruction is great. It is not difficult to understand the interest shown in ATI by researchers. What is difficult to explain, however, is the widespread rush of special educators to put into classroom practice something that cannot be reliably produced in the laboratory. One explanation is that special teachers really aren't interested in the idea of ATI at all; a quick survey will probably reveal that few are even familiar with the term. It is equally unlikely that many can state the basic assumptions upon which ability testing relies. Their interest lies not in the idea but in the tools. ATI, as it has been presented to the field of special education, offers a "cookbook" path to instruction which is extremely appealing to practitioners. The emphasis is on finding "types" of students through the use of the various tests. These types of students are then matched to programs which seem logically to compliment their particular label. In reality, teachers should be skeptical of any program which is titled *Methods for* ____ (LD, MR, BD, EMH). Similarly, they should demand validation studies for testing instruments which try to summarize (or profile) children's cognitive or perceptual functioning.

If a teacher really intends to make use of ATI in teaching, then certain measurement requirements must be met: (1) the teacher must be able to accurately measure aptitudes; (2) the teacher must be able to recognize treatments which will interact with these aptitudes; and (3) if the teacher decides to train aptitudes himself ("We need to strengthen the student's auditory sequential memory"), then a variety of instructional requirements and assumptions must also be met (Mann, 1975).

In dealing with aptitudes, there has been a tendency in special education to define them with the test designed to study them. The reasoning goes something like this: "I believe there is such a thing as form constancy—therefore I have devised a paper and pencil test involving tasks logically related to form constancy. I can now tell when a kid has a form constancy problem because the kid will score low on my test."

Ample evidence exists to indicate that researchers, both inside and outside special education, have indeed tailored the definition of aptitudes to fit their own needs and/or frames of reference. For teachers, the problem is finding aptitude measures that are good evaluative tools. Such measures must be both reliable and highly predictive of future task performance. Unfortunately, many test scores are too narrow to generalize beyond the laboratory, while others may be too broad to produce the specific results needed for influencing instruction.

Definitional problems in the ATI field are not limited to aptitudes. Treatments have frequently been defined in broad terms, too. In the case of treatments, many of the measurement problems inherent in the assessment of abilities should not exist because treatments seem open to view in ways which cognitive processes are not. But treatments may not be as observable as they seem.

Many researchers seem to assume that student abilities don't change although treatments do. In reality, it is quite possible that aptitudes are not stable at all and that the relationship of abilities to treatments may vary a lot more than anyone would ever wish. For example, initial success at most tasks is highly related to general ability. If treatments do not last across time, then general ability may be the only aptitude related to mastering the task. In order to avoid the confounding influence of general intelligence, it has been suggested that ATI studies take place over long periods of time. Unfortunately, the instrumentation necessary to identify individuals who are unique with respect to specific abilities for long periods of time is not available. This is particularly true of psycho-educational testing instruments, many of which have low test-retest reliabilities (Ysseldyke & Salvia, 1974).

Another consideration pertaining to treatments is that the tasks themselves are not one-dimensional. Any given task, learning multiplication facts for example, may require using a variety of cognitive abilities from the time the

task is first attempted until it is mastered (Tobias, 1976). This means that learning a task may require auditory abilities at one time and visual abilities at another, or as already mentioned, initially high general ability followed by some form of specific ability (Figures 4.3, 4.4). The use of ATI in instruction assumes long-term, parallel relationships between tasks and aptitudes. These relationships may not exist.

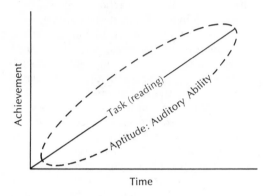

Figure 4.3

ATI assumes a long-term, parallel relationship between tasks and aptitudes.

Because treatments vary, their precise definition is difficult. Classroom treatments are particularly hard to define as any number of influences may serve to alter a treatment from day to day, such as the teacher's mood, the sequence of the instructional material, the type of presentation, the amount of time spent on the task, the reliance on memory, the types of visual cues used, and other characteristics (Rhetts, 1974).

It's possible that currently popular treatments may not be sufficiently unique from one another to interact with specific abilities at all. Few teachers would be willing to subject students to treatments contrived in such a way as to be different at the expense of being educational. Yet the most efficient model for using ATI demands significantly different treatments. The indications are that radically different programs don't sell in the conservative school market. Even if a teacher were able to recognize an auditory learner, there is no scale available that will tell the teacher just how "auditory" or how "visual" any given program is.

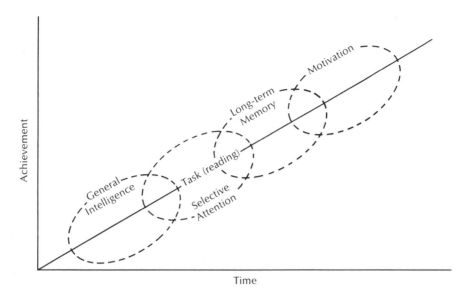

Figure 4.4

Aptitudes may only play an important role during a small part of task acquisition.

An Alternative to Prediction

In deciding *how* to teach kids tasks, special educators have become bogged down in attempts to predict what kids will do best in what programs. In many cases, these predictions have far surpassed the reliability of existing testing instruments and the validity of learning theories. As the science of ATI evolves, it is possible that both the reliability and validity of interaction prediction will improve. In the meantime, educators should be asking if there is an alternative strategy for matching students to methods—and there is.

At present, the best way to match a student to a method is to place the student in the method and see how she does. In the past, this technique was not used because the tools were not available to evaluate *quickly* the effectiveness of the placement. The risk of misplacing a student for months or even weeks wasn't acceptable. Due to the advances in formative evaluation and applied behavioral analysis, which will be discussed later in this chapter, this is no longer the case. It is now possible to place a student in a program and decide in a matter of days as to the validity of the placement. Essentially, this procedure is ATI backwards. Instead

of looking for aptitudes to interact with treatments, the teacher looks for treatments to interact with aptitudes. The result is a movement away from attempts to measure and define abilities and toward the exact measurement of student behavior and tasks.

Using applied behavior analysis in the assessment of academic growth and the selection of appropriate curriculum is not new. The essential component of the system is accurate, continuous measurement of student behavior. The resulting data can be analyzed for evidence of acceptable or unacceptable growth toward a specific objective, and comparisons can easily be made between a student's growth in one treatment as opposed to another treatment. Much of the classroom application of this method was developed by Dr. Ogden Lindsley under the label of *precision teaching* (Kunzelmann et al., 1970) and has been elaborated on by White and Haring (1976).

To give a basic example, Figure 4.5 shows a student's reading behavior in two treatments. Each dot represents a timed oral reading test showing the number of words read in 1 minute. In this case, the student is in each treatment for 1 week, and the superiority of treatment *B* over treatment *A* is obvious. This is a type of evaluation in which data is collected throughout the instruction and used to make decisions to change the instruction.

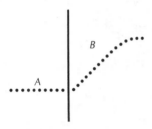

Figure 4.5

Increase in reading performance.

Table 4.1 shows the process of formative evaluation, and it differs dramatically from traditional evaluation, which is called summative evaluation. Summative evaluation takes place after the instruction.

Table 4.1 lists a few of the characteristics of posttest only, pretest-posttest, and continuous measurement. The most frequently used method of summative evaluation is undoubtedly the posttest only system. In this system, the teacher teaches a unit and then tests. The resulting test score may or may not indicate the effectiveness of the instruction; there is no way to tell because there is no comparison to make. Similarly, because the results are after the fact, the testing has no diagnostic implications.

The pretest-posttest system is considerably better than the posttest only system. By using a pretest, the teacher can screen-out students for whom a particular lesson is probably not applicable. The system doesn't actually affect the resulting instruction, it only controls the type of student who receives the instruction. In addition, it allows the teacher to calculate the student's gain by subtracting the pretest score from the posttest score. However, in actual practice, gain scores mean almost nothing, particularly those calculated by comparing a student's scores on norm-referenced tests (Tallmadge & Horst, 1974; Cronbach & Furby, 1970).

When a teacher decides to teach a unit and administers a pretest, he is merely summing up the kid's knowledge of the material prior to that point (Figure 4.6). The posttest does the same thing and must be compared to the pretest in order to obtain the gain score. The pretest score is summative, the posttest score is summative, and the gain score is summative. They all reflect past instruction and may give no indication of future performance.

In Figure 4.7a, the score for one test is supplied. Whether or not the student is improving or getting worse can't be told from one summation of her total performance.

In Figure 4.7b, two posttests have been added to the design, which increases the descriptive power of the testing. However, there is still a lot of slack in the system, and a teacher could easily make the wrong interpretation of the data.

In Figure 4.7c, a series of tests has been given

Table 4.1

Characteristics of Three Evaluative Procedures

	Posttest Only	Pretest Posttest	Continuous
1. Type of evaluation	Summative	Summative	Formative
2. Students tested	All	All pretested Only those taught post-tested	All students tested until they reach criteria
3. Effect on instruction	None	Sort students who do or don't need instruction	Guides instruction by showing trends in learning
4. Result	Nonspecific After the fact	General gain scores After the fact	Gain plus learning trends

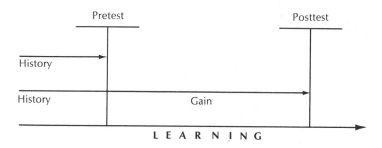

Figure 4.6

Determining gain.

and the ability to predict where the next score will fall is greatly increased. When enough data points are available, the importance of each individual test score is decreased. In Figure 4.7a, Test Score 1 is totally important. In Figure 4.7c, the importance of Test Score 1 is minimized, whereas the value of Line A is increased.

One advantage of using several data points to establish a trend (Line A) is that the trend becomes a predictor of the next data point. But if prediction is all teachers are interested in, then they might just as well use a one-shot achievement test which correlates highly to future test performance, that is, a test with high test-retest reliability coefficients. There are other uses for trends.

Figure 4.8a shows the typical pretest (1) posttest (2) evaluation. In this case it might be assumed that the student's acquisition of multiplication facts was shown in a smooth line connecting tests 1 and 2. However, by administering several tests between points 1 and 2, as

in Figure 4.8b, it can be seen that the learning may not have been so smooth.

In Figure 4.8b, it can be seen that no learning took place at all until the final stage of instruction. In this case, had the teacher been able to examine the learning trend (which was flat for some time), he could have taken steps to provide more effective instruction. In Figure 4.8c, the student actually made a greater gain than that indicated in 4.8b. Unfortunately, after learning the material, the student's performance fell. It doesn't matter why the performance fell; all that matters is that if a teacher had seen this decelerating trend he may have been able to stop it.

One last example. In Figure 4.9a, we see the data on a student's "talk out" behavior. The previous examples may have covered as much as a full year's instruction; this example is to show the dangers of summative evaluation, even for short periods of time. Note that the time period in Figure 4.9a is only 2 weeks (5 days data

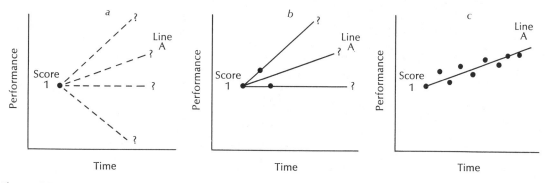

Figure 4.7

Descriptive power increases with the number of tests given.

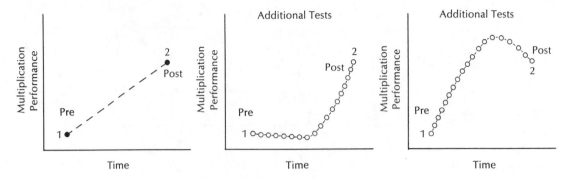

Figure 4.8

Three possible patterns of reaching the same posttest level.

per week) and that the number of "talk outs" increases routinely throughout each week. This is known as a "week effect" and it is very common in the school behavior of both teachers and students. The student is quiet on Mondays and loud on Fridays. In Figure 4.9b, the trend for talk outs was calculated only on the basis of point A (the first Monday) and point B (the last Friday); as a result, the behavior appears to be getting worse. Actually, on the average, the behavior is staying the same, as shown in Figure 4.9c.

Because formative evaluation allows the teacher to observe trends in how the student is learning, it can be used to guide instruction, even to the point of indicating which method is most effective for which student. Once a teacher has mastered formative evaluation, he can quickly compare the utility of various teaching methods, including those same methods associated with ATI studies. The difference in this case is that the evaluator doesn't look for audi-

tory and visual learners, but for auditory and visual reading programs. The child can then be tried out in both, and a decision can quickly be reached as to which is the most effective program for that student on that particular task. This type of decision is basic to diagnosis.

Although there are a lot of different treatments in the world, these treatments are all composed of a limited number of instructional variables combined in different fashions. For example, suppose a teacher wanted to devise eight different treatments, all of which were intended to teach a list of spelling words. Some common variables which influence the effectiveness of instruction are length of lessons, use of rewards, and mode of response. These three variables (there are many others) can be placed into a grid like that in Figure 4.10 and used to generate different treatments. The eight possible ways of varying a spelling lesson on just these three variables are these:

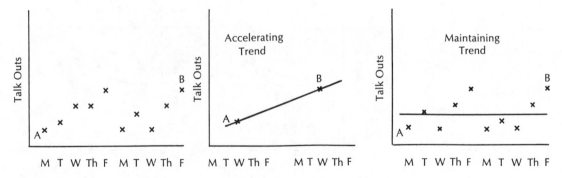

Figure 4.9

A week effect.

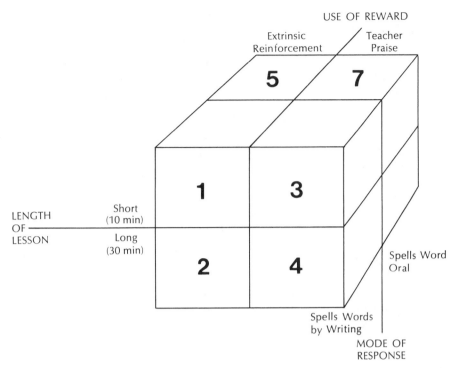

Figure 4.10

Common instructional variables.

1. Short Lesson, Extrinsic Reinforcer, Written Response
2. Long Lesson, Extrinsic Reinforcer, Written Response
3. Short Lesson, Teacher Praise, Written Response
4. Long Lesson, Teacher Praise, Written Response
5. Short Lesson, Extrinsic Reinforcer, Oral Response
6. Long Lesson, Extrinsic Reinforcer, Oral Response
7. Short Lesson, Teacher Praise, Oral Response
8. Long Lesson, Teacher Praise, Oral Response

It is reasonable to suspect that a student might do very well in one of these programs and not well at all in another.

Educators have had to learn to write specific behavioral objectives rather than general goals; they may also need to learn to be specific in describing treatments. It is an oversimplification to assume that a "visual" program is really any different from an "auditory" program. There are many instructional variables, task variables, and kid variables. Kid variables (abilities such as intellect, perceptual skills, past knowledge, etc.) are difficult to measure and hard to change. Task variables (prerequisite skills, cognitive operations, psychomotor operations, etc.) are stable, easier to isolate than kid variables, and can be changed. Instructional variables (teacher style, length of lesson, grouping of students, textbooks, etc.) are easy to observe and manipulate. Adjusting instructional variables is what teachers are paid to do. Considering that attempts to measure and change kid variables have been largely unsuccessful, maybe it's time to give them up, at least in the classroom. In place of attempting to guide instruction by training kid variables, teachers should begin paying attention to the instructional and task variables which they can actually control. This means continuously monitoring student progress while systematically varying instruction. In short, the way to find out how to teach the student is to teach the student in different ways and see which way is best by how well the student improves.

Choosing a Treatment

A teacher who is going to select a treatment to try on a student should be interested in making

Table 4.2

Best Guesses to Guide Initial Treatment Selection

First: Treatments which research has shown to be effective for groups of students.
Second: Treatments which make use of variables shown to be related to achievement.
Third: Treatments which make use of instruction shown to be related to learning.

the best possible choice. He should choose the treatment with the highest probability of being successful. As it turns out, there is quite a bit of information available indicating which types of interventions are usually the most effective. These interventions are the "best guesses" of what type of programming the students belongs in. Table 4.2 illustrates a hierarchy of best guesses which a teacher could use to select treatments.

Treatments Supported by Research

The first way to select a treatment is to go back to the horse race research described earlier. Some specific treatments are consistently shown to be better than others when tested on groups of students. By reviewing the literature according to subject area (reading research, math research, language research, etc.), it is possible to find studies which test the utility of published and original treatments. This body of research is invaluable to the teacher who is trying to decide how to teach a particular subject. For example, research consistently indicates the superiority of code emphasis programs for teaching decoding. If a student isn't decoding, the intervention with the highest probability of success is a code emphasis program. By using formative evaluation a teacher can quickly tell if a student is an exception to the code emphasis generalization.

If a child does not learn in one method that doesn't mean the teacher should throw out the method. Instead, the teacher should adapt the method. The treatment was originally selected because research had shown it to be an effective technique for most students. There is no reason to assume, however, that it cannot be made more effective. If the method is known to be a good one it makes more sense to try and modify it than to replace it with a method which is less effective.

Because there are unlimited numbers of ways to modify instruction, the teacher needs guidance. This guidance can be obtained by returning to the research literature and identifying variables which have been shown to relate to good instruction. The teacher should be able to make use of these variables to modify the unsuccessful treatment.

Instructional Variables Related to Achievement

In addition to studies on specific programs, there is another body of information of great importance. Many variables have been examined in order to determine the general characteristics of effective instruction. Some of these variables are consistently correlated to academic achievement. Rosenshine (1976) reviewed information on a series of variables which can be controlled by the classroom teacher. A competent teacher should be able to modify nearly any instructional program in order to accommodate these findings. The variables reported on by Rosenshine were (1) time spent, (2) content covered, (3) child work group, (4) teacher questions, (5) student reactions, and (6) teacher reactions. The conclusions reported on these variables are briefly summarized in Table 4.3. Many of these conclusions are limited to certain age groups and settings. Before trying to apply these conclusions the reader is advised to do additional reading beginning with Rosenshine (1976, p. 371), then Brophy and Good (1974), and Stallings and Kascovitz (1974).

Regarding the variables summarized in Table 4.3, the most interesting results reported by Rosenshine seem to be these:

1. The greater the emphasis on academics the greater the academic growth.
2. How a thing is taught (what method is used) is not as important as what is taught and how long it is taught.
3. Individualization alone is not sufficient to guarantee academic growth.
4. Adult feedback which is unrelated to a task (including praising the student) is negatively correlated to increased task achievement.

Table 4.3

Selected Summary of Conclusions Reported by Rosenshine (1976)

Variable	*General Conclusions*
1. Time Spent	1. Increased total time in school is related to increased achievement.
	2. Increased time spent on academics is related to increased academic achievement.
	3. Increased time spent on nonacademics (arts, music, play, classroom management, etc.) is related to decreased academic achievement.
2. Content Covered	1. Different programs covering different content produce different results.
	2. Opportunity to learn content is related to increased achievement.
	3. Teacher emphasis on content is related to increased achievement.
3. Child Work Groups	1. Unsupervised work is negatively correlated to achievement.
	2. Teacher working with 1 or 2 children is negatively correlated to achievement.
	3. Teacher working with small and large groups is positively correlated to achievement.
4. Teacher Questions	1. Direct academic questions are positively correlated to achievement.
	2. Open-ended and nonacademic questions are not correlated to achievement.
	3. Personal questions are negatively correlated to achievement.
5. Student Reactions	1. Student response to direct academic questions is positively correlated to achievement.
	2. Student response to nonacademic and open-ended questions is negatively correlated to achievement.
	3. There appears to be an interaction between socioeconomic status and the effect of giving incorrect answers.
6. Teacher Reactions	1. The topic of feedback (academic or nonacademic) is more important than the type of feedback (positive or negative).
	2. Positive feedback on nonacademic topics (student behavior or other tasks) is negatively correlated to achievement.
	3. There appears to be an interaction between socioeconomic status and the effect of feedback.

NOTE. From "Classroom Instruction" by B. Rosenshine. In N. L. Gage (Ed.), *Psychology of Teaching: The 77th Yearbook of the National Society for the Study of Education,* 1977. Copyright by the National Society for the Study of Education. Reprinted by permission.

One additional variable which has been found to relate to achievement is rate of presentation. If instruction is presented in a fast-paced manner, the result is less off-task behavior and more correct responses (Carnine, 1976). Fast-paced instruction also allows for an overall increase in both teacher and student responses. As long as the interactions between the teacher and student are "on task," this increase should correlate positively to achievement (Stallings & Kascovitz, 1974).

Each of these conclusions has implications for deciding how to teach the student. For example, it appears that the most influential variables are not method variables at all, but teacher variables. Therefore, selecting a good method in which to place a student could be less important than improving the teacher's use of feedback, questioning behavior, and scheduling policies.

When an instructional method is selected, that method should be specific to the instructional objectives. Methods which teach the task directly and make use of task-specific feedback should be used. In addition, programs which

	S$_1$	R	S$_2$
	Before	**Response**	**After**
Treatment 1	Flashcard = $\begin{array}{r}8\\ \times\,6\\ \hline\end{array}$ Teacher says, "What is 6 × 8?"	"48"	Teacher says, "Good" for every correct response.

Figure 4.11

A lesson plan.

lend themselves to fast-paced, small-group instruction are probably the best for basic skills. The methods used to identify students for grouping should be task specific in order to take advantage of the relationship between content covered and content learned.

Instructional Variables Related to Learning

The third body of information which can help a teacher make an initial treatment choice comes out of the area of learning research. This area seems removed from the "real world" to many teachers, but to disregard it is an error. Some educators believe that special students learn differently from normal students, but few educators can describe the ways normal students or retarded students attack a problem. If they do solve problems differently, then this information would be of great importance to a teacher.

There are many learning theories. Each theory proposes the existence of cognitive dimensions that influence learning. Some of the dimensions are beyond the control of teachers and some

are not. Two cognitive dimensions which can be influenced through instructional design are attention and reinforcement preference.

It has been suggested that special students differ from normal students in their attention to preceding stimuli and their responses to consequent stimuli. Teachers can allow for differences in attention and reinforcer effectiveness by altering the way they present a task and/or the way they react to a student's behavior.

It is possible to divide an instructional situation into three sections. The following is the traditional S$_1$-R-S$_2$ model: S$_1$ comes before the response; R is the response; and S$_2$ is what comes after the response. If a teacher wants to increase the likelihood of the response, he can do so by changing either the way he presents the task or the way he reacts to the student. For example, Figures 4.11 and 4.12 show two treatments which differ only in what comes after the response (the consequent stimuli).

Since the popular acceptance of contingency management, a possibly disproportionate amount of attention has been given to the consequences of behavior (S$_2$). But the preceding

	S$_1$	R	S$_2$
	Before	**Response**	**After**
Treatment 2	Flashcard = $\begin{array}{r}8\\ \times\,6\\ \hline\end{array}$ Teacher says, "What is 6×8?"	"48"	Teacher gives the child another problem for every correct response.

Figure 4.12

A change in consequent stimuli.

stimuli (S_1) are also important to changing behavior.

In the case of slow learners, the inability to master a task has been linked to problems in attending (Zeaman & House, 1963; Ross, 1976; Broadbent, 1977). In order to learn a task, a student must be able to select out the important task stimuli and attend to them. Learning which stimuli are important and which are not is one of the first stages in acquiring any skill. A student who doesn't attend to the correct stimuli would be unable to form a stimulus-response association. Therefore, a reasonable guess as to why a student who is otherwise ready to learn has not learned is that the student is not using selective attention.

Ross (1976) suggests that slow learners (specifically, learning disabled students) can benefit from instruction which is designed to offset differences in their ability to selectively attend. Ross does not recommend trying to train attention in isolation or suggest that training a student to attend in reading will necessarily increase her attention in math. Some ways in which the presentation of stimuli can be altered to increase attention are to build in novelty, complexity, uncertainty, surprise, conflict, and change (Berlyne, 1960). From an instructional point of view, an attention problem is easier to overcome than is a problem in an area like memory. The teacher can draw attention to important stimuli by altering them in the ways suggested above.

Treatment decisions can be based on the research evidence in attention. The best treatment for some students is one which is designed to aid the student in selective attention. This is probably truer of students who are very poor at a task than it is of those who are accurate but who have failed to completely master the task. For example. the successful reader can decode consonant sounds at a rate of 60–80 correct with 0–2 errors per minute. Suppose Ralph can only decode 5 correct with 10 errors while Fred decodes 35 correct with 1 error. Although neither student has mastered the task they do not necessarily need the same instruction on it. For students like Ralph who are inaccurate at a task the best guess for modifying a treatment is to change the preceding stimuli; for example, doubling the time spent in instruction. This kind of treatment may compensate for the possibility that the student is having problems attending. While low levels of performance suggest altering the preceding stimuli, higher levels suggest altering the consequent stimuli. For students who are well on their way to criteria or who may be accurate but slow, the best choice is a change in reinforcer type or schedule.

These suggestions are general guidelines for making a best guess. Once the guess has been made, it is essential that the student's progress be monitored in order to validate or change the initial treatment choice. In the absence of tests which predict best treatments, the teacher can only select a treatment and try it out. The teacher's first treatment choice will always be a guess no matter what testing procedures are used. The quality of the guess can be improved by using information on the effectiveness of treatments, their relationship to achievement, and their relationship to learning.

5

The Diagnostic Evaluation

The Purpose

When a student is failing at school because of academic or behavioral problems, he becomes a candidate for special education. One of the first steps in special education placement is the comprehensive diagnostic evaluation. Frequently this evaluation reflects a number of factors which have very little to do with the student. One such factor is the confusion between classification and diagnosis.

The purpose of educational evaluation is to answer two questions: (1) What is wrong with the kid? and (2) How can the kid be fixed? Although it is an oversimplification, psychological and educational tests can almost be divided into explaining and remediating categories. Explaining tests could be thought of as tests which try to find the source of the student's problem. Remediating tests would then try to find out how to cure the problem. The specific disability categories used so extensively in special education are linked to tests which deal with failure by looking for its source. Special students are classified according to source variables (Quay, 1973). Many of the controversies which exist concerning evaluation in special education can be traced to the mistaken assumption that knowledge of cause must precede cure.

Tests which classify and tests which diagnose both follow from the same fact. The student is failing. Given this fact, the evaluator begins to test out ideas which can explain or change the failure. The tests selected and the ideas checked by the evaluator dictate the evaluation's ultimate usefulness. If the evaluator selects tests which can be used as proof of a categorical disability, the product of the evaluation may be additional funding to help the student. If the evaluator selects tests which can be used to determine the student's skills, the product of the evaluation may be a statement of what and how to teach that student. If the evaluator selects both types of tests, it is possible to obtain both results.

The Evaluation Format

Educational evaluation follows a format very similar to that followed in any other field. It is composed of four steps:

1. Facts are gathered about the student's behavior.
2. An assumed cause of the student's behavior is hypothesized.

48

Table 5.1

A Further Comparison of the Psycho-educational and Task Analytical Models of Evaluation

Evaluative Steps	Psycho-educational	Task Analytical
1. Facts pertaining to failure	General normative information such as "below grade level."	Specific criterion-referenced information such as "works written math problems slowly."
2. Assumed cause	Something is wrong with the student, preventing him from succeeding.	The student lacks the necessary skills to succeed.
3. Test	Test to find out what is wrong with the student.	Test to find out what skills the student does or does not have.
4. Repeat	Stop once the test results conform to a learning theory.	Stop once the test results indicate what to teach the student.

3. A test is given to find out if the assumed cause is correct.
4. The procedure is repeated.

In the first chapter a comparison was made between the psycho-educational (psycho-medical) and task analytical (behavioral) models of evaluation. The differences between the two models can be seen again by looking at each of the four steps as illustrated in Table 5.1.

A Sample Evaluation

Perhaps the best way to explain the funtioning of the two models is to examine a typical psycho-medical evaluation. The evaluation as presented here is an example which pertains to the mildly handicapped student. The severely handicapped student would not be expected to take paper and pencil tests in the search of an appropriate category.

Name—Ralph	Age—9 years 3 months
	Grade—4th

Reason for Referral: Ralph was referred by his teacher for poor academic progress.

Educational History: Ralph has never been a good student. When he was 8 years old he was referred for an extensive vision and hearing examination but no evidence of any sensory disability was found. He does not attend well in class. He is currently behind in all academic areas, particularly reading.

Tests Administered:

1. Wide Range Achievement Test (WRAT)
2. Wechsler Intelligence Scale for Children–Revised (WISC-R)
3. Bender Gestalt Test
4. Neurological examination
5. Illinois Test of Pyscholinguistic Abilities (ITPA)
6. Behavior Checklist

Test Results:

1. WRAT. A quick test of general academic achievement.

	Grade Equivalency Scores
1.1 Spelling	3.5
1.2 Arithmetic	3.9
1.3 Reading	2.9

Interpretation of WRAT Scores: Ralph is significantly behind in all academic areas.

2. WISC-R. A test of general intellectual function. The test has two areas—verbal and performance. Each area is composed of five subtests and one alternate.

Verbal Subtests	Scaled Score	Significant Deviation
2.1 Information	9	
2.2 Comprehension	12	
2.3 Arithmetic	7	
2.4 Similarities	6	+
2.5 Vocabulary	12	
2.6 Digit Span	9	

Verbal IQ 95

Performance Subtests	Scaled Score	Significant Deviation
2.7 Picture Completion	14	+
2.8 Picture Arrangement	12	
2.9 Block Design	11	
2.10 Object Assembly	6	+
2.11 Coding	8	
2.12 Mazes	10	

Performance IQ 101

Full Scale IQ 97

Interpretation of WISC-R Scores: Ralph scored in the normal range indicating that he is not retarded. His low scores on the verbal tests indicate that he is unable to effectively use his auditory-vocal channel. The scatter (variability) of his subtest scores is indicative of learning disabilities.

3. Bender Gestalt Test. A test of design copying.

Test Results: Ralph's scores were equivalent to those of a much younger student. His work was disorganized and crowded into the corner of the paper. Some of his drawings were slightly rotated. Ralph was very slow in completing his drawings.

Interpretation of Bender Gestalt Test: The results of the Bender Gestalt were consistent with the low scores Ralph obtained on two WISC-R performance subtests. His visual-motor perception seems to be poor. Based on his performance on the Bender Gestalt, Ralph should have a neurological examination.

4. Neurological examination. An examination given by a physician. The purpose of the examination is to identify indications of abnormal brain wave patterns, physical movements, or reflexes associated with brain damage.

Test Results:

4.1 Neurological—Deep tendon reflexes +2 and equal. No abnormal movements. Good muscle tone. Occular movements complete. Cranial nerves intact.

4.2 EEG (Electroencephalogram)
Hyperventilation normal.
No spikes.
Normal sleep activity.
Medium Voltage—awake.

Interpretation of neurological: Ralph is alert and cooperative. His EEG is normal.

5. ITPA. A test of general achievement and psycholinguistic ability. It is divided into two areas, the representational level and the automatic level.

Test Results:

Representational Level	Scaled Score	Deviation from Mean
5.1 Auditory Reception	41	+3
5.2 Visual Reception	36	−2

5.3	Auditory Association	38	0
5.4	Visual Association	28	− 10
5.5	Verbal Expression	45	+7
5.6	Manual Expression	37	−1

Automatic Level

5.7	Grammatic Closure	39	+1
5.8	Visual Closure	38	0
5.9	Auditory Sequential Memory	30	−8
5.10	Visual Sequential Memory	31	−7
5.11	Auditory Closure	45	+7
5.12	Sound Blending	45	+7
	Mean Scaled Score	37.75	

Interpretation of the ITPA: Ralph's weakest areas are Visual Association, Auditory Sequential Memory, Visual Sequential Memory. Ralph's strongest areas are Verbal Expression, Auditory Closure, Sound Blending. Overall, Ralph seems to be better at the auditory subtests than at the visual subtests. This indicates that he may be instructed most effectively by using auditory methods. Steps should be taken to remediate Ralph's sequential memory.

6. Behavioral Checklist. A series of questions given to the classroom teacher and parents. The test is actually an informal interview designed to determine if the student is well adjusted in school and at home.

Test Results and Interpretation: Ralph's parents could not supply any information pertinent to his learning problems. Ralph's teacher reported that Ralph often does not attend to his work. She reported that he has no problems with peers.

It would seem that Ralph's problems are situational in that the classroom is the only situation on which his behavior is unusual.

Conclusions:

1. Ralph appears to be average in all respects except in his academic work.
2. Previous testing indicated that Ralph had no vision or hearing problems.
3. His WISC–R scores are within the normal range but subtest analysis suggests poor verbal skills. Scatter on his WISC–R profile is indicative of learning disabilities.
4. His Bender Gestalt test suggests poor visual-motor integration possibly associated with brain damage.
5. A neurological examination refuted the presumption of brain damage.
6. The ITPA results suggest that Ralph is an auditory learner with sequential memory deficits.
7. With the exception of the lack of organization on the Bender Gestalt there is no evidence of behavior disorders.

Recommendations:

1. Ralph should be placed into a self-contained special education classroom for the learning disabled.
2. He should be taught primarily through his auditory channel.
3. Steps should be taken to remediate his sequential memory problems.
4. Ralph needs one-to-one instruction in order to compensate for his inattention.

Discussion of the Evaluation

Conclusions

In this section each of the statements from the conclusion portion of the diagnostic evaluation will be reviewed.

STATEMENT 1. "Ralph appears to be average in all respects except in his academic work."

Statement 1 is based on the results of the WRAT and the failure to find any gross handicapping condition. The WRAT or some other achievement test is routinely given to verify the referral. In other words, the diagnostician is simply confirming that the student is academically behind.

General achievement tests are a good way to sample a wide variety of student behavior in a short time. However, the resulting test scores and grade level equivalencies are of no value in determining what or how to teach the student. Normative test scores and their limitations are discussed in Appendix A.

STATEMENT 2. "Previous testing indicated that Ralph had no vision or learning problems."

Statement 2 begins a pattern of testing in which the evaluator tries to place Ralph within one of the traditional special education categories. This procedure is outlined in Figure 5.1. A series of tests are given. If Ralph fails a particular test he is placed into the corresponding category. The first tests given are usually those associated with severe and/or physical handicaps.

If the student passes one set of examinations then another will follow. The unwritten rules are that categories are mutually exclusive, and that severe and physical handicaps absorb mild handicaps. Therefore, should a child be identified as unable to see, he would probably not be given any of the tests associated with learning disabilities or behavior disorders.

STATEMENT 3. "His WISC-R scores are within the normal range but subtest analysis suggests poor verbal skills. Scatter on his WISC-R profile is indicative of learning disabilities."

The IQ test is by far the most influential test in use today. The ramifications of IQ testing are so great that the practice is under constant discussion. Anyone who administers or routinely

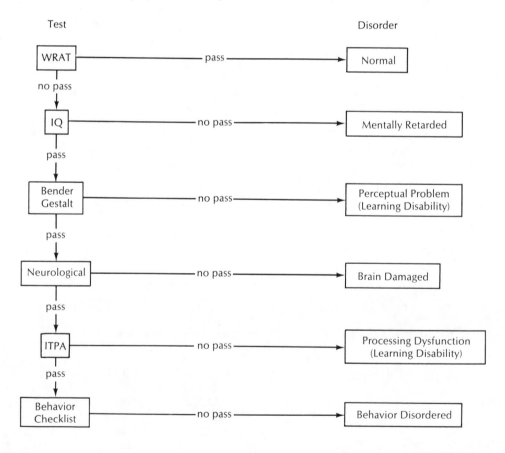

Figure 5.1

Testing for categorical placement.

interprets IQ scores is encouraged to pursue this discussion. For the time being we will deal with only two major points.

First of all it is important to remember that IQ tests are normative devices. Like other normative tests they tend to discriminate for or against individuals who are unlike their norming populations.

Second, the tests were originally developed as prognostic instruments. Their primary use was and is to predict the future performance of a student. As the use of IQ tests has continued, a mass of information and speculation has accumulated regarding them. No set of diagnostic rules has yet to emerge from this mass.

Suppose that Ralph had obtained a full scale IQ score of 75. In the 1960s he would have been retarded; today he would be normal. This is because the most widely accepted definition of mental retardation has recently changed from one (85) to two (70) standard deviations below the mean.

Fortunately Ralph did score within the normal range although his subtest scores showed some scatter or variability. The scatter is determined by finding the mean of the subtest scores and then seeing how far above (+) or below (−) the mean each subtest is. This scatter is often referred to as an indicator of learning disabilities. But the degree of scatter should not be determined informally. Refer back to Ralph's subtest scores. While they may appear to be scattered if one uses the usual criterion of plus or minus 3 scale scores from the mean (9.7), only three of Ralph's subtest scores are significantly deviant. This number of deviant subtest scores can be expected to occur about 20 times out of every 100 tests given. Therefore, while the scores may seem quite variable, it turns out that the odds are 1 in 5 of finding a student with a similar degree of scatter. WISC–R subtest scatter should not be used to diagnose learning disabilities (Kauffman, 1976). In fact, there are no WISC–R subtest patterns which can be used reliably to place students into diagnostic categories (Tittle, 1975). Neither subtest analysis or the total test score can be used to tell about the cognitive processes of the student. In the words of Baumeister and Muma (1975), "The IQ test cannot, or at least should not, be used to 'diagnose' anything" (p. 297).

STATEMENT 4. "His Bender Gestalt test suggests poor visual-motor integration possibly associated with brain damage."

The Bender Gestalt test involves design copying. It is used to assess students for disorders in personality and perceptual functioning as well as for brain damage. The test has been used for so many diverse purposes that its exact place in evaluation has become somewhat obscure. However, a few points do need to be made about the Bender.

First, the test does not have high test-retest reliability or predictive validity. Therefore, it should not be used to justify long-term placement into any treatment. The visual-motor skills which the test samples have not been shown to be related to academics. The test results can't be used to guide remediation except perhaps in the area of handwriting. The same is true of other visual-motor tests. Finally, the link between tests such as the Bender and brain damage is correlational (For a discussion of correlation, read Appendix A, Unit 3.) Test scores should never be used to categorize students as brain damaged or brain dysfunctioned. Psychological tests cannot be used to separate even grossly impaired brain damaged students from normal students, let alone normal students from minimally brain damaged ones (Ross, 1976).

For years special education has been preoccupied with the assessment and treatment of various perceptual-motor and/or sensorimotor deficits. Despite a growing amount of literature which discredits this preoccupation, the sales of perceptual-motor tests and materials continue to flourish. The Bender Gestalt test has become associated with perceptual-motor training and is used as an example here because, of all similar tests, it has been researched the most extensively.

STATEMENT 5. "A neurological examination refuted the presumption of brain damage."

It is logical to assume that since learning occurs in the brain, nonlearning may result from brain damage. Working from this logic, evaluators may examine failing students for evidence of brain damage. In Ralph's case some suggestion of brain damage was found in his poor Bender Gestalt scores. The suggestion was then checked out with a neurological examination. Ralph passed the neurological but, interestingly enough, it is possible for someone to pass an EEG even when he has brain damage. Individuals with severe structural damage to the brain may still have normal EEG patterns. Conversely an abnormal EEG is no real proof that there is damage. Figures vary but as much as 20% of the general population would have abnormal EEG patterns if tested (Freeman, 1967).

There are no clearcut relationships between neurological data and student behavior. Psychological tests which purport to identify brain damaged students do not appear to do so reliably. EEG patterns cannot be used to predict how a student will behave or what kind of treatment he needs. The so called "soft signs" (mixed dominance, letter reversals, clumsiness, etc.) offer no insight into the treatment or cause of behavioral abnormalities. The diagnosis of brain damage, minimal brain dysfunction, and/or neurologically related perceptual handicaps is usually arrived at after all other options have been tried. In short, the categories of brain damaged and minimal brain dysfunction are educationally irrelevant (Bateman, 1972).

STATEMENT 6. "The ITPA results suggest that Ralph is an auditory learner with sequential memory deficits."

This statement represents the classic aptitude treatment interaction assumption. ATI has already been discussed in some depth as has the ITPA. There are a large number of perceptual and/or modality preference tests on the market. These tests claim to be tests of specific psychological abilities and can be recognized by titles containing terms like visual perception, auditory discrimination, perceptual-motor or visual-motor integration as well as psycholinguistic abilities. As Waugh (1975) has pointed out, the ITPA is the best of these tests. She also concluded that it was not a test of psycholinguistics at all and cannot be used effectively to select materials for students or to assess their modality preferences.

STATEMENT 7. "With the exception of the lack of organization on the Bender Gestalt there is no evidence of behavior disorders."

Unlike the other disability categories, behavior disorders has not been overwhelmingly reliant on the paper and pencil test. Frequently, observations are made of the student's actual behavior and/or questions are asked of individuals who know the student. In Ralph's case physical/sensory handicaps and retardation were ruled out as explanations for his failure. Once this was done the only choices left were learning disabilities and behavior disorders. With learning disabilities it is necessary to put up with vague definitions. With behavior disorders it is necessary to put up with situational definitions. What is disturbed behavior in one setting may be quite normal in another.

When Ralph passed the questionnaire screening for behavior disorders he had nowhere to go but into learning disabilities. He passed the questionnaire in part because he apparently was exhibiting no "acting out" or extremely disruptive behavior. Ralph also passed because his behavior was not uniformly bad. A truly disturbed individual would probably have trouble at home as well as at school. The obvious conclusion is that something about school makes Ralph misbehave. That something is probably the fact that he is called on in school to do things he cannot do—academics.

Recommendations

Ralph's diagnostic write-up is a fairly typical one. It started with general statements of fact such as "academic failure" and resulted in general statements of treatment such as "needs special class placement." Many school psychologists or educational diagnosticians will supply a much larger set of remedial recommendations but these usually come from observing the child's work and not actually from the test scores. Such observations could be better made by observing in the classroom rather than in the testing room.

There is some danger for the diagnostician in that she must avoid suggesting specific remedial techniques which have already been tried. In the absence of detailed information about past treatments there is a risk of looking foolish by recommending that the teacher use a treatment which has already proven worthless. For these reasons the recommendation sections of most psycho-educational evaluations fall into one of three categories.

TYPE 1—GENERAL STYLE. Because the tests are usually normative they give little specific information about what the student can or cannot

Table 5.2

General Assumption of Cause Leads to General Conclusions

Fact	Assumed Cause	Test	Conclusion
Poor academic achievement	Fact Incorrect	WRAT	General achievement information only.
	Mental Retardation	WISC-R	The IQ test is a prognostic instrument.
	Visual Perception Problem	Bender Gestalt	Too general for academic conclusion.
	Brain Damage (minimal brain dysfunction)	Neurological Examination	No established relationship between EEG abnormalities and specific academic behaviors.
	Processing Dysfunction (psycholinguistic disabilities)	ITPA	Conclusions suspect due to low test reliability and assumption of predictable ATI.
	Behavior Disordered	Behavior Checklist	Informal checklists tend to confirm what is already known.

do. The recommendation section may also be general because the tests seek to measure variables which are beyond the control of the teacher such as intelligence, brain damage, processing dysfunctions, emotional disturbance, or sensory impairment. Task-specific remedial recommendations cannot follow from tests which are not task specific.

In order to get task-specific information it is necessary to task analyze the test items to find out what skills the student must have to pass the items. This kind of analysis could just as easily be done on the student's homework assignment. In addition, there are two dangers to analyzing normative test items: (1) the analysis of test items assumes the items themselves are of curricular importance—which they may not be and (2) such analysis increases the probability that the teacher will teach to the test, making any future use of the test worthless.

TYPE 2—COOKBOOK STYLE. Many diagnosticians will look at test results as if they were the index to a book. Some test authors and publishers have developed remedial programs which are keyed to tests. This is true of tests such as the ITPA, the Frostig Development Test of Visual Perception, and the Detroit Tests of Learning Aptitude. Other tests such as the WISC-R have accumu-

lated large bodies of similar literature and recommendations without necessarily consulting the authors of the tests.

The cookbook approach to educational diagnosis is extremely appealing to teachers and evaluators. However, teaching is seldom as predictable as the sun rising. The reader is advised to be skeptical of programs which try to relate test scores to specific remedial techniques. Such programs place almost absolute faith in the power of the test score. In such cases it is wise to carefully review the test items to see if they seem relevant to what you are teaching. It is also necessary to review the reliability of the test including its stability over time. Guidelines for such a review are available in *Standards for Educational and Psychological Tests* (American Psychological Association, 1974).

One other caution about the cookbook method should be noted. Many of the tests which lend themselves to this technique are intended to group students into treatment types, for example, auditory learners and visual learners. These tests are based on the assumption that predictable, long-term aptitude treatment interactions can be accurately identified and used. Research using existing tests has failed to support this assumption either for groups of students or for individuals.

TYPE 3—JARGON STYLE. The final type of recommendation section involves nothing more than paraphrasing. In these write-ups, the diagnostician will take the easily identified behavioral symptom of the student and rename it with educational jargon. The following examples show the behavioral symptom and the name given to the symptom (conclusion):

Poor at math (discalculia)

Poor handwriting (disgraphia)

Can't repeat sounds (auditory sequential memory deficit)

Reverses letters (strephosymbolia)

The quality of diagnostic evaluations would improve considerably if the evaluator would say what a child does instead of applying a label. It is easier to treat a student who can't complete line drawings than one who has a visual closure deficit. In the meantime, the way to translate the terminology is to look at what the student was expected to do on the test.

The Utility of a Psycho-educational Evaluation

A psycho-educational evaluation seeks to explain student failure. It does not give sufficient information on how to change behavior. It tries to locate the cause of the student's failure by asking a series of questions then testing for an answer. This list shows several psycho-educational questions and the instruments chosen for diagnosis:

1. Is the kid really behind? (WRAT)
2. Is the kid retarded? (WISC–R)
3. Does the kid have visual-motor discrimination problems? (Bender Gestalt)
4. Is the kid neurologically impaired? (EEG)
5. Does the kid have psycholinguistic or information processing problems? (ITPA)
6. Is the kid disturbed? (Bender Gestalt, Behavioral Checklist)

Once again it is important to note that each of the psycho-educational questions assume that there is something wrong with the kid. There are other questions which could be asked. This list shows several task analytical questions and the tests chosen to answer them:

1. Was the material worth learning? (Assess the curriculum)
2. Did the teacher present the lesson clearly? (Observe the teacher)
3. Did the teacher use appropriate feedback and reinforcement techniques? (Observe the teacher)
4. Were the materials used related to the content? (Compare materials to content)
5. Was the instruction properly sequenced? (Task analyze the lesson)
6. Was the test used to ascertain failure valid? (Analyze test items)

Any question from either list could be used to explain why Ralph didn't learn. Failure to give feedback can account for nonlearning just as well as retardation. The important issue is which list can be used to guide instruction. The psycho-educational causes are not necessarily linked to treatments whereas the task analytical questions are.

As has already been discussed, the psycho-educational evaluation hinges on the power of tests to summarize cognitive and perceptual characteristics within the kid. These characteristics are not directly observable, and their relationship to specific behaviors has not been proven.

Teaching is a process of behavior management. The only tool available to the teacher is the ability to change the learning environment. This is done by altering the way a task is presented or the way the student is treated. Teachers can't alter brain damage, and even if they could, they would still have to do it through behavioral interventions. Therefore, the most useful information is that information which is directly related to specific behaviors.

The techniques for collecting useful diagnostic information will be explained in Part 2. You will find that the task analytical approach lacks the quasi-psychological and medical vocabulary of the psycho-educational model. The task analytical model is not limited to any category of handicapping condition or to any severity level. This means that the teacher who uses it may miss out on the use of terms which impress regular classroom teachers and/or parents. However, they can still impress them with excellent teaching.

Part Two

Methods of Evaluating Exceptional Children

Introduction

Diagnosing a child's learning problem requires that you answer two basic questions—What? and How? What skills and/or knowledge do I need to teach the child so that he will be able to successfully perform a given task? How do I teach him so that I can be sure he will learn? Over the years, professionals have attempted to answer both questions through a variety of assessment techniques. In the applied section of this text, we cover three of these techniques. The first is discussed in Chapters 6, 7, and 8. It is called the *task analytical model* and it is used to determine WHAT a child needs to be taught. Chapter 6 describes the task analytical (TA) model and how it works. Comparisons are made with the traditional model of educational diagnosis. Hypothetical cases are used to demonstrate the model's procedural aspect. The two major components of the TA model, task analysis and criterion-referenced testing, are covered in Chapters 7 and 8.

The assessment technique discussed in Chapter 9 is referred to as *learner/treatment interaction,* and its purpose is to determine HOW a child should be taught.

The last assessment technique is called *precision teaching,* and it is described in Chapters 10, 11, 12, and 13. Precision teaching is used to evaluate the efficacy of a treatment plan based upon the data collected through the TA model and learner/treatment interaction.

The relationship between these three assessment techniques may be seen in the following table which is a simple procedural outline of the process of educational diagnosis as advocated by the authors of this text. We suggest that you refer to it periodically. We hope it will give you a sense of continuity as you move from chapter to chapter.

Chapters 6, 7, and 8 are divided into two units each, one concerned with knowledge and the other with acquisition of skills. The units may be said to be competency based since each requires successful completion before moving on to the next. The reader has to meet a prespecified criterion for acceptable performance (CAP) on a unit assessment. If this criterion is not met, you have some options. One may be to reread the material in the unit and then take the assessment again. Another may be to apply the task analytical model to your own learning problem to determine why you may be experiencing difficulty with the text material. This

The Process of Educational Diagnosis as Advocated by the Authors

The Four Sacred Pedagogical Questions	Evaluative Method Used to Answer the Four Sacred Questions
1. Where is the child now? (translation) What is the child's current level of educational performance?	The task analytical model: A form of curriculum-referenced evaluation; its two major components are task analysis and criterion-referenced testing.
2. Where do I want him to be? (translation) What are the child's *long-* and *short-term objectives?*	Same as above.
3. How do I get him there? (translation) What methods and/or materials should I use to teach him?	Learner/treatment interaction: A form of treatment-referenced evaluation; its major component is formal and informal observation of what works and what doesn't work with a particular child.
4. How will I know when he's arrived? (translation) How will I know when he's learned what I want him to learn?	Precision teaching: A type of formative evaluation; its major components are specifying behaviors, planning, testing, charting behaviors, and estimating learning trends.

will not only help you to solve your own problem, but it will enable you to learn how the model works so that you can more readily apply it to your students' learning problems. Sections of the text are designed as competency based units. To insure maximum understanding of these sections, you should follow the steps listed below.

I. Read the objective(s) at the beginning of each unit.
   A. If you feel that you already have the competency stated in the objective, take the test at the end of the unit without completing the reading assignment.
   B. If you do not feel that you have the competency stated in the objective, look to see if there are prerequisite(s) listed at the beginning of the unit.

1. If you feel that you have completed the prerequisite(s), begin the reading assignment.
2. If you have not completed the prerequisite(s), do so before you begin the reading assignment.

II. Complete the reading assignment.

III. Take the test at the end of the unit.
   A. If you pass the unit test without completing the reading assignment, go on to the next unit.
   B. If you do not pass the unit test, complete the reading assignment, and then take the assessment again.
   C. If you do not pass the unit test and you have completed the reading assignment, you may wish to apply the task analytical model to your own test results and try to determine what your problem is.

6

The Task Analytical Model

Unit 6.1: What it's all about.

Objective: Given 12 statements pertaining to the task analytical and psycho-medical models of educational diagnosis, the learner will correctly label each.

Prerequisite: None.

Reading Assignment

Although the literature is replete with methods for diagnosing learning problems, it is not our intention to deal with them in this text. Instead we have incorporated all of these methods into two basic contrasting models as covered in Part One of this text. These models were the psycho-medical (PM) and the behavioral, or task analytical (TA), models. First we will briefly review the philosophies of each.

The underlying philosophy of the PM model is, *if the kid hasn't learned, there must be something wrong with the kid.* Therefore, evaluation always begins with the learner. If Juanita can't read, it must be her fault. It can't be the teacher's fault. Refer her to the school psychologist or psychometrist so she can be tested to see how she differs from her peers. Maybe she's retarded. Perhaps there is a personality problem caused by some long-forgotten psychological trauma that has resulted in an emotional block to learning. Or maybe Juanita is one of those learning disabled children with minimal brain damage, ill-defined laterality, or heaven forbid, the dreaded Strephosymbolia.

The TA model takes a completely different view. *If the kid hasn't learned, there must be something wrong with the way she was taught.* If Juanita can't read, maybe there is a prerequisite knowledge or skill that she hasn't acquired either because it wasn't taught properly or wasn't taught at all. The best way to determine this is to sit down and analyze the task that you expect Juanita to perform, making sure that you have identified all of its components, and then, only after task analysis, determine whether or not Juanita has mastered them.

In the TA model, teachers do most of the testing since there is no psychological or medical evaluation involved. Labeling is considered irrelevant simply because it has no educational usefulness. Telling Juanita's teacher that Juanita has an intelligence quotient that is more than two standard deviations below the mean or that she suffers from dyslexia or "ego deprivation" does not help her teacher write Juanita's educational plan.

Differences between the two models extend into the area of how to test as well as what is tested and which instruments are used. Assessment tends to start at the "bottom" of the developmental ladder in the PM model in terms of the complexity of abilities measured. If a child has difficulty reading, testing might start in the readiness areas, for example, visual and auditory perception, to see if there are any processing deficits. Since Juanita has difficulty reading words, the hypothesis is that she will have the same problem with geometric shapes. To verify this, she is given a test in visual perception. If she "fails" the test, this is often interpreted as the reason for her reading problem. She may be assigned the label "learning disabled" and, if there is room, Juanita is provided with a special educational program. It doesn't make any difference that the perceptual-motor test she was given might not have enough test-retest reliability to make these educational decisions or that there isn't any empirical data to support the theory of a causal relationship between perceptual disability and reading disability. The tests are given and the decisions are made, based upon normative interpretations, by examiners who are often medical people and/or psychologists. Their advanced degrees tend to intimidate people with little knowledge of the literature in the field. How many parents or teachers really understand enough statistics, have read enough of the research, or understand enough of the psychological or medical jargon to question the relevance of the test given their child or the interpretations of such assessment?

Since the TA model does not accept the relevance of perceptual-motor tests, or any process-oriented testing for that matter, assessment does not begin at the bottom of the developmental ladder but at the top. *Testing is concentrated on reading behavior,* using the same words

and letters that the child is experiencing difficulty with in the classroom rather than using circles, triangles, and squares.

Perhaps we should make something clear at this point. We are not minimizing the importance of psychologists, social workers, speech clinicians, pediatricians, school nurses, optometrists, or teachers. What we are criticizing is the way in which many of these professionals are used in the diagnostic process of the psychomedical model. It is our bias that before children are automatically subjected to a parade of examiners and a countless array of tests, there should be some behavioral data to indicate that all of this testing is necessary. Again it is not the number of tests administered that we object to, but rather the amount of irrelevant testing done. For example, psychologists know that there is a high correlation between achievement scores and intelligence quotients. IQ is often used as a reliable predictor of achievement. However, IQ tests don't explain why a child is failing in school; they simply predict that she will fail. Therefore, if we already know that the child is failing in reading, why do we need to give the child a test that tells us what we already know? The answer, of course, may be found in the underlying philosophy of the PM model. If the kid hasn't learned, there's something wrong with the kid. Maybe she's retarded. Give her a WISC–R to find out. And while you're at it, give her a Bender and a California Test of Mental Maturity too. She might be LD or emotionally disturbed. Again, keep in mind that while we are not condemning doctors and psychologists, neither are we condemning the tests they use. We are condemning the way in which they are used. We are suggesting that tests are often used inappropriately and that this tends to make the information we get from them irrelevant since our major purpose for testing children should be to determine what and how to teach. The California may be given because an emotional block is suspected as the cause of Juanita's problem. After all, she does refuse to read for the teacher, the psychologists, or any adult who hands her a book. But what if her refusal to read is not the cause of, but rather the symptom of, her reading disability? May we not hypothesize that Juanita's refusal to read is a result of her anxiety and frustration that have made the act of reading aversive? The only problem with this hypothesis is that in order to test it, we have to go back to a diagnostic assessment of Juanita's reading behavior; this may be difficult because in order to evaluate in the area of reading, the psychologist would need to have a knowledge of reading instruction.

In the behavioral model, emphasis is placed upon the child's performance on individual test items rather than on overall scores. Comparisons are not made between a child and her peers. The important question is not how Juanita differs from her peers, but rather what skills and/or knowledge she lacks. Because of this emphasis, criterion-referenced testing is stressed rather than normative and, as explained in Chapter 8, such testing provides data from which an educational plan may be constructed.

To summarize all of the above, the underlying philosophy of the PM model is, if the kid hasn't learned, the assumption is made that there is something psychologically or physically wrong with the kid. In direct contrast, the basic philosophy of the TA model is, if the kid hasn't learned, then she is lacking a prerequisite skill or knowledge.

Checkpoint 6.1

Directions: Mark "PM" for psycho-medical or "TA" for task analytical next to each of the statements below. Take no more than 6 minutes to complete the task. You may not use reference aids. Criterion for acceptable performance (CAP) is 100% accuracy.

_____ 1. The underlying philosophy is, if the kid hasn't learned, there must be something wrong with the way she was taught.

_____ 2. Etiology and labeling are emphasized.

_____ 3. The trend is for a number of specialists to administer whole batteries of tests to a child whether she needs them or not.

_____ 4. Emphasis is placed on scores from norm-referenced tests (e.g., intelligence quotients, percentiles, standard scores).

_____ 5. The underlying philosophy is, if the kid hasn't learned, there must be something wrong with her.

_____ 6. Teachers do most of the assessment.

_____ 7. Criterion-referenced assessment is stressed over normative testing.

_____ 8. Assessment tends to start at the "bottom" of the developmental ladder.

_____ 9. Etiological factors and labeling are de-emphasized since they serve little purpose in programming.

_____10. Assessment begins at the top of the developmental ladder and follows a step-by-step progression until the child reaches a point where she is successful.

_____11. Psychologists and medical people do most of the assessment.

_____12. Tests are given only when prior testing suggests it is necessary.

Acceptable Responses

1. TA	4. PM	7. TA	10. TA
2. PM	5. PM	8. PM	11. PM
3. PM	6. TA	9. TA	12. TA

Options

1. If you scored 100% on this checkpoint, you may go on to the next unit in this chapter.
2. If you scored less than 100%, go back and reread the reading assignment. Then take the checkpoint again.

Unit 6.2: How the task analytical model works.

Objective: Given the directions to list and describe each of the steps in the task analytical process, the learner will do so in writing.

Prerequisite: None.

Reading Assignment

The TA model requires four basic competencies: (1) the ability to appropriately choose, accurately administer, and score tests; (2) the ability to identify a task and analyze it; (3) the ability to design a criterion-referenced test; and (4) the knowledge of how the model works.

Many classroom teachers already know how to administer and score a standardized norm-referenced test, e.g., the WRAT, the Spache, or the Key Math. If you don't, you can easily learn. Simply borrow a copy of the test from someone in the school district and start practicing. Make sure that you have a knowledgeable person check your administration and scoring procedures before you start using the test "for real." Often you will find that administering and scoring a test is easier than determining what test to use. As far as the TA model is concerned, the rule of thumb is to choose a test that will provide a sample of the child's behavior in the area or areas you wish to diagnose. Do not use a test that will only provide you with a guess as to the behavior actually shown. For example, if you wish to test spelling behavior, do not choose a test that requires the learner to pick the correct spelling of a word from a group of words. Instead, choose one that requires writing the word from memory. Likewise, tests of reading behavior should follow a see-to-say format instead of hearing a sound or word and underlining it on the recording sheet. Again, *always be certain that the behaviors required on the test are the same as those required in your class.*

As far as the other competencies in the TA model are concerned, successful completion of Chapters 7 and 8 should enable you to identify and analyze tasks as well as design criterion-referenced tests. This chapter will be devoted to the fourth competency, knowing how the model works.

In operation, the TA model follows a cycle of fact finding, task analyzing, hypothesizing, and validating that continues until the examiner is reasonably certain that he has diagnosed the student's problem. This cycle is presented as a flowchart in Figure 6.1.

Fact Finding

The purpose of the initial fact finding is to identify tasks which are the areas of concern. Unless the child is severely handicapped, the best procedure is to compare her to classroom tasks on which she is failing. This usually means regular classroom assignments, because regular class success is the ultimate long-term goal of special education. Sometimes, however, the school assignment may be so difficult that no behavior other than random guesses can be obtained. Schoolwork may also be too limited in that it doesn't ask the child to work on many tasks. In these cases the evaluator may want to use a general achievement measure to obtain many different behaviors at varying levels of difficulty. When an achievement test is used, the tester should closely examine the items to see if they ask the student to do things similar to what she needs to learn to do. In these cases the tests are not given to get a score but to get a behavior sample.

The first phase of the cycle, fact finding, relates the student's responses to a stimulus or set of stimuli. Billie sees 4 − 1 on a test (stimulus) and writes 5 as the answer (response). This is a fact. As the diagnostician, it is your job to find out why she made that response. Fact finding usually requires testing and always requires specifying errors. The purpose of fact finding is to collect a sample of student behavior which can be analyzed in subsequent phases.

Testing

In testing you simply provide the student with a specific stimulus or set of stimuli and require her to make a response. Obviously you must first decide what it is you want to measure and, as stated earlier, choose an appropriate instrument or lesson. Is the student's problem in arithmetic, reading, writing, spelling, or in another area of the curriculum? The TA model may be applied to many different problem areas, e.g., social behavior, academic knowledge or skills, and perceptual-motor readiness. Is the problem a specific one or is it so diffuse you will need to examine more than one area? You should be able to answer these questions before choosing the test(s) for the initial assessment.

It is important that you understand that the initial assessment does not necessarily have to include a commercially prepared norm-referenced test. The test choice depends upon what behaviors you want to measure. There are some skills for which there are no commercially prepared tests available. Lack of experience in administering or scoring certain tests may also influence your choice. It is quite possible that you may have a test in mind, be able to administer it (or know someone who can), but not be able to use it because it is not readily available. Should you find yourself in this situation, don't give up. Simply design your own test. (For information on designing tests, see Chapter 8.) You may also feel that the child has had enough testing, and you know her behavior well enough to describe it already. The important thing is to be able to specify in writing what the child does (or does not do) during her performance of the task. What you are interested in doing is summarizing how the student responds to specific stimuli. This can be done by following a stimulus-response format like the one seen in Table 6.1.

Specifying Errors

Assuming that you have completed the initial assessment or that you are familiar with the child's behavior when she performs the task, you are now ready to describe the student's response(s) in writing. Simply identify and specify all of the errors (i.e., incorrect responses) that the subject made on the test(s) or what she does during the task's performance that is not acceptable. You may do this without writing anything down, but if you are new to educational diagnosis, we suggest that you record it on paper as shown in Table 6.1. In fact, if you are a true novice, we strongly urge you to not only write things down but to summarize them in a prescribed manner. You might want to use our recording system. It is easy to remember, and it will help you follow the TA model and organize your thinking. It also helps you interpret the results of your testing. We call it a F–AC–T sheet (see Table 6.2). F–AC–T is an acronym for the three headings you use: F is for Fact, AC is for Assumed Cause, and T is for Testing. Simply divide a sheet of paper into three columns using the three headings just mentioned. Briefly describe the child's incorrect responses (errors) on the test you gave her. Do this in

Table 6.1

A Format for Summarizing Student Behavior

Problem Area	Stimulus	Response	Comment
Reading	hope	hop	final e
	either	other	vowel combination
	rob	robe	vowel–final e
	butter	buter	double consonant
Math	$\begin{array}{r} 4 \\ \times 3 \\ \hline \end{array}$	7	Signs (slow)
	$\begin{array}{r} 27 \\ -9 \\ \hline \end{array}$	$\begin{array}{r} {}^{1}\!\!/_{\!}27 \\ -9 \\ \hline 8 \end{array}$	Borrowing (slow)

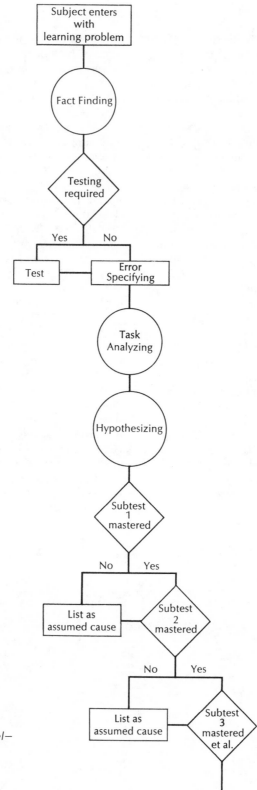

Figure 6.1

*The task analytical model—
how it works.*

Figure 6.1 *(cont.)*

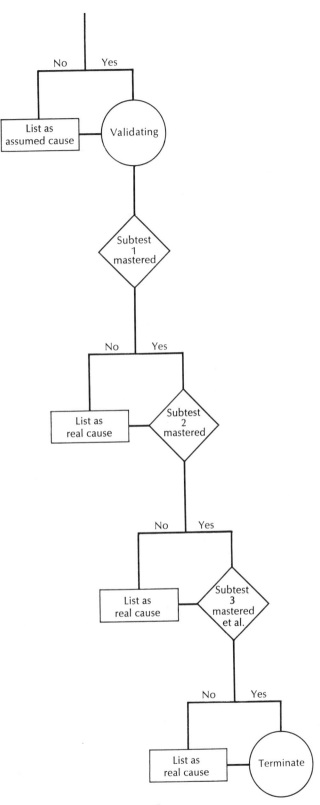

Table 6.2

F–AC–T Sheet

Fact	Assumed Cause	Test
A description of the child's incorrect responses (errors) on the test (i.e., stimulus or set of stimuli) you gave her.	A list of the subtasks (from the task analysis) that you think (i.e., hypothesize) the subject may not have mastered.	The stimulus or set of stimuli you present to the child to validate an assumed cause.
Example:	*Example:*	*Example:*
Writes 5 to 4 − 1 or 4 − 1 = 5. or Given 4 − 1 in writing, child writes 5 as the difference.	1. Does not read operation sign or doesn't know what it says. 2. Doesn't know what sign means. 3. Doesn't know this subtraction fact.	1. Point to sign and ask her what it is (minus or take away). 2. Ask her what she should do when she sees the sign. (subtract). 3. Say, "Four take away one equals____?" (three)

writing on the F–AC–T sheet under the heading "Fact." These incorrect responses are facts. They are examples of the child's behavior on a task. At this point you may not know why the child made these errors, but you do know that she behaved in this way. If more than one error needs to be specified in writing, you should list each one in the order in which it was made on the test.

Task Analyzing

The second phase in the cycle is task analyzing. Remember, we stated that the underlying philosophy of the TA model is that *a child fails a task because she does not possess a skill or knowledge essential to the successful completion of that task.* Therefore, before you hypothesize as to the reason for the child's error, you need to analyze the task (i.e., behavior required of the child on the test). By isolating subtasks essential to the successful completion of the task, you will have produced a list of possible "assumed causes" from which to choose. While a complete task analysis requires that you describe the subtasks by writing performance objectives for each, we suggest that you do not do this until you are ready to test your assumptions. If you have 10 subtasks and you write a performance objective for each, you may later find that there are only three or four subtasks that qualify as assumed causes and that you have

wasted a lot of valuable time. *Don't write a performance objective for a subtask unless you plan on listing the subtask as an assumed cause.*

Hypothesizing

The next phase in the cycle is hypothesizing. We should mention here that we are using the terms *hypothesis* and *assumed cause* synonymously. Under the heading "Assumed Cause" on the F–AC–T sheet, write why you think the child made each error or incorrect response. Again, use the subtasks from your task analysis as the basis for all assumed causes.

If one subtask is "ability to write the numbers 0 through 9" and you suspect that the child does not have this skill, you should state "not able to write the numbers 0 through 9" in the "Assumed Cause" column. It goes without saying that you do not list a subtask as an assumed cause if it is obvious that the child has this particular skill or knowledge. For example, if it has been demonstrated in the past that the child can write the numbers 0 through 9, you would not list this as one of your assumed causes even though it is one of the subtasks in your task analysis. The rule of thumb in hypothesizing or assuming cause is to *use only those subtasks where competency is in doubt.* Also, if you are listing more than one possible cause for each error, list them according to probability, with the most probable cause listed first. The reason for this will become clear as we continue to describe the task analytical model.

Validating

The cycle becomes complete (not finished necessarily, just complete) when you begin the second testing phase. This time you are testing the validity of each of your assumed causes to see which one(s) is the reason for the student's inability to successfully perform the task. Until you do this, you cannot say for sure what the child needs to be taught. You can only hypothesize. Once you have listed those subtasks as assumed causes, you are now ready to write a performance objective for each subtask that will describe how you intend to test the child. It may be that you will need to give the complete test or subtest of a norm-referenced, commercially prepared instrument in order to validate one or more of the assumptions. However, most of the time you will be able to administer an informal, teacher-prepared, criterion-referenced test that can be tailor-made for the situation. If you are using the F–AC–T sheet, describe any future assessment you plan to conduct in the "Testing" column. For expediency, you may wish to simply list the number of the performance objective to identify the test you will use. As you will learn in Chapter 8, *a performance objective is the basis for all criterion-referenced tests*. When you are ready, administer the test(s) until you have satisfactorily assessed the validity of each of the assumed causes. Continue through the cycle as many times as is necessary to identify the cause of the child's learning problem. You'll know it's

time to stop when the child reaches a level where she starts passing all tests.

We are now ready to apply the TA model to some hypothetical cases. Our first example is that of a child with a gross-motor coordination problem manifested by an inability to skip properly. Following the cycle of the TA model, you first need to do some fact finding by testing and error specifying. Remember, don't bother to test if you are already able to describe the child's incorrect responses. If you can't, you should test the child. Testing will give you the opportunity to observe skipping behavior and record exactly what the child does. Since there are few (if any) commercially prepared tests for skipping, you will probably have to design one yourself. All you need to know is how to skip and how to write a performance objective. Most people know how to skip, but if writing performance objectives is not one of your strong points, you should complete Appendix B. In the meantime, we'll supply the performance objective for you. "Given the directions, 'skip to me,' the child will skip (i.e., step-hop-slide) a distance of 15 feet without breaking rhythm (L–R–L–R, etc.) or losing her balance. The examiner will model skipping for the child." This performance objective is your skipping test. It includes everything you will need to assess the child's skipping behavior.

Let's assume that you go ahead and administer the test and find that the child was not able to skip but instead hopped on one foot in an irregular pattern, e.g., L–R–L–L–R–L–L–L, etc. Using our F–AC–T sheet, we would specify in writing the child's behavior on the skipping test exactly as she performed it (see Table 6.3).

Table 6.3

F–AC–T Sheet/able to skip

Fact	Assumed Cause	Test
On test for terminal objective: Child hopped on one foot in irregular pattern (e.g., L-R-L-L-R-L-L-L).	Not able to *hop on alternate feet.*	See objective 1, Table 6.4.
On test for objective 1: Child hopped on L,R,R,L, R,L,L,R.	Not able to *stand on alternate feet.*	See objective 3, Table 6.4.
On test for objective 3: Child met criterion for acceptable performance.	....	....

The next step is to task analyze skipping. We need to do this so that we may identify those subtasks that are essential to the successful completion of the task. Stated in another way, if the learner lacks these subtasks, she will probably not be able to successfully perform the task. Therefore, by listing all of the essential subtasks, we are actually identifying all of the possible assumed causes for her failure.

Given all of the essential subtasks for skipping (Table 6.4), we must decide which of them are missing and thus are keeping the learner from successfully performing the task. Since subtasks are sequenced according to complexity (from most to least) and success on each depends upon success on a previous subtask, we should begin the hypothesizing process with the most complex subtask. If we find that the learner has the most complex skill, she therefore must have the other (lower) skills. In the TA model, the evalua-

tor "tests down" from most complex to least complex. Whenever testing children, it is important to avoid upsetting them. This is true for the obvious humanistic reasons and because when upset they may not behave in a representative manner on the test. It is hard to say if starting with hard items and working down to easy ones is more disturbing than starting with easy items and working up to harder ones. In either case the competent evaluator will take a break or insert an extraneous but enjoyable task whenever the child seems upset.

We wouldn't necessarily try to order all lists of subtasks since they are not all "task ladders" in the sense that success at each level is contingent upon success at a lower level. Given that our child can hop on one foot in an irregular L–R pattern, we may conclude that she is able to hop on one foot at a time. Given that she can hop on one foot at a time, we should expect

Table 6.4

Task Analysis/able to skip

Task: able to skip
Terminal Objective: Given the directions, "Skip to me," the learner will skip (i.e., step–hop–slide) up to the instructor from a distance of approximately 15 feet without balance aids. The student will alternate feet without losing her balance or rhythm. The examiner will model skipping for the learner.

Subtask 1: able to hop on alternate feet
Objective 1: Given the directions, "Hop to me," the learner will hop up to the instructor on one foot, alternating the left and right foot, from a distance of approximately 15 feet without balance aids. She will not lose her balance or rhythm nor will she break the left-right pattern at any time. The examiner will model hopping for the learner.

Subtask 2: able to hop on one foot
Objective 2: Given the directions, "Hop to me on one foot," the learner will hop on one foot up to the instructor from a distance of approximately 15 feet without balance aids. She will not touch the raised foot to the floor at any time nor will she stop for more than one second at a time. The examiner will model hopping for the learner.

Subtask 3: able to alternate standing on one foot
Objective 3: Given the directions, "Stand on one foot until I say 'Switch' and then stand on the other," the learner will stand on one foot at a time for 5 seconds on each foot without balance aids and without touching the raised foot to the ground until the examiner says 'Switch.' She will perform in this manner 5 times on the left and 5 times on the right (i.e., L-R-L-R-L-R-L-R-L-R). She may begin with either foot. The examiner will model standing on alternate feet for the learner.

Subtask 4: able to stand on one foot
Objective 4: Given the directions, "Stand on one foot until I say stop," the learner will stand on one foot for 5 seconds without balance aids and without touching the raised foot to the floor. She may use either foot. The examiner will model standing on one foot.

---

her to be able to stand on one foot. However, since she has difficulty skipping (alternate step–hop–slide), we may not conclude that the learner can hop on alternate feet. Therefore, we would list this under "Assumed Cause" on the F–AC–T sheet.

The next phase in the cycle is validating each of the assumed causes. To do this we need a test for hopping on alternate feet. Again, we simply write a performance objective that goes with the subtasks (as in Table 6.4) and use it as our test. Given that we administer the test for alternate hopping and the child fails, we might then assume that she cannot stand on alternate feet and administer a test for alternate standing. Let's say that she passes this test. An assumed cause has been validated, and the diagnosis for the child's inability to skip is cited as an inability to hop on alternate feet. This information has educational utility because it tells the teacher *what to teach*. Alternate hopping must be mastered before we may expect the learner to master skipping.

Remember that an educational diagnosis is not complete until an attempted intervention is found to be successful. In this case, confirmation of the diagnosis is subject to instruction. If the child is taught to hop on alternate feet, and acquisition of this skill results in successful performance of the terminal objective, we may say that our diagnosis was accurate.

Let's try another hypothetical example of the TA model applied to a specific problem in the classroom. This time we'll apply it to the cognitive task of looking up words in the dictionary. Let's suppose that every time a child asks you how a word is spelled, you suggest that she look it up in the dictionary. The child's response is to sit there doing nothing or to write the word incorrectly. At this point you decide to find out why she refuses to use the dictionary. For your initial assessment you might use a test similar to the one in Table 6.5. After administering this test you would specify the behavior and describe it in writing on the F–AC–T sheet (see Table 6.6). Let's suppose that the child was able to locate only three words in 20 minutes without any errors.

Table 6.5

Initial Assessment/able to locate words in the dictionary

Directions: Look up each of these words in the dictionary. When you find each, circle it and write the page number on the line next to it. Take no more than 20 minutes to complete the task. CAP is 100% accuracy.

1. majesty	_____	6. basic	_____
2. caterpillar	_____	7. tension	_____
3. majestic	_____	8. ballistic	_____
4. appliance	_____	9. chrome	_____
5. flannel	_____	10. flammable	_____

Table 6.6

F–AC–T Sheet/able to locate words in the dictionary

Fact	Assumed Cause	Test
On initial assessment: Child located three words in 20 minutes with no errors.	Able to match words but slow.	See objective 1, Table 6.7.
	Not able to alphabetize words.	See objective 2, Table 6.7.
	Not able to estimate location of word in dictionary.	See objective 3, Table 6.7.

Table 6.6 *(cont.)*

On test for objective *1:* Child met CAP.	....	....
On test for objective *2:* Child did not meet CAP; had difficulty with words beginning with same first two letters; accurate with words that began with different letters.	Doesn't know how to alphabetize words with same first two letters; hasn't been taught?	....
On test for objective *3:* Child did not meet CAP; child was nowhere near word in dictionary.	Doesn't know how; hasn't been taught?	....

The next step would be to analyze the task (see Table 6.7). After this, you would look at each subtask and decide whether or not it might be a possible cause of the problem. Let's suppose that you didn't sit with the child and watch her carefully. This makes it more difficult to make any assumptions regarding the cause of the problem. Therefore, you must list all three sub-tasks as possible causes. Unlike the task ladder in skipping, the subtasks identified are not dependent upon one another. This means that passing the test for the most complex subtask is no guarantee that the subject will pass the tests for less complex subtasks. Therefore, all three of the tests must be given regardless of the child's performance on the first or the second. Let's suppose that the child is able to pass the test for matching words but fails the test for alphabetizing words with similar spellings as well as the test for estimating the location of a word in the dictionary. You diagnose the student's problem as *an inability to estimate the location of a word in the dictionary and not being able to alphabetize words with similar spellings.* The obvious solution would be to teach the child both of these skills. Considering that she already can match words, mastery of the two missing subtasks should result in the task's successful completion.

So far we have used specific behaviors, e.g.,

Table 6.7

Task Analysis/able to locate words in dictionary

Task: able to locate words in the dictionary
Terminal Objective: Given a list of 10 words and a dictionary, the learner will look up each word in the dictionary and write the corresponding page number next to each. She will also circle the word in the dictionary. CAP is 100% accuracy in 20 minutes or less.

Subtask 1: able to match words
Objective 1: Given a list of 10 words with 2 similar and 1 matching word next to each, the learner will circle the matching word with 100% accuracy. She will do so within 60 seconds.

Subtask 2: able to alphabetize words
Objective 2: Given a list of 10 words, the learner will write them in alphabetical order, taking no more than 10 minutes and with 100% accuracy.

Subtask 3: able to estimate where the word is in the dictionary
Objective 3: Given a list of 10 words and a dictionary, the learner will open the book to a page not more than five letters away from the letter the word begins with. She will do this for 8 out of the 10 words.

---

skipping and looking up words in the dictionary, to provide examples of how the TA model might be applied. Suppose you have a child who has diffuse academic deficits. Where would you begin testing? You could start with tests in reading, spelling, writing, arithmetic, and language. On the other hand, you could simply give the student one test that provides you with a sample of her behavior in all of these areas. As discussed earlier in this unit, be sure that you do not use a test that requires different test behavior from that required of the child in the classroom. A single test that provides a sample of valid spelling, writing, arithmetic, and reading behaviors could be administered at one sitting to get you started on fact finding. An example of such a test is the Wide Range Achievement Test (Jastek, Bijou, & Jastek, 1965). On the WRAT spelling subtest, the child must write dictated words from memory just as she would be required to do in the classroom. This provides a sample of both writing and spelling behavior. In arithmetic she is required to compute the answers in writing to various problems, and in reading the child must pronounce the words she sees. It takes less time to administer this one test than to administer a battery of three or four.

Suppose that you administer the WRAT to one of your students and she performs poorly in spelling (see Figure 6.2). Again, simply look at the TA cycle. What are the facts regarding her spelling? You have already tested the student. All you need to do is to specify in writing the test behavior on your F-AC-T sheet (see Table 6.8). Next, you need to task analyze the spelling dictation test (see Table 6.9). After looking at each subtask you should be in a position to list an assumed cause or causes. Again, please note that the subtasks are not interdependent, and failure (or success) on one does not ensure failure on another.

Now you are ready to hypothesize. Taking the subtasks in the order listed, would you say that the subject was able to discriminate words dictated? Some of the mistakes are sound alikes, e.g., *much* for *must*, *rich* for *reach*, and *mate* for *make*. Given this type of performance, we would have to be suspicious of the student's auditory discrimination. Did she write *rich* instead of *reach* because she heard (i.e., perceived) *rich* or because she knew how to spell it and

didn't know how to spell *reach*? Since we won't know for sure unless we test her ability to discriminate words dictated, we'll list this under "Assumed Cause."

Another essential skill is the ability to revisualize the words dictated. Unless the learner remembers what the word looks like, she will be hard-pressed to spell it. If she was able to remember what similar-sounding words looked like, why couldn't she revisualize the dictated words? Of course, it helps the learner to remember what a word looks like if she has been recently exposed to it. Let's say that in this particular case the learner was a third grader, which means that she would have been exposed to a number of the words on the test that she misspelled. Was she able to remember what they looked like? Another rule of thumb: when in doubt about a competency, list it as an assumed cause.

What about the ability to spell words phonetically? According to Spache (1940), better spellers are able to make phonetic rather than nonphonetic substitutions for vowels, consonants, and syllables. Logically (and empirically), it would follow that children who are able to spell phonetically have fewer and less severe spelling problems. It is obvious that the learner did not attempt to spell the misspelled words phonetically. Why not? Was it because she didn't know how? List it under "Assumed Cause" and we'll find out.

Finally, is the learner able to spell and write words at the same time? Some children do not have the skill of writing developed at the automatic level where they can concentrate on the spelling of a word and automatically write the correct letters without thinking about what the letter looks like. Given that the learner was able to write a number of words correctly, we may assume that this skill is intact. We are, therefore, left with three of the four subtasks as assumed causes of the learner's spelling problem. Our next step will be to validate each of these by administering the informal criterion-referenced test (CRT) described by the performance objective written for each subtask, as in Table 6.9.

Given that we administer all of these tests, let's suppose that the child passes the tests for revisualization and discrimination of words dictated but fails phonetic spelling. Normally we

WIDE RANGE ACHIEVEMENT TEST

Reading, Spelling, Arithmetic from Pre-School to College

By J. F. Jastak, S. W. Bijou, S. R. Jastak

COPYRIGHT, 1965 by
Guidance Associates
of Delaware, Inc.
1526 Gilpin Avenue
Wilmington, Delaware

Printed in U.S.A.
1937, 1946, 1963
Revised Edition
1965

Name................................

School.................... Grade........

Referred by...............

Date.............. Examiner..........

Birthdate............... M. F. Chron. Age.........

Reading Score....... Grade...... Stand-Sc..... %ile.....

Spelling Score....... Grade...... Stand-Sc..... %ile.....

Arithmetic Score...... Grade...... Stand-Sc..... %ile.....

Percentiles and Standard Scores corresponding to grade ratings and age may be found in the Manual.

Level I—Spelling—Grade Norms.

Score	Grade	Score	Grade	Score	Grade	Score	Grade	Score	Grade	Score	Grade
1	N.5	12	Kg.4	23	1.5	34	3.0	45	5.7	56	10.3
2	N.8	13	Kg.5	24	1.6	35	3.2	46	6.0	57	10.9
3	Pk.1	14	Kg.6	25	1.7	36	3.5	47	6.3	58	11.5
4	Pk.2	15	Kg.7	26	1.8	37	3.7	48	6.5	59	12.2
5	Pk.3	16	Kg.8	27	2.0	38	3.9	49	6.8	60	13.0
6	Pk.5	17	Kg.9	28	2.2	39	4.2	50	7.2	61	13.8
7	Pk.7	18	Gr.1.0	29	2.3	40	4.5	51	7.7	62	14.5
8	Pk.9	19	1.1	30	2.5	41	4.7	52	8.2	63	15.2
9	Kg.1	20	1.2	31	2.6	42	5.0	53	8.7	64	15.9
10	Kg.2	21	1.3	32	2.7	43	5.3	54	9.2	65	16.7
11	Kg.3	22	1.4	33	2.9	44	5.5	55	9.7		

Level II—Spelling—Grade Norms.

Score	Grade	Score	Grade	Score	Grade	Score	Grade	Score	Grade
0	Kg.2	11	4.0	21	6.7	31	9.0	41	12.4
1	Kg.6	12	4.3	22	6.8	32	9.3	42	12.8
2	Gr.1.0	13	4.6	23	7.0	33	9.6	43	13.2
3	1.3	14	4.9	24	7.2	34	9.9	44	13.6
4	1.6	15	5.2	25	7.4	35	10.2	45	14.0
5	1.9	16	5.5	26	7.6	36	10.5	46	14.4
6	2.2	17	5.8	27	7.8	37	10.8	47	15.0
7	2.6	18	6.1	28	8.1	38	11.2	48	15.7
8	3.0	19	6.3	29	8.4	39	11.6	49	16.4
9	3.3	20	6.5	30	8.7	40	12.0	50	17.2
10	3.7							51	18.0

Spelling Scores

	Level I		Level II	
Test		Cumul Score	Test	Cumul Score
Copying 1 point per mark		1 to 18	Copying 4-9 / 10-17 / 18	1 / 2 / 3
Name 1 letter / 2 letters		19 / 20	Name 1 letter / 2 letters	4 / 5
Spelling 1 point per word		21 to 65	Spelling 1 point per word	6 to 51

Name _____

31. _____

1. (go) _go_   16. (order) _or_   32. _____

2. (cat) _cat_   17. (watch) _wish_   33. _____

3. (in) _in_   18. (enter) _into_   34. _____

4. (boy) _boy_   19. (grown) _going_   35. _____

5. (and) _and_   20. (nature) _nice_   36. _____

6. (will) _will_   21. _____   37. _____

7. (make) _mate_   22. _____   38. _____

8. (him) _him_   23. _____   39. _____

9. (say) _sat_   24. _____   40. _____

10. (cut) _cat_   25. _____   41. _____

11. (cook) _coat_   26. _____   42. _____

12. (little) _let_   27. _____   43. _____

13. (must) _mush_   28. _____   44. _____

14. (dress) _doors_   29. _____   45. _____

15. (reach) _rich_   30. _____   46. _____

Figure 6.2

Wide Range Achievement Test—spelling.

* The words in parentheses are dictated by the examiner; the child's written response to each follows.

NOTE: From *Wide Range Achievement Test* by J.F. Jastek, S.W. Bijou, and S.R. Jastek. Copyright 1965 by Guidance Associates of Delaware. Reprinted by permission.

73

Table 6.8

F–AC–T Sheet/able to spell words from dictation (WRAT spelling)

Fact	Assumed Cause	Test
On WRAT spelling dictation wrote *mate* for *make; sat* for *say; cat* for *cut; coat* for *cook; let* for *little; much* for *must; doors* for *dress; rich* for *reach; or* for *order; wish* for *watch; into* for *enter; going* for *grown; nice* for *nature.*	Child not able to discriminate words dictated.	See objective 5, Table 6.9.
	Not able to spell phonetically.	See objective 3, Table 6.9.
	Not able to revisualize words.	See objective 2, Table 6.9.
On test for objective 5: Child met CAP.	----------------------	------------------
On test for objective 3: Child did not meet CAP.	It is assumed the child lacks phonetic skills so she is given a phonetic spelling inventory as seen in Table 6.10.	------------------
	Not able to isolate syllables.	See objective 2, Table 6.10
	Not able to isolate sounds.	See objective 5, Table 6.10.
	Not able to associate sounds with corresponding letters.	See objective 6, Table 6.10.
	Not able to recall the sequence of the syllables or sounds.	See objective 3, Table 6.10.
	Not able to identify order of syllables.	See objective 4, Table 6.9.
	Does not know the operation (i.e., procedure) for spelling a word phonetically.	See objective 7, Table 6.9.

Table 6.9

Task Analysis/able to spell words from dictation (WRAT spelling)

Task: able to spell words in written form
Terminal Objective: The learner will correctly write each word dictated on the WRAT spelling test, taking no longer than 15 seconds per word.

Subtask 1: able to spell words verbally
Objective 1: The examiner will dictate each of the misspelled words from the WRAT, and the learner will correctly spell each verbally within 15 seconds after each dictation and with 100% accuracy.

Subtask 2: able to revisualize words
Objective 2: The learner will be given four different versions of the spelling of a word from the WRAT, one of which will be correct, along with the directions, "Point to the correct spelling of the word _____." The learner will correctly comply in all cases and within 5 seconds after hearing the word.

Table 6.9 *(cont.)*

Subtask 3: able to spell words phonetically
Objective 3: The learner will be able to write all misspelled words on the WRAT phonetically correct.

Subtask 4: able to write words
Objective 4: The examiner will spell each of the words on the WRAT out loud and the learner will correctly write each, taking no more than 2 seconds per letter with 100% accuracy.

Subtask 5: able to discriminate words dictated
Objective 5: The examiner will dictate each of the words on the WRAT and the learner will correctly repeat each within one second and with 100% accuracy.

would say that our diagnosis is complete and that the solution would be to teach her to spell phonetically. However, let's take the diagnostic process one step further. We do this to demonstrate that the TA cycle may be repeated over and over until you have found a place to start teaching. We are assuming that our student did poorly on the WRAT spelling dictation test because she is not a phonetic speller. We then need to find out why she is not able to spell words phonetically. Again, what are the facts? Do we need to give more tests? No! A test has

already been given. The student has already failed the informal CRT for phonetic spelling. Going back to our original F–AC–T sheet again, we would first specify the test behavior (*see* Table 6.10) and then task analyze phonetic spelling. Notice that phonetic spelling, formerly a subtask, is now the main task.

Using the subtasks listed in Table 6.10, we would again find assumed causes. Can the learner discriminate words dictated (subtask 1)? Remember she has already passed this test. Can she isolate syllables (subtask 2) in polysyllabic

Table 6.10

Task Analysis/able to spell words phonetically

Task: able to spell words phonetically
Terminal Objective: Given each of the misspelled words on the WRAT by dictation, the learner will write each word phonetically correct, taking no more than 15 seconds per word with 100% accuracy.

Subtask 1: able to discriminate words dictated
Objective 1: Given each of the misspelled words on the WRAT by dictation, the learner will correctly pronounce each word without hesitation.

Subtask 2: able to isolate syllables
Objective 2: Given each of the misspelled words on the WRAT by dictation, the learner will say each word, with a pause between each syllable. To be correct, the pause must be of at least one-second duration and correctly divide the word into syllables. CAP will be 100% accuracy, taking no more than 5 seconds per word.

Subtask 3: able to recall syllables (also applies to sounds)
Objective 3: Using the misspelled words on the WRAT, the examiner will say a word by syllable (i.e., with a one-second pause between each) and the learner will repeat the syllables in the correct order and with the one-second pause in the appropriate place. CAP is 100% accuracy, taking no more than 10 seconds per word.

Subtask 4: able to identify temporal order of syllables (also applies to sounds)
Objective 4: Using the misspelled words on the WRAT, the examiner will say a word by syllable (i.e., with a one-second pause between each). The examiner will then ask the learner, "What is the first syllable?" and "What is the last syllable?" The order of these questions may be reversed. The learner must answer correctly for each syllable in the word without any hesitation.

Table 6.10 *(cont.)*

Subtask 5: able to isolate sounds
Objective 5: Using the misspelled words on the WRAT, the examiner will say a syllable from a word and the learner will correctly say each sound in the syllable with a one-second pause between each sound. This will be done with 100% accuracy, taking no more than 10 seconds per syllable.

Subtask 6: able to associate sounds (phonemes) with corresponding letters (graphemes)
Objective 6: Given a sound (phoneme) in isolation, the learner will write the corresponding letter (grapheme) within 3 seconds and with 100% accuracy.

Subtask 7: able to state procedure used for spelling words phonetically
Objective 7: When asked to do so, the learner will verbally state each step in the procedure for spelling words phonetically. To meet CAP, all of the steps must be present and in proper sequence.

words? We're not sure about this one, so we will list it as an assumed cause. Can she isolate the sounds in syllables (subtask 5)? According to the test behavior specified in the "Fact" column, she was only able to do this with initial sounds. Therefore, we'll have to list it under assumed causes. Can she associate phonemes or sounds with the corresponding grapheme or letters (subtask 6)? It could be that she is able to isolate sounds but associates the wrong written symbol with each. This would make it appear that she is unable to isolate sounds in a word or syllable. We'll have to test this also.

Having given the informal CʳTs to validate each of our assumptions, let's suppose that the student passes all of them. What then? This usually is a signal that we have left out one or more subtasks when we did our task analysis. When this happens, it's usually a good idea to try the task yourself. Do this slowly and carefully, recording each of the subtasks as you think of them. We'll simply take a word that we don't know how to spell and try to spell it phonetically. You pick your word and we'll pick ours. It doesn't make any difference if the words are not the same as long as we use the same technique. Just make sure that it is a polysyllabic word. Imagine that you are taking a spelling test, the teacher has just finished dictating the word, and you have 15 seconds to write it on your paper. Probably the first thing you would do is to say the word to yourself. This demonstrates your ability to discriminate words dictated, which was already listed in our task analysis. The next step would be to break the word down into syllables. Syllable isolation was also listed as a subtask. Next you would have to identify the first syllable

in the word. This was a separate subtask that was not previously listed. It is actually different from isolating syllables since it requires you to retain the syllables in a first-to-last sequence and to isolate the first syllable. The next step, sound isolation, was already listed as a subtask. So was sound-symbol association. Once the steps of sound isolation and sound-symbol association are repeated until all of the sounds in the syllable are represented by letters on the page, the process begins again with the next syllable in the original sequence of syllables. Given that there is more than one syllable in the word, the learner would have to be able to recall the sequences of syllables and sounds in order to facilitate the process and complete the task within 15 seconds. This is a new subtask.

Another subtask as yet unmentioned is the knowledge of the operation or process of spelling words phonetically. A student might conceivably pass all of the CRTs for each subtask and still not be able to spell words phonetically because she doesn't know how to put them together.

Now we have identified three new subtasks. Given that we administer the CRTs for each to our student, let's suppose that she passes all but the test for knowledge of the operation. You may now say that the student is functioning below expectations in spelling because she can't spell phonetically, and the reason for this is that she was never taught the operation. Once she is taught how to spell phonetically, she will probably make fewer mistakes. Given that she has adequate revisualization, she should also be able to recognize the correct spelling of a word after using the phonetic spelling process.

Checkpoint 6.2

Directions: In writing, list and describe (in sequence) each of the steps in the TA model of educational diagnosis. Take no more than 10 minutes to complete the task. You may not use reference aids. All of the steps must be present, in the correct sequence, and accurately described.

Acceptable Responses

1. Fact Finding: Describe the student's incorrect responses (errors) to a stimulus or set of stimuli (test) on the F–AC–T sheet in the "Fact" column.
2. Task Analyzing: Isolate the subtasks essential to the successful completion of the task (i.e., the behavior required of the child on the test).
3. Hypothesizing: Identify all of the subtasks that you think the child may not have mastered and list them on the F–AC–T sheet under "Assumed Cause."
4. Validating: Test the validity of each of the assumed causes to see which of them is (are) the reason(s) for the child's inability to successfully perform the task.

Options

1. If you score 100% on the assessment for this unit, you may go on to the next chapter.
2. If you score less than 100% without completing the reading assignment, go back and read it before you retake the checkpoint.
3. If you score less than 100% after completing the reading assignment, apply the TA model which follows to help you diagnose your problem.

While you may already know why you did not pass the checkpoint, remember that by applying the TA model to your own problem you can learn how it works more easily than if you simply read about it. We therefore encourage you to read the material in the section below.

Applying the TA Model to Your Learning Problems

Phase I/Fact Finding

Since you already took Checkpoint 6.2, we have a set of behaviors and can complete the first phase of the TA model by specifying your errors. Simply describe in writing your incorrect responses on the test. We suggest that you use a F–AC–T sheet. We have provided a sample F–AC–T sheet with a number of possible incorrect responses described in the "Fact" column (Table 6.11). One or more of them may apply to you.

Phase II/Task Analyzing

Next you need to do an analysis of the task (i.e., test behavior) required in the checkpoint. We realize that many of you will not be able to do this until you complete Chapter 7 so we have provided a task analysis for you, complete with subtasks and corresponding performance objectives (Table 6.12).

Phase III/Hypothesizing

You should now be ready to start the hypothesizing process of the TA cycle. Look at your test behavior described in the "Fact" column of Table 6.11 and at each of the subtasks in the task analysis in Table 6.12. See if you can determine

Checkpoint 6.2 *(cont.)*

which essential competencies you may be lacking. If you find a subtask which you may be lacking, list it as an assumed cause for your failure on Checkpoint 6.2.

Phase IV/Validating

After you have listed the assumed cause(s), either find (or design) an appropriate test for each.

Table 6.11

F–AC–T Sheet/able to list and describe the steps in the TA model

SAMPLE

Fact	Assumed Cause	Test
You were able to list all of the steps in the correct sequence but *none of the steps were described accurately.*	Do not understand the procedural steps.	Paraphrase the appropriate section of the text.
You were able to list all of the steps and describe them accurately but the *steps were not in the correct sequence.*	Not able to recall the sequence of procedural steps.	List steps on cards and put them in order.
You were able to accurately describe all steps listed but *there were some steps missing.*	Not able to recall all of the procedural steps.	Write steps from memory.
You were able to list all of the steps in the correct sequence but *the descriptive statements were written for the wrong steps.*	Not able to associate the procedural steps with the corresponding description.	Write out step descriptions and match them to step labels.

Table 6.12

Task Analysis/able to list and describe all of the steps in the TA model

Task: able to list in sequence and describe all of the procedural steps used in the TA model
Terminal Objective: Given the directions to do so, the learner will list in correct sequence and accurately describe in writing all of the procedural steps used in the TA model. Reference aids may not be used and CAP is 100% accuracy, taking no more than 10 minutes for the task.

Subtask 1: able to list all of the procedural steps in sequence
Objective 1: Given the directions to do so, the learner will correctly list in writing the procedural steps used in the TA model. All steps must be included and in the correct sequence. Reference aids may not be used and CAP is 100% accuracy, taking no more than one minute to complete the task.

Table 6.12 *(cont.)*

Subtask 2: able to list all of the procedural steps
Objective 2: Given the directions to do so, the learner will correctly list in writing the procedural steps used in the TA model. All steps must be included, but they do not necessarily have to be in the correct sequence. Reference aids may not be used and CAP is 100% accuracy, taking no more than one minute for the task.

Subtask 3: able to recall sequence of procedural steps
Objective 3: Given all of the procedural steps used in the TA model *out of sequence,* the learner will write them in the correct sequence without using reference aids. The task will be completed in 45 seconds with 100% accuracy.

Subtask 4: able to accurately describe all of the procedural steps
Objective 4: Given each of the procedural steps used in the TA model one at a time, the learner will write an accurate description for each. Reference aids may not be used and CAP is 100% accuracy, taking no more than 7 minutes for the task.

Subtask 5: able to demonstrate an understanding of the procedural steps through paraphrasing
Objective 5: Given a written description for each of the procedural steps in the TA model, the learner will write a paraphrased description for each. CAP is 100% accuracy, taking no more than 10 minutes for the task.

Subtask 6: able to associate procedural steps with corresponding descriptions
Objective 6: Given all of the procedural steps in the TA model in one column and the descriptions in another column, the learner will correctly match each procedural step with its corresponding description. CAP is 100% accuracy, taking no more than one minute.

7

Task Analysis

Unit 7.1: What is a task analysis?

Objectives: 1. Given instances and not instances of tasks that could be analyzed, the learner will correctly discriminate between each.
2. Given an incomplete operational definition of task analysis, the learner will correctly fill in the missing words.

Prerequisite: Successful completion of Unit 6.2.

Reading Assignment

In order to analyze a task, you must first be able to recognize one. Before you can do this, it helps to know what a task is. Any job or activity that a student engages in during the school day may be referred to as a task. Since we are using task analysis in an evaluative context, we have chosen to define task as *any behavior or set of behaviors that a child must engage in to demonstrate the acquisition of skill or knowledge.* Stated in an evaluative context, a task may be defined as the behavior required of a student on a test.

For example, a teacher may wish to measure a student's knowledge of addition facts. Is it possible to write a task analysis for "knows addition facts"? We doubt it. First of all, "knows addition facts" is not a task, it is an ability. You

don't analyze an ability, you analyze a task. A statement of a task should include a verb and describe some action or observable behavior that the learner will engage in. How about "writes the answers to addition problems"? That's more like it. It doesn't describe the ability (i.e., knowledge), but rather the task that indicates the ability. By writing the answers to addition problems, the student is demonstrating whether or not he knows his addition facts. There's only one problem. We would have to know a little bit more about the task before we can analyze it. For instance, is it a see-to-say task, e.g., teacher shows flashcard and student says answer? Is it a see-to-write task, e.g., writing on a ditto? Is it a hear-to-write task, e.g., teacher says "2 + 2 =" and the student writes "4" or is it a hear-to-say task where the student says "4"?

Does the student have to copy the problem from a book or a blackboard or have the problems been written for the student? While all of these measure the same "ability" (albeit to different degrees), they each suggest a different task because they each require different test behavior. Before you can begin to analyze the task of "writes the answers to addition problems," you will need to know more of the details. Suppose we told you that the student was given a ditto of 50 simple addition problems with the directions to write the correct sums to as many as possible in one minute. Given this additional information, you can now write the task analysis.

To summarize, remember that a task is any behavior or set of behaviors that a child must engage in to demonstrate the acquisition of skill or knowledge. Used in the evaluative context, a task may be defined simply as the test behavior required of the learner. It should not be confused with the ability it measures and it should provide enough information to make an analysis feasible.

Now that you know what a task is, we may begin to discuss the process of task analysis. An operational definition of task analysis is *the process of isolating, sequencing, and describing all of the essential components of a task.* When the components have all been mastered, the learner should then be able to perform the task. Task components are called *subtasks,* and an essential subtask is one that is necessary for the learner to successfully complete the task. To illustrate, we will use the following example of a teacher who wants to know if her students have acquired a knowledge of U.S. geography. More specifically, the teacher wishes to determine if they know the capitals of the 50 states. The teacher gives them a ditto with the states listed in alphabetical order. Next, the teacher directs the students to write the name of the capital city on the line next to the corresponding state. Conditions for the test include a 30-minute time limit and prohibited use of reference aids such as an atlas or dictionary. What is the task in this example? Is it "knows U.S. geography"? Is it "knows the capitals for each of the 50 states"? Neither is correct. Both are abilities, not tasks. How about "associates capital cities with states"? Much better. Except how will the association be made? Is it matching? Multiple choice? In this particular case, it happens to be fill-in. Therefore, the best

statement of task would be "identifies *in writing* the capital city for each of the 50 states." This describes the test behavior required of the student if he is to demonstrate acquisition of the ability being measured. Now that we have a task statement, we need to isolate, sequence, and describe all of the essential components which, when mastered, enable the learner to successfully perform that task. There's only one problem. We still need more information for our task analysis. Unfortunately, this will be the case most of the time. It is virtually impossible to write a task statement that provides enough information to enable you to write a task analysis without the statement becoming a short novella. We suggest that you write a performance objective to go along with a short statement of the task. The latter may be used to quickly convey the essence of the task to others while the former will provide enough data for the task analysis. In the above example, our task statement was "identifies in writing the capital city for each of the 50 states." The performance objective that goes with this task statement is referred to as a *terminal objective* because it describes the behavior required of the learner at the end of a period of instruction. It may be stated as "Given a ditto with the 50 states listed in alphabetical order, the learner will correctly write the name of the corresponding capital city next to each state. The task will be completed in 30 minutes without reference aids and with 100% accuracy. A response will be considered correct if it is readily distinguishable as the name of the capital city of the state it is written next to." Quite a mouthful, isn't it? You can see why it is impractical to use this as a statement of the task. Still, because it describes the task in such detail, the task analysis may not be completed without it. We can use this terminal objective to isolate our essential subtasks. In the example above, these subtasks would be (1) able to read (i.e., decode) the names of the 50 states listed on the test, (2) able to write the names of the 50 capital cities, (3) able to spell the names of the 50 capital cities well enough so that they can be distinguished as such, (4) able to write the names of the 50 capital cities in the correct place, and (5) able to name (i.e., say) a capital city for each state.

Our next step is to list these subtasks in order of complexity, if possible, from most to least difficult. The reason for this is that we want to "test down" when we diagnose a student's learning problem. By testing the student on the most difficult task first, we may save lots of valuable time in the diagnostic process. If the student is able to perform the first or second most difficult task, we may assume (notice we said assume) that he is capable of performing tasks requiring less complex skills and/or knowledge. This is the advantage of sequencing the subtasks. Of course, not all subtasks can be easily sequenced. It often depends upon the interdependence of the subtasks. We are not suggesting that acquisition of a subtask in every hierarchy is *always* dependent upon acquisition of a preceding subtask. All subtasks can't be arranged into a "task ladder." Often a group of subtasks resembles a "task tree" with many branches of subtasks all at the same difficulty level. Still, all subtasks may be necessary for the task's successful completion. In these cases, all subtasks must be tested.

We sequenced our example as follows: (1) able to name (i.e., say) a capital city for each state, (2) able to spell the name of the 50 capital cities well enough so that they can be distinguished as such, (3) able to read the names of the 50 states, (4) able to write the names of the 50 capital cities in the correct places, and (5) able to write the names of the 50 capital cities.

Now that we have isolated and sequenced our subtasks, we are ready for the third step in the task analysis process—describing the subtasks. This is simply a matter of writing a performance objective which, along with directions and test materials, becomes a criterion-referenced test. Since we will not cover performance objectives and criterion-referenced tests until Chapter 8, you will not be required to describe any subtasks in this unit. Instead we have described them for you in Table 7.1 so that you may see what a completed task analysis looks like. As you look over Table 7.1, remember the steps in the task analysis process: isolate, sequence, and describe (i.e., write performance objectives for) all essential subtasks.

Table 7.1

Task Analysis/identifies in writing the capital city for each of the 50 states

---

Task: identify in writing the capital city for each of the 50 states
Terminal Objective: Given a ditto with the 50 states listed in alphabetical order, the learner will correctly write the name of the corresponding capital city next to each state. Task will be completed in 30 minutes without reference aids and with 100% accuracy. A response will be considered correct if it is easily distinguishable as the name of the capital city of the state it is written next to.

Subtask 1: able to name (i.e., say) a capital city for each state
Objective 1: Given the name of the state, the learner will say the correct name of the capital city for that state within 5 minutes and with 100% accuracy for all 50 states.

Subtask 2: able to spell the names of the 50 capital cities
Objective 2: Given the names of each of the 50 capital cities verbally, the learner will correctly spell each within 15 seconds. To be correct, each response when written by the examinee should be distinguishable by a third party as the name of the city it represents.

Subtask 3: able to read the names of the 50 states
Objective 3: Given the name of each of the 50 states on a flashcard, the learner will correctly pronounce each within 5 seconds and with 100% accuracy.

Subtask 4: able to write the names of the 50 capital cities in the correct places
Objective 4: Given the task described in the terminal objective (see p. 81) and told the correct answer for each item, the learner will write the answer in the correct place for each of the 50 items, taking no more than 15 seconds per item.

Table 7.1 *(cont.)*

Subtask 5: able to write the names of the 50 capital cities
Objective 5: Given the name of each of the 50 capital cities on a card, the learner will accurately copy each onto a piece of paper, taking no more than 15 seconds per card and with 100% accuracy. Responses will be considered accurate if they are legible enough to be accurately decoded by a third party.

Checkpoint 7.1

This checkpoint consists of two parts. Complete them according to the directions for each.

Part 1: able to identify a task for which a task analysis may be written.

Directions: Look at each of the following items and decide whether or not it would be possible to write a task analysis for it. The responses are as follows:

a. A task analysis could be written.

b. A task analysis could not be written because it is not a task.

c. A task analysis could not be written because not enough information about the task has been provided.

Write either *a, b,* or *c* in the blank provided after the task. You have 10 minutes to complete this task with 100% accuracy.

Task 1. Write the answers for each of the following:

4	6	3	7	5	7	
-1	-2	-0	-4	-4	-6	Response:_____

Task 2. Knows subtraction facts.   Response:_____

Task 3. Able to tell time.   Response:_____

Task 4. Given a ruler and a piece of plywood, the learner will use the ruler to measure the length, width, and thickness of the wood, saying each within one minute, and being accurate to within ⅛ of an inch.

Response:_____

Task 5. Match the opposites (antonyms) by drawing lines from one column to the other.

boy   down
big   cold
hot   girl
night   little
up   day

Response:_____

Task 6. Knows the concept "opposite."   Response:_____

Task 7. Given a toy clock and the question, "What time is it?" the learner will say the correct time when shown each of the following: 12:00, 2:30,

Checkpoint 7.1 *(cont.)*

> 6:15, 8:02, 7:20, 4:13, and 9:45. Responses will be made within 5 seconds and with 100% accuracy.

Response:_____

Task   8. Able to use a ruler.   Response:_____

Task   9. Writes his/her name.   Response:_____

Task 10. Follows directions.   Response:_____

Part 2: knows the operational definition of task analysis.

Directions: Complete the following operational definition of task analysis by filling in the missing words. You have one minute to complete this task with 100% accuracy.

Task analysis is the process of _____, _____, and _____ all
$\qquad\qquad\qquad\qquad\qquad$ (1) $\qquad\qquad$ (2) $\qquad\qquad\qquad$ (3)

of the essential _____ which, when mastered, enable the learner to
$\qquad\qquad\qquad\qquad$ (4)

successfully complete the task.

Acceptable Responses

Part 1		Part 2
1. *a*	6. *b*	(1) isolating
2. *b*	7. *a*	(2) sequencing
3. *b*	8. *b*	(3) describing
4. *a*	9. *c*	(4) subtasks
5. *a*	10. *c*	

Options

1. If you met CAP on both parts of the checkpoint, go on to the next unit.
2. If you failed to meet CAP, reread the text and retake the checkpoint.

> Unit 7.2: Writing a task analysis.
>
> Objective: Given 10 tasks (each written as a performance objective), the learner will write an acceptable task analysis for each.
>
> Prerequisites: Successful completion of the preceding unit in this chapter as well as the units on writing performance objectives (Appendix B).

Reading Assignment

In the last unit we operationally defined task analysis as the process of isolating, sequencing, and describing all of the essential subtasks. We will now attempt to demonstrate the first step in the process with the following example.

Suppose you want a child to cut a pattern out

of paper with a pair of scissors. You provide the learner with scissors and a piece of paper with the pattern of a triangle drawn on it in ¼-inch solid blue lines and require that the task be completed within one minute and without going off the blue lines at any time.

The subtasks essential to the successful completion of this task may be listed as follows:

1. Able to hold the paper in the nondominant hand
2. Able to cut with scissors
3. Able to move the paper with the nondominant hand while simultaneously operating the scissors with the dominant hand
4. Able to follow a pattern

Each of the above subtasks must be mastered before the learner can successfully complete the task. However, some would argue that the list is not complete. True, we could add a number of other subtasks distantly related to the terminal task, like being able to open and close scissors and holding scissors properly. These would certainly be necessary for successful completion of the terminal task. However, they are *implicit* in subtask 2 above. If we found through subsequent testing that the learner was unable to perform subtask 2 (i.e., cut with scissors) we would task analyze it and then we could list "holds scissors properly" and "opens and closes scissors." *The point is you go only as far as you need to in listing essential subtasks.* Try not to get carried away in listing too many subtasks that are implicit in subtasks already identified, or your task analysis will take too long to complete and be much too unwieldy to be of any real value. Also be certain to include only those subtasks that are essential to the completion of the task. For example, is it necessary for the learner to know the name of the object he is cutting out of paper? It certainly couldn't hurt, but is it essential to the successful completion of the task? We don't think so. Whenever you are in doubt about the "essential quality" of a subtask, it is a good idea to perform the task yourself and carefully list all of your actions. This will help you to separate the essential from the nonessential.

Look at the following terminal objective and the corresponding list of subtasks below it. Which of these subtasks are essential and which are nonessential to the successful completion of the task? Terminal objective: "Given a pencil, a piece of 8½-by-11-inch ruled paper, and a

3-by-5-inch card with his name written on it in manuscript, Ralph will write (i.e., copy) his name once on the ruled paper, meeting the criterion for acceptable performance within 60 seconds. To meet CAP, he must have done the following:

1. Formed all letters correctly so that they are legible
2. Made letters the correct size in relation to one another
3. Not allowed an inordinate amount of space between letters
4. Written the letters on one line, not going above or below that line more than ⅛ of an inch
5. Put the letters in the proper sequence

Now you decide which of the following are essential subtasks. After reading each subtask, write "E" for Essential and "NE" for Nonessential in the space provided. The discussion which follows will give you the correct answers.

_____ 1. Can hold a pencil
_____ 2. Can copy letters in sequence (i.e., more than one letter shown)
_____ 3. Can copy letters in isolation (i.e., one letter shown)
_____ 4. Can copy letters in isolation on a line
_____ 5. Knows the names of the letters in his name
_____ 6. Knows the alphabet
_____ 7. Can write letters on a line with the proper space between each
_____ 8. Can read his name
_____ 9. Can copy a triangle, a square, and a circle
_____10. Can focus on one letter at a time

There certainly may be more essential subtasks. However, that is not important now. What is important is that you can identify the essential subtasks from the nonessential. Let's take them one at a time.

1. Is it essential that the learner be able to hold a pencil if he is to write (i.e., copy) his name? Yes. An "E" should be next to 1 for essential.
2. Is it essential that the learner be able to copy letters when he is shown more than one at a time? Sure is. That's the terminal objective. Another "E."
3. Is it essential that the learner be able to copy letters when he is shown them one at a time? Sure, if you expect him to be able to copy when more than one letter is shown. An "E" should be next to 3.
4. Is it essential that the learner be able to copy letters in isolation on a line? Yes, if you want him to stay on the line as in your objective. Another "E."
5. Is it essential that the learner knows the names of the letters in his name? Don't be so quick to answer this one. Think now. Do you really have to know the names of the letters in order to copy them on

another piece of paper? You could get the student to copy in Russian or Chinese. The names of the letters would be different and he probably wouldn't know them, but Ralph could still copy them even if he didn't know what he was copying. An "NE" for nonessential should be next to 5.

6. Is it essential that the learner know the alphabet? Remember what we discussed in 5. Letters are no more than squiggly and straight lines at tangents to each other. In the objective we simply ask that the child transfer these squiggly and straight lines to another piece of paper by means of writing (i.e., copying). Surely Ralph doesn't have to say the alphabet or say the names of the letters in order to copy them; does he? Another "NE."

7. Is it essential that he write letters on the line with the proper space between each? Sure, otherwise you would have to drop proper spacing as one of the CAPs in the terminal objective. An "E" should be next to 7.

8. Is it essential that he read his name? "NE" please. "Reading" here means saying the name of the word (i.e., written symbol) that one sees. We are not requiring that he say the name of the word on the 3-by-5-inch card but simply that he write (i.e., copy) it, letter by letter, on another piece of paper. Another "NE."

9. Is it essential that he be able to copy a triangle, square, and a circle? Although some children learn how to copy triangles, squares, and circles before they learn to write (i.e., copy) their names, countless others were taught to copy letters, numbers, and words before they became proficient at copying simple geometric shapes. An "NE" should be next to 9.

10. Is it essential that he be able to focus on one letter at a time? You bet. It is especially essential if we are not requiring that he be able to read the word, know it's his name, and then write the letters from memory. An "E" should be next to 10. How can a kid copy an "R" if he can't separate it from an "A"?

Get the idea about essential and nonessential? Don't worry about any conflicts we may have had over the best 10 subtasks. The nonessential ones were not so obvious. If you missed the obvious ones, there are two likely explanations for your trouble: (1) you don't understand the process and need to review this chapter or (2) you lack the necessary knowledge about handwriting and need to read about it.

So far we have discussed only the isolating process in task analysis. Since this is by far the most difficult and most important process, it requires the most attention. Once you have accurately identified all of the essential subtasks, it should require less effort on your part to sequence them. Also, mistakes in sequencing subtasks will not dramatically affect the diagnostic process as will errors in isolating and describing them. Therefore, we will not deal with the sequencing process here except to provide you with some examples of subtasks listed both

Table 7.2
Sequencing Subtasks

Subtasks for "writes sums to simple addition problems":

Listed Randomly	*Sequenced According to Complexity*
1. Writes numbers from memory	1. Reads add sign
2. Reads number	2. Reads numbers
3. Reads add sign	3. Writes numbers from memory
4. Demonstrates comprehension of addition sign	4. Demonstrates comprehension of addition sign
5. Demonstrates knowledge of addition facts	5. Demonstrates knowledge of addition facts

Subtasks for "ties shoelaces":

Listed Randomly	*Sequenced According to Operation*
1. Folds one bow under the other	1. Crosses laces
2. Folds one lace under the other	2. Folds one lace under the other
3. Crosses laces	3. Pulls each lace in opposite direction simultaneously
4. Pulls each lace in opposite direction simultaneously	4. Folds each lace into a bow
5. Folds each lace into a bow	5. Folds one bow under the other
6. Pulls each bow in opposite direction simultaneously	6. Pulls each bow in opposite direction simultaneously

randomly and in sequence according to complexity and operation (see Table 7.2).

As for the process of describing subtasks, we expected you to complete the units on writing performance objectives in Appendix B before you began work on this unit. Given that you have successfully completed this material and you feel confident in your ability to isolate and sequence essential subtasks, we invite you to try Checkpoint 7.2.

Checkpoint 7.2

Directions: Write a task analysis for *any five* of the tasks described below. Isolate, sequence, and describe as many essential subtasks as you can for each task. Take no more than 5 minutes per task.

1. Given a 16-inch playground ball, the learner will bounce the ball on the floor within a 12-inch square target area, catching the ball with two hands after one bounce. The learner will do this for 10 consecutive bounces without missing the target area or failing to catch the ball after one bounce.

2. Given a page of nonsense trigrams (consonant-vowel-consonant words), the learner will correctly read at least 90 trigrams in one minute with two errors or less.

3. Given 10 pictures of the faces of clocks with hands set at different times (i.e., hour, ½ hour, ¼ hour), the student will give the correct time with 90% accuracy, taking no more than 5 minutes per clock.

4. Given 9 different strips of colored paper (i.e., black, white, red, blue, green, yellow, orange, purple, brown), the student will say the correct color for each with 100% accuracy, taking no more than 5 minutes per color.

5. Given a nail, a hammer, and a piece of wood, the learner will hammer the nail all the way into the wood in 10 seconds without bending the nail.

6. Given a piece of paper with a triangle drawn on it and scissors, the learner will cut out the pattern in 30 seconds without going off the line more than ¼ of an inch.

7. Given a dictionary and a list of 10 unknown words, the learner will locate each in the dictionary and write the corresponding page number next to each with 90% accuracy in 30 minutes.

8. Given a page of short division problems, with no remainder, the learner will correctly write the answer to 50 in one minute with no more than two errors.

9. Given the instructions "Hop on one foot to the wall," the learner will do so without balance aids and without touching the raised foot to the floor more than once.

10. Given a reader at grade level, the learner will orally read 100 words correctly per minute with two errors or less.

For each subtask you have listed, ask this question: Is it possible to complete the total task if the student does not possess the subtask skill? If the answer is *no,* then you have isolated an essential subtask. Check your opinion with other students, teachers, or your instructor.

8

Criterion-Referenced Testing

Unit 8.1: What is criterion-referenced testing?

Objective: Given statements pertaining to criterion-referenced and norm-referenced testing, the reader will be able to discriminate between each.

Prerequisite: Successful completion of preceding units.

Reading Assignment

In order to understand what a criterion-referenced test is, you must first know something about normative testing. In the paragraphs below, both types of testing are compared with regard to purpose, construction, standardization, and the relative advantages and disadvantages of each. We suggest that you read the material carefully before you take the posttest. However, if you feel that you already know the characteristics of both types of testing, you may skip the reading assignment and go directly to the posttest. Normative and criterion-referenced testing were briefly discussed in Chapter 3, and are also discussed throughout Appendix A.

Purpose of NRT

The major purpose of the norm-referenced test (NRT) is to help educators see how a student compares with other students of the same age. This may be accomplished by comparing an individual's performance on a NRT with the average performance or norm of her peer group. For example, suppose you taught third grade and 8½-year-old Kathi entered your class in the middle of the school year with a note from home explaining that her records have been sent to the wrong place and may not turn up for another two weeks. How would you know what work to assign her? Is she an average student? Above average? Below? You don't want to waste a lot of time in trial-and-error teaching to identify her present level of functioning in each subject area. What would you do? You might administer a norm-referenced achievement test such as the Wide Range Achievement Test (WRAT). The raw score norms on the WRAT for an 8½-year-old child are 36 in spelling, 29 in arithmetic, and 54 in reading. This simply means that a child who is 8 years, 6 months old should be functioning on an academic level commensurate with the sixth month of third grade. Theoretically, the average student at this level achieves the respective raw scores 36, 29, and 54 to attain the grade equivalency of third grade, sixth month. For argument's sake, let's make Kathi's scores 29 in spelling, 40 in reading, and 30 in arithmetic. These scores indicate that Kathi is below the norm for this age in spelling and reading, but is functioning above the norm in arithmetic. Although this information might help you begin to make the necessary group and/or book assignments for Kathi, it won't tell you *why* she is functioning below the norm in spelling and reading. All it tells you is how Kathi compares with her peers. However, since this is what you wanted to know in the first place, the norm-referenced WRAT has served your purpose well. A thorough discussion of normative test scores can be found in Appendix A.

Purpose of CRT

To find out *why* your new student is not performing as well as her peers in spelling and reading, you will have to do some further testing to find what particular skills and/or knowledge she is lacking. This is where the criterion-referenced test (CRT) becomes useful. The purpose of the CRT is to help educators determine whether or not a student has certain skills or knowledge. Once it is determined what a student should be taught, you may begin instruction, and, because some CRTs don't lose reliability if given every day, you will be able to test your student daily to determine when to end instruction.

Construction

Tests are constructed according to the purposes they are designed for. Because the NRT is used

to determine how one student compares with her age-mates, it is important that the test is contructed with a wide range of difficulty among test items. For example, going back to Kathi and the WRAT, you will recall that her scores placed her below the norm in spelling and reading and above the norm in arithmetic. Her actual grade equivalencies were 2.3 (second grade, third month) in spelling, 2.1 (second grade, first month) in reading and 3.9 (third grade, ninth month) in arithmetic. If we had given her a test with items that did not vary greatly in difficulty, we would not have been able to identify her academic level of functioning. If the WRAT only included items taught at the third grade level, all we would know from her performance is that she is functioning below grade level in spelling and reading. We would not know *how far below* grade level because the test would not include items below third grade. This is why it is necessary to include items that vary in difficulty, from those performed successfully by preschoolers to those taught in high school. Because of this, the NRT is able to provide us with information regarding a student's performance in relation to her peers. Figure 8.1, which is the Level I arithmetic subtest of the WRAT, provides you with an example of the types of progressively difficult items found on NRTs. Notice the wide variety of items beginning with something as simple as counting dots all the way up to finding the square root. There are items on this page that "average" third graders would pass, and there are others that few third graders, if any, would pass. Remember that the test was designed this way on purpose so that it becomes possible to measure a student's academic level of functioning in relation to her peers.

The criterion-referenced test, on the other hand, is composed of items that are all at the same level of difficulty. Because this results in less variation in performance, you would not use a CRT to see how a student compares with her age-mates. A wide variety of items ranging from easy to hard is not always necessary. The CRT is used to determine whether or not a student has a particular skill or knowledge, so it includes only those items that measure the skill or knowledge in question. Student performance

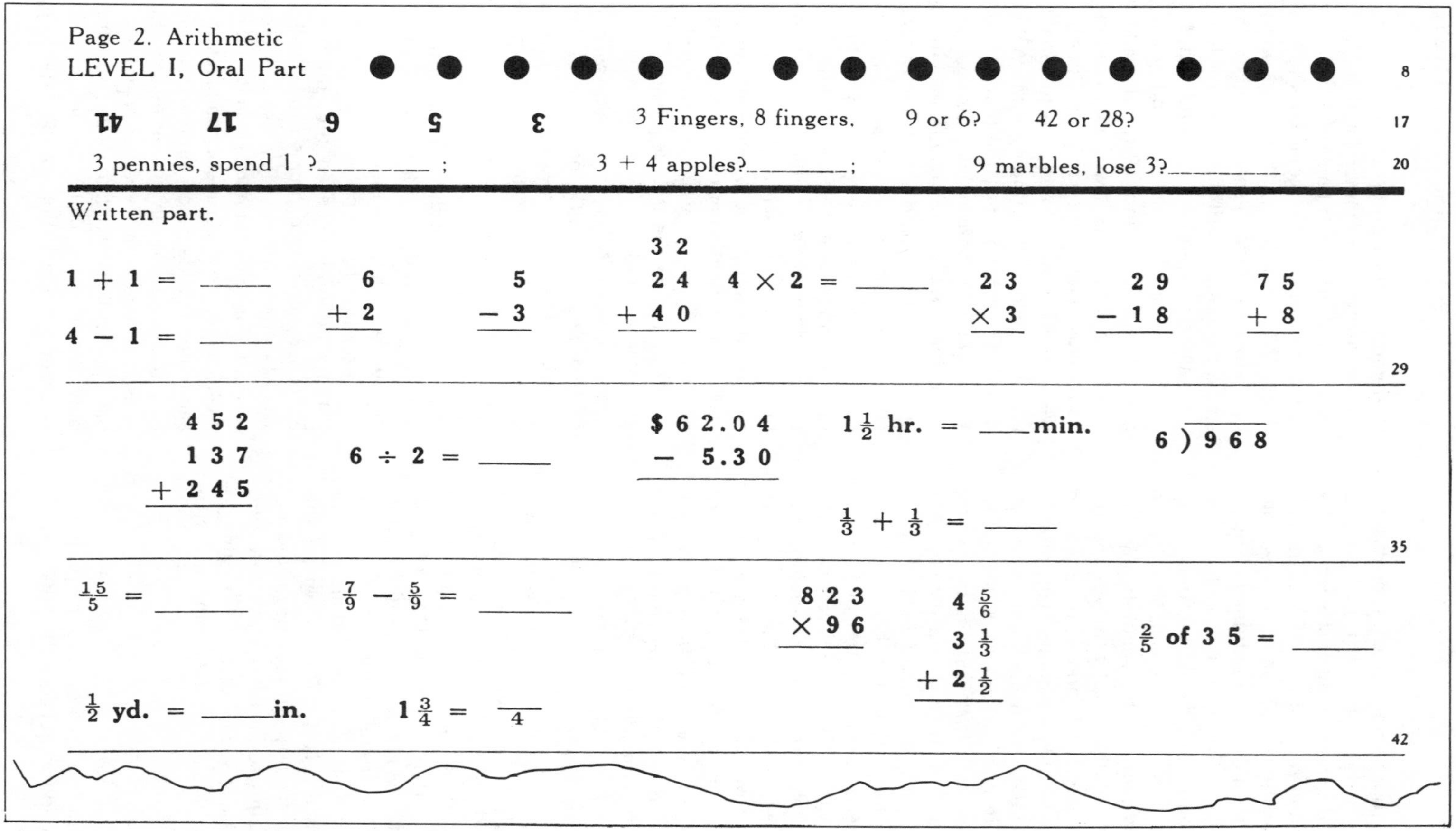

Page 2. Arithmetic
LEVEL I, Oral Part

● ● ● ● ● ● ● ● ● ● ● ● ● ●

8   17   20   29   35   42

3 pennies, spend 1? _____   3 + 4 apples? _____ ; _____   3 Fingers, 8 fingers.   9 or 6?   42 or 28?   9 marbles, lose 3? _____

3   5   6   17   41

Written part.

$$1 + 1 = \text{_____} \qquad 6 \qquad 5$$
$$4 - 1 = \text{_____} \qquad +2 \qquad -3$$

$$\begin{array}{r} 4\,5\,2 \\ 1\,3\,7 \\ +\,2\,4\,5 \\ \hline \end{array} \qquad 6 \div 2 = \text{_____}$$

$$1\tfrac{5}{9} = \text{_____}$$

$$\tfrac{1}{2}\ \text{yd.} = \text{_____ in.}$$

$$\begin{array}{r} 3\,2 \\ 2\,4 \\ +\,4\,0 \\ \hline \end{array} \qquad 4 \times 2 = \text{_____} \qquad \begin{array}{r} 2\,9 \\ -\,1\,8 \\ \hline \end{array} \qquad \begin{array}{r} 7\,5 \\ +\,8 \\ \hline \end{array}$$

$$\begin{array}{r} 2\,3 \\ \times\,3 \\ \hline \end{array}$$

$$\begin{array}{r} \$\,6\,2\,.\,0\,4 \\ -\,5\,.\,3\,0 \\ \hline \end{array} \qquad \begin{array}{r} 8\,2\,3 \\ \times\,9\,6 \\ \hline \end{array}$$

$$\tfrac{7}{9} - \tfrac{5}{9} = \text{_____} \qquad 1\tfrac{3}{4} = \dfrac{\text{_____}}{4}$$

$$6\,)\overline{\,9\,6\,8} \qquad 1\tfrac{1}{2}\ \text{hr.} = \text{_____ min.}$$

$$\tfrac{1}{3} + \tfrac{1}{3} = \text{_____} \qquad \tfrac{2}{5}\ \text{of}\ 3\,5 = \text{_____}$$

$$\begin{array}{r} 4\tfrac{5}{6} \\ 3\tfrac{1}{3} \\ +\,2\tfrac{1}{2} \\ \hline \end{array}$$

Figure 8.1

An example of a norm-referenced test.

NOTE: From *Wide Range Achievement Test* by J. F. Jastek, S. W. Bijou, and S. R. Jastek. Copyright 1965 by Guidance Associates of Delaware. Reprinted by permission.

will not vary greatly on the CRT because the item difficulty does not vary. Students either pass or don't pass the CRT. They either have the skill or knowledge being measured or they do not. Figure 8.2 provides an example of the kinds of items one might expect to find on a CRT. Notice that they are all the same type of example: simple addition equations written in vertical fashion with sums no greater than 18. This happens to be first-grade material. If a student passed this test (sometimes called a *probe sheet*), does it mean that she is working on a first-grade level in arithmetic? Not necessarily. All it tells us is that she possesses the skill being measured, regardless of grade or age. Since this is all we really wanted to know, it is not necessary to include any other items on the test.

Standardization

In order to determine how a student compares with her peers, it is obvious that you need a sample of the student's behavior as well as a sample from her peers. The way to obtain those samples is to gather a representative group of the student's peers, test them, and then calculate the mean performance of the group. The mean is usually represented by a number or score which thereafter may be designated as the performance expected of a child that age. This process is called *norming*. Now that you have a sample of the group's behavior, you can administer the same test to other students and see how their performance compares with the norm. The key word used above is "representative" because it is the selection of the standardization sample that separates NRTs and CRTs.

A representative sample used in the standardization of a NRT should include a relatively *large* number of individuals of the same age and/or grade. These individuals are selected at random with no prior attention paid to their ability in the skill or knowledge being measured. If only the fast or slow child were selected, we would wind up with a high or low norm that was not truly representative of the age group being tested. Therefore, the standardization group for the NRT is chosen at random from the population to ensure an even distribution of skills. For example, if you wanted to standardize a math test that might be used with *all*

college freshmen, you would not go to the Massachusetts Institute of Technology for your sample. Average MIT freshmen might have superior interest, training, and aptitude in math. They are a select group and not representative of the major population who would be taking the test. If your test was standardized on this group, it would have limited value because the norms could only be used to compare a special group of students with the norms (e.g., engineering, math, and science majors).

In direct contrast, the criterion-referenced sample need only include a *small* number of individuals. The individuals may differ widely according to age and/or grade. However, they all would have one thing in common—they would possess the skill or knowledge being tested. This is important, since the CRT is used to assess whether or not a student has a particular skill. This is accomplished by comparing the student's score with the score achieved by individuals possessing the skill or knowledge being measured. We can't use a random sample here because the students picked by chance might not have the skill tested. For example, if we wanted to find out if a student knows consonant sounds, we would construct a CRT made up only of consonant sounds and then pick our representative sample on which to standardize the test. If we chose students at random, we would be liable to include some who did not know their consonant sounds, and their performance would lower the score we eventually came up with. Therefore, we would be careful to select a group of individuals who did know their consonant sounds. We would then proceed to give them the test. Next, we would rank the scores from lowest to highest and find the lower half of these *successful* students. The average score of the lower half of these students is called the "minimum criterion for acceptable performance." This score would become the standard against which future scores are compared.

After establishing a minimum criterion, we can give the test to other students to see if they know the consonant sounds. If they score at least as well as the standard for the test, we may say that they have the skill being measured. If not, this is an area that they will need work in. Notice the difference between the standardization samples in the two examples we have used. On

Behavioral Objective

That the student demonstrate the ability to add single digits to single digits at a rate of 35 digits correct per minute for three successive days.

NAME________________ TEACHER__________ SCHOOL__________
GRADE________________ TIME________ CORRECT______ ERROR______
ADMINISTERED BY ________________________ DATE__________

4	2	4	6	2	3	3	5
+2	+3	+0	+1	+2	+0	+4	+1
0	7	1	2	6	1	1	5
+0	+2	+9	+8	+4	+1	+7	+9
2	5	0	0	7	8	8	7
+4	+5	+8	+9	+7	+7	+9	+9
6	7	3	8	4	7	8	5
+5	+6	+7	+5	+9	+4	+3	+7
2	6	5	3	6	4	1	5
+9	+8	+5	+3	+9	+4	+2	+4
9	7	9	2	1	2	3	7
+5	+8	+9	+6	+4	+10	+9	+2

Figure 8.2
An addition probe.

the norm-referenced math test for college freshmen, we didn't want to pick a select group of successful math students. We were looking for the typical college freshman. On the criterion-referenced consonant test, we wanted to pick a select group of students. We were looking for students who had the skill being measured. Remember this, because it is probably the most basic difference between the two types of testing.

Advantages and Disadvantages

To be sure, both normative and criterion-referenced tests have disadvantages. However, it is our opinion that for educational diagnosis the disadvantages of normative testing far outweigh those of criterion testing. For one thing, the NRT provides us only with "static" data. Because most NRTs lose their reliability if given more than twice in a school year, it is not likely that we will get more than two test scores for a child, and these are usually recorded before (pre) and after (post) instruction. We then determine academic growth by calculating the differences between a student's pre- and postscores to evaluate the effectiveness of our instruction (see Appendix A, Unit 5). However, if at the end of the year our instruction appears to have been ineffective, it is often too late to do anything about it. One of the disadvantages of the normative test is that it tells us only what has happened, not what is happening. It provides us only with static data and therefore does not allow us to make changes in our instruction while we are still teaching the child.

The CRT, on the other hand, can provide us with "dynamic" data because the data are collected over time. Since CRTs may be given every day without losing their reliability, it is possible to make a chart of a student's performance in one particular area of the curriculum. The chart then enables us to see movement or growth from day to day while we are still teaching the child. If the "movement" is too slow for us, we still have time to change our instruction and continue to collect data over time until we are satisfied with a program. This is one of the major advantages of the CRT.

Another disadvantage of the normative test is that its test items vary so much in complexity that there is often only one or two samples of each (see Figure 8.1). It then becomes necessary to analyze the child's errors and conduct further testing to determine specifically what the problem is. In direct contrast, the CRT includes test items that are all at the same level (see Figure 8.2). By using a CRT, a teacher can see the same error more than once, which makes it easier to see what the child needs to be taught. Task analysis and further testing are usually not necessary, since it becomes readily obvious what the child needs to be taught. This also means that educational planning may be constructed from the test itself, all of which saves you precious time for instruction.

Occasionally, there is a disparity between the behavior required on the norm-referenced test and the behavior expected of the child in the classroom. We can best describe this with the following hypothetical case. Billy was a third grader who, after taking a norm-referenced achievement test, scored at the 3.6 level in spelling. At first glance, there was nothing unusual about this, except that Billy had failed every spelling test given to him that year. Every Friday he brought home an "F" on his spelling paper. When his parents heard about his achievement scores, they were dumbfounded at first, then angry. They complained to the principal that Billy's teacher wasn't motivating him in school and that was why he wasn't "working up to his potential." His teacher's confusion and frustration were evidenced by contradictory remarks that Billy was both lazy (in class) and lucky (on the test). Who was right? Billy's parents or his teacher? In this case, neither. Billy's teacher was doing everything he knew how to motivate Billy in school. So it wasn't his fault. But neither was it Billy's. In fact, Billy should have gotten a medal for persevering in the face of failure. However, his teacher was right about his being lucky on the test. You see, the behavior expected of Billy on the spelling section of the achievement test was different from the behavior expected of him on his Friday quizzes. As part of the achievement test, Billy was given a page with rows of words on it. In each row were four words, one of which was the correct spelling of a word dictated to him. The teacher said, "In the first row, underline the correct spelling of the word *enough*." Billy looked at each of the four words in the row and underlined one of them. The same procedure was used for the other items on the page. Sometimes Billy actually recognized the correct word and sometimes he just guessed. Since there was always a 25% chance of guessing the correct answer on this test, it was conceivable that Billy's score in spelling was more a result of guessing skill than spelling skill. The test behavior was in marked contrast to the behavior expected of Billy on Friday's quiz, when his teacher dictated a word and he was to write it from memory. Needless to say, this disparity caused a great deal of confusion, not to mention friction, between school and home with the child caught in the middle.

This would never happen with a well-designed CRT because there is no disparity between test and classroom behaviors. Since the best CRTs are teacher-prepared, they may be tailor-made for each setting. For example, instead of using a normative achievement test, Billy's teacher could have taken the words from Billy's word list and made a CRT. Instead of counting the whole words correct or incorrect, the teacher could have counted the total letters correct and the letters in correct sequence. The teacher wouldn't need to standardize the test to determine the minimum criterion for acceptable performance because obviously instruction on the words would continue until Billy reached 100% accuracy. Billy could be tested daily after each period of instruction. As his performance improved, the teacher could send his CRTs home to show his parents that good things were happening in school. If there wasn't any improvement in his spelling performance on the CRTs, it would alert the teacher to make changes in his instruction while there was still time left to teach. If there was improvement in Billy's performance on the CRTs, everyone would be reasonably certain that it was due to effective instruction and not the result of a disparity between test and curriculum behaviors.

The interpretation of a child's performance as above average, average, or below average may change depending upon the standardization group the performance is compared with. This can happen even though the student's raw score does not change. We'll use another hypothetical case to illustrate this. Jim was the fastest runner in his eighth grade class. He won all of the 100-yard dashes in an average time of 18 seconds, but when he ran against the boys in the other eighth-grade class, he lost every race and looked slow in the process, even though his average of 18 seconds remained the same. Is Jim fast or just the fastest among a group of slow runners? Looking at the situation more closely, we see that the average time for the 100-yard dash in Jim's class is 20.5 seconds while the average for the same distance in the other eighth-grade class is 15 seconds. His performance against his classmates was interpreted as "above average" (i.e., 18 seconds compared to a mean of 20.5) while his performance against the faster class was interpreted as "below average" (i.e., 18 seconds compared to a mean of 15). Anyone who makes an interpretation of a child's performance on a normative test must first know something about the makeup of the standardization group and about how the norms for that group were derived. This is not a problem with a CRT because the interpretation of an individual's performance on a CRT does not change regardless of the group the student is compared with. This is because performance is always compared against a *fixed* standard, representing what's good, instead of the average, which in many instances, is not always good. In Jim's case, if we had used his average time and compared it with the standard of 10 seconds for the 100-yard dash, we would have known immediately that while Jim was the fastest runner in his class, he was not a fast runner. There is a difference. The CRT makes this distinction and, in so doing, allows educators to make more reliable interpretations of a child's test performances.

Checkpoint 8.1

Directions: Mark "CR" for criterion-referenced or "NR" for norm-referenced next to each of the 25 statements about testing below. Take no more than 9 minutes to complete the task. You may not use reference aids. CAP is 100% accuracy.

Checkpoint 8.1 *(cont.)*

_____ 1. Educational planning may be constructed from the test itself.

_____ 2. Helps educators see how a student compares with other students her own age.

_____ 3. Is used to assess whether or not a student has a particular skill or knowledge.

_____ 4. It is important that in the test's construction there is a wide range of difficulty among test items.

_____ 5. Composed of items that are all at the same level of difficulty.

_____ 6. The WRAT is this type of test.

_____ 7. There is usually a disparity between the test behavior and the expected curriculum behavior.

_____ 8. Provides us with "dynamic" data because the data are collected over time.

_____ 9. Uses "static" data collected before and after a period of instruction has occurred.

_____10. Consists of individual test items that include several behaviors requiring further analysis to determine specific deficits.

_____11. Is constructed so that all individuals within a group may either pass or fail.

_____12. The learner's performance is always compared against a fixed standard representing what's good instead of what's average.

_____13. Is standardized on a random sample drawn from a population of individuals having age and grade in common, but not the skill or knowledge to be measured (i.e., some have the skill or knowledge and some do not).

_____14. Is standardized on a sample drawn from a population of individuals who all possess the measured skill or knowledge but who are not necessarily the same age.

_____15. The interpretation of an individual's performance as above average, average, or below average may change depending upon the standardization group it is compared with.

_____16. It allows you to make changes in your instruction while you are still teaching the child.

_____17. The child is given the opportunity to make the same error more than once, which makes it easier for you to see what she needs to be taught simply by looking over her errors.

_____18. It may be tailor-made for each child since it is usually teacher-prepared.

_____19. Billy was made a pitcher in Little League because he's the tallest boy on his team.

_____20. Billy was made a pitcher in Little League because he can throw a baseball harder than his teammates.

_____21. Billy was made a pitcher in Little League because he always throws strikes (i.e., pitches the ball within a defined target area).

_____22. She got an "A" on the test because she made fewer errors than her classmates.

Checkpoint 8.1 *(cont.)*

_____23. She passed the test because she made less than the quota of errors allowed.

_____24. Karna is reading on a third-grade level.

_____25. Karna is in the top reading group in her class.

Acceptable Responses

1. CR	6. NR	11. CR	16. CR	21. CR
2. NR	7. NR	12. CR	17. CR	22. NR
3. CR	8. CR	13. NR	18. CR	23. CR
4. NR	9. NR	14. CR	19. NR	24. NR
5. CR	10. NR	15. NR	20. NR	25. NR

Options

1. If you scored 100% on this checkpoint, you may go on to the next unit in this chapter.
2. If you scored less than 100%, go back and reread the reading assignment. Then take the checkpoint again.

Unit 8.2: How to write a criterion-referenced test.

Objective: Given the directions to do so, the learner will be able to write an acceptable criterion-referenced test.

Prerequisites: Successful completion of preceding units as well as the units on writing performance objectives (Appendix B).

Reading Assignment

Writing a CRT does not require that you hold a Phi Beta Kappa key. More teachers would be writing CRTs if they weren't so conditioned about commercially prepared tests. They seem to think that in order for a test to be of any value, it has to be written by a psychologist, standardized on a population of thousands, and published by a large corporation. To be of value, any test, whether it be criterion- or norm-referenced, should provide you with answers to questions you might have about a student's skills. As long as a test can consistently provide you with accurate answers to these questions, it should not make any difference who wrote it, who published it, or how much it cost.

As stated in the first unit of this chapter, the major purpose of the CRT is to tell you whether or not a child has a particular ability (i.e., skill or knowledge). For this purpose you do not need a commercially prepared test. You can write one yourself. By following the directions listed below, you should be able to write CRTs for any curricular area.

Developing a CRT

1. Decide what specific questions you want answered about a student's behavior. What ability (i.e., skill and/or knowledge) do you want to test?
2. Write a performance objective which describes how you are going to test the student. It should include *(a)* what the student must do (i.e., what behavior must be engaged in); *(b)* under what conditions the student will engage in this behavior; and *(c)* how well the student must perform in order to pass the test. If the performance objective is relevant, your CRT will be valid. If the performance objective is complete and comprehensive, your CRT will be reliable. CRT reliability and validity are discussed later in this unit and in more detail in Appendix A.
3. Use the performance objective to help you construct

(i.e., write) your CRT. All of the necessary components of a CRT may be found in your performance objective. These components are *(a)* the directions for administration and scoring, *(b)* the criterion for passing the test, and *(c)* the materials and/or test items necessary.

4. Identify those individuals who you (or a qualified "expert") feel possess the skill being measured by the CRT. Administer the CRT to these individuals and use the minimum level of their performance as a standard for passing your test. This standard may be referred to as the *criterion for acceptable performance* (CAP). It is important that you consistently administer and score your CRT according to the prespecified directions.

We will now construct a CRT using each of the steps listed above. First, we need a question to answer regarding a child's behavior. We have arbitrarily chosen "knowledge of eight basic colors." Next, we will write a performance objective that includes the behavior expected of the child on the test, the conditions under which the child will take the test, and how well she must perform in order to pass it. Let's start with behavior. The behavior we want is, "says names of the colors." This seems like a reasonable request to make of a child when you want to test knowledge of colors. Next, we'll list the conditions under which she will say the names of the colors.

Should the child say the names of the colors when asked? Is this what you want to know . . . if she can say the names without making associations between name and color? Since we chose the questions in the first place, we should explain what we mean by "knowledge of eight basic colors." We want to know if the child can recognize (i.e., name) each of the eight basic colors when she sees them. Therefore, we think our student should say the name of each basic color when the teacher holds up each color of crayon. We also want the student to respond to each request within 3 seconds. Now for the criterion for acceptable performance. Remember in the first unit of this chapter we said that CAP should come from a group of individuals who all possess the knowledge or skill being measured. Since our example is knowledge of colors, we need to find a group of individuals who possess this ability and see how well they do on our test. We would then use their performance as our CAP. Actually we don't need to do this in our example, since most of us would agree that 100% accuracy (eight out of eight) should be used. After all, we can't really say that a child knows the eight basic colors unless she gives the correct response for each.

We are now ready to look at all of the components of our performance objective. *For behavior:* "says the names of the eight basic colors." *For conditions:* "when the teacher holds up each crayon and within 3 seconds of each request." *For CAP:* "100% accuracy."

The complete performance objective may be stated as "Given a box containing crayons representing the eight basic colors, the child will say the correct color name, within 3 seconds, for each crayon that the examiner holds up. The student will give the names with 100% accuracy." Now that we have our performance objective, we are ready to construct the actual test. Instead of preparing a lengthy test manual like those usually associated with normative tests, simply take a 3-by-5-inch card and write the following headings down the left-hand side: Skill, Task, Materials, Directions, and CAP. Then use the performance objective in this paragraph to help you fill in the necessary information to the right of each heading. Check this against the sample CRT filled out in Table 8.1.

Table 8.1

Sample Criterion-Referenced Test

Task: Names each of the eight basic colors when shown

Materials: One box of crayons (to include eight basic colors). One scoring sheet (see Table 8.2).

Directions (to student): "Say the name of each crayon as I hold it up. You have only three seconds to give me your answer, so pay close attention. (Pick up the first crayon.) What color is this?" Repeat procedure for each of the eight colors. Do not tell the subject if she

Table 8.1 *(cont.)*

is correct or incorrect. Do not let the student see what you are marking. Use a stopwatch or a sweep second hand out of the subject's field of vision. Timing should begin immediately following the word *this* in the directions.

Scoring: Wait 3 seconds for response. If the response is incorrect, put the crayon back in the box and mark "incorrect" on the scoring sheet. If the response is correct, put the crayon back in the box and mark "correct" on the scoring sheet. If the child hesitates, wait the full 3 seconds before putting the crayon back in the box and mark "incorrect."

CAP: 100% accuracy

You may ask what happened to the performance objective we wrote. If you look carefully, you will see that we have incorporated all of the information under separate headings. For example, the behavior in the objective is listed as the task and appears again in the directions to the child. The conditions under which the behavior will occur are written next to materials and appear also in the directions to both subject and examiner as well as in the scoring sheet (see Figure 8.3). And, of course, CAP is listed separately. So you see all of the components of our objective have been used in the development of the CRT.

Before going on we should briefly discuss reliability and validity. A criterion-referenced test, like a normative test, is valid if it measures what you want it to (Appendix A, Unit 4). In other words, if the CRT is based upon a relevant performance objective, it has validity. A question

often asked is "Relevant to what?" If the behavior described in the performance objective will answer your original questions regarding the learner's performance, the performance objective is relevant, and therefore the CRT based upon that objective is valid. For example, the CRT we just wrote is valid because the performance objective we based the test on was relevant. The performance objective described a test that would answer our question regarding knowledge of colors. This is assuming that we all interpret "knowledge" in the same way. We think that "knowledge" implies the ability to name (among other things). Suppose we wrote a test based upon the following objective: Given two boxes of crayons representing the eight basic colors, the child will hold up the same color that the examiner holds up. Responses must be made within 3 seconds and with 100% accuracy. If you gave this test and the student

---

Skill: Knowledge of the eight basic colors
Task: Names each of the eight basic colors when shown

Subject _____   Age _____

Examiner _____   Date _____

Stimulus   *Response* (check one)
                                                     (correct)   (incorrect)

1. red   1_____   1_____
2. blue   2_____   2_____
3. yellow   3_____   3_____
4. green   4_____   4_____
5. black   5_____   5_____
6. orange   6_____   6_____
7. brown   7_____   7_____
8. purple   8_____   8_____

Figure 8.3

Scoring sheet (to go with sample CRT).

met CAP, would you then know if she had "knowledge" of the eight basic colors? Naming colors is not the same as matching them. Matching colors implies discrimination, which is only one facet of knowledge. If the question is, "Does she know her colors?", you'll probably want a test that requires *naming* behavior, not just *matching* behavior. A test is valid only if it provides you with an answer to a question you want answered. If it doesn't provide you with a complete answer to your question but instead provides an answer to a different question, then the test is not valid *for you*.

If your test is valid, it must be reliable. To ensure that your CRTs are always reliable, construct them from performance objectives that are complete and comprehensive. A complete performance objective contains all three components described in this unit (i.e., behavior, conditions, CAP). To be comprehensive, an objective must include components that are not open to interpretation and that are easily understood by different examiners. The behavior must be described in such a way that everyone knows exactly what the child is expected to do. For example, we described the behavior in our performance objective as "says the names of the colors." "Says," from the verb "to say," is not open to interpretation. Everyone knows that the child is required to speak a word and that word should be the name of the color. What color? The color of the crayon. What crayon? The crayon held by the examiner. What if there were no limits on the time allowed to complete the behavior? One day a child, given no time constraints, might achieve 100% accuracy while the next day, with a time limit, she might only get 50% correct. Such a test would not be reliable because it would produce different results with the same child. It is not only important to use time constraints to build in test reliability, but critical that you state them exactly and require the consistent use of a monitoring instrument (e.g., a stopwatch or a sweep second hand) when administering the test. Counting the seconds in your head one day and using a timepiece on the next may give the appearance of different performances. To summarize, your CRT will be valid if your performance objective is relevant. It will be reliable if your performance objective is complete and comprehensive. A more detailed

discussion of relevancy, completeness, and comprehensiveness in writing performance objectives appears in Appendix B.

For another example of the construction of a CRT, we refer you to Checkpoint 8.1. The question we wanted answered was "Does the reader have the ability to recognize criterion-referenced and normative testing?" To help us construct a CRT that would provide us with the answer, we first wrote a performance objective which would, in essence, describe the ultimate test. Remember that in order to ensure the validity of our test, the performance objective must be relevant, and in order to be relevant, the objective must describe behavior that provides an answer to our original question. Therefore, the behavior in our objective must have indicated whether or not you had the ability to discriminate between criterion- and norm-referenced testing. The behavior we described in our objective was "labels statements as criterion- or norm-referenced." The implication here was that the reader would be given statements to label. However, in writing performance objectives, one must be explicit and leave nothing to the imagination. The complete objective upon which the checkpoint was written was as follows: "Given 25 written statements pertaining to criterion- and norm-referenced testing, the learner will correctly label each in writing as "CR" or "NR." Task to be completed in 9 minutes without using reference aids and with 100% accuracy." This objective was complete because it included the behavior, the conditions under which the behavior would occur, and the criterion for acceptable performance. It was comprehensive because all three components were described in enough detail to eliminate any confusion. Nothing was left open to interpretation. Because the objective was complete and comprehensive, it was reliable. However, we know that being reliable does not make it valid. Again, we must go back to the relevancy of the objective. Did it describe behavior that would tell us what we wanted to know about the student? We felt that labeling statements in the manner described above would help you determine your knowledge of criterion- and norm-referenced testing. Therefore, we felt that our objective was relevant. Given that the objective was relevant, complete, and comprehensive, we went ahead and constructed our CRT. Remember that a CRT is nothing more than a performance objective with directions to the child and examiner as well as the test items or descriptions of materials. After we wrote our test items and our directions, we standardized our test. This was done to determine our time limits. We felt that in order to be able to discriminate between criterion- and norm-referenced testing, it was necessary to answer all 25 items correctly. We identified a population (students) who were knowledgeable in this area and standardized the test on them, using the minimum test score from this group for our CAP. One of the authors took the test first to determine an appropriate time constraint. It took him 3 minutes to complete the test in writing. However, since he was hopefully more familiar with the test material than you were, we felt obligated to provide you with more time. Having written the test items, the author was in a position to "anticipate" the meaning of an item by reading only the first few words. You would be new to the material and might need to read each statement *more than once* in order to get its full meaning. Therefore, 3 minutes as a time constraint did not seem realistic. It was then decided to administer the test to a small population of students whose knowledge of the subject was well-known to the authors. The longest time necessary to complete the test was 9 minutes and, we might add, everyone in the standardization group met the 100% CAP. Once we had our time constraint, we could use our CRT and it was ready for this text.

To review, we first identified what we wanted our test to measure. Second, we wrote a performance objective that was relevant, complete, and comprehensive. Third, we constructed our CRT based upon the objective by writing test items and directions to persons taking the test. Finally, we administered our test to a population of individuals who (we knew) had the skill being measured. This was done not so much to determine CAP but to identify an appropriate time constraint. (Time statements can appear in either the conditions or criterion section of a performance objective.)

Having given you the steps for writing a CRT as well as an example, we feel that you should now be ready to attempt to write your own CRTs. Remember, in order to write a CRT you must be skilled at writing performance objectives. If you aren't, we suggest that you complete the material on performance objectives in Appendix B. Otherwise, go ahead and take Checkpoint 8.2.

Checkpoint 8.2

Directions: Choose two of the questions below and write a criterion-referenced test for each. Take no more than 15 minutes to complete each test. Both tests must be valid and reliable and include all of the components of CRTs. Be sure to include any and all test materials that may be necessary as well as a statement indicating the source of your CAP (i.e., who you will standardize your test on).

1. Does the learner know how to use the telephone book to find someone's telephone number?

2. Does the learner know how to solve an arithmetic problem involving the addition of mixed numbers such as $5\frac{1}{2} + 2\frac{3}{4}$?

3. Is the learner able to tell time to the nearest minute?

4. Is the learner able to feed herself?

5. Is the learner able to hit a baseball?

Acceptable Responses

Please keep in mind your CRTs need not match ours word for word. They don't even have to resemble ours. We have provided them merely as a source of reference.

1. Does the learner know how to use the telephone book to find someone's telephone number?

Checkpoint 8.2 *(cont.)*

CRT (Sample)

Task: Able to use the telephone book to find and write a telephone number

Materials: A list of 5 names (see below)
A telephone book

Directions (to student): "Locate each of the names listed below in the telephone book. When you find the name, circle it in the book. Then write the corresponding telephone number on your paper on the line next to the name. You have 5 minutes to complete the entire task."

Directions (to examiner): None

Scoring: Count each correct if the telephone number written next to the name is *in fact* that person's number as it appears in the telephone book.

CAP: 100% accuracy (standardized on 25 third-grade students)

Name	*Telephone Number*
Breshahan, John T.	_____
Williams, Clarence R.	_____
Philomath, I. R.	_____
Johnson, E. A.	_____
Monroe, Cecil B.	_____

* * * * *

2. Does the learner know how to solve an arithmetic problem involving the addition of mixed numbers such as $5\frac{1}{2} + 2\frac{3}{4}$?

CRT (Sample)

Task: Able to write the answers to problems involving addition of mixed numbers

Materials: 10 problems (see below)

Directions (to student): "Write the answers to each of the problems below. You have 10 minutes to complete the task. Show all work."

Directions (to examiner): None

Scoring: Count each problem correct if correct answer is written legibly in the appropriate place and all work is shown (e.g., finding common denominator).

CAP: 100% accuracy (standardized on 15 eighth-grade math students)

1. $5\frac{1}{4}$ $+3\frac{2}{3}$	5. $6\frac{3}{4}$ $+3\frac{3}{5}$	8. $2\frac{1}{2}$ $+8\frac{3}{4}$
2. $6\frac{7}{8}$ $+4\frac{1}{2}$	6. $9\frac{1}{16}$ $+1\frac{3}{8}$	9. $6\frac{2}{3}$ $+1\frac{3}{4}$
3. $2\frac{2}{3}$ $+5\frac{3}{4}$	7. $7\frac{2}{3}$ $+4\frac{2}{5}$	10. $2\frac{1}{4}$ $+4\frac{2}{3}$
4. $5\frac{1}{2}$ $+8\frac{2}{3}$		

* * * * *

Checkpoint 8.2 *(cont.)*

3. Is the learner able to tell time to the nearest minute?

CRT (Sample)

Task: Able to read time from wall clock to nearest minute when requested

Materials: One wall clock within view

Directions (to student): "What time is it now?"

Directions (to examiner): Ask the subject what time it is 10 times within a 6-hour period. Be sure to vary the times to the hour, half hour, quarter hour, and minute.

Scoring: Count correct if the time is stated accurately and within 5 minutes. Accept responses for the hour only if "o'clock" is stated after the number. The half hour may be stated as "half past _____," "30 minutes after _____" or "_____ thirty." Acceptable quarter-hour responses are "_____ 15," "15 after _____," "a quarter past _____," or "a quarter to _____." Responses to the minute may be stated in any fashion as long as they convey the accurate time. *Note:* Not acceptable are responses such as, "the big hand is on the three and the little hand is on the six."

CAP: 100% accuracy (standardized on 10 third graders)

* * * * *

4. Is the learner able to feed herself?

CRT (Sample)

Task: Able to feed herself

Materials: Glass of liquid, for example, juice or milk; plate containing food already cut for eating; cup containing liquid (e.g., juice or milk); bowl containing cereal or soup; fork and spoon.

Directions (to student): See below

Directions (to examiner): Place glass of liquid in front of the child and say, "Take a drink of _____ from this glass." Put plate of cut (bite size) food in front of the child and, giving her a fork, say "Use this fork and show me how you eat this food with it." Give the child a bowl of soup or cereal and a spoon and say, "Show me how you eat your_____." Put a cup of liquid in front of the child and say, "Pick up the cup and drink from it." *Note:* Modeling by the examiner may be used in cases where receptive language is impaired.

Scoring: Count as acceptable if the child is able to transfer liquid and/or solid food from plate, bowl, glass, and cup to mouth without "excessive" spillage. All food must be ingested *without aid* within one minute of each request.

CAP: 100% accuracy (standardized on four Arizona State University faculty members at the "Dash-in" Restaurant, Tempe, Arizona)

* * * * *

5. Is the learner able to hit a baseball?

CRT (Sample)

Task: Able to hit a pitched baseball

Materials: Six baseballs; one bat

Directions (to student): See below

Directions (to examiner): Have the student stand in the batter's box while you stand on

Checkpoint 8.2 *(cont.)*

a regulation pitcher's mound 60 feet 6 inches away. Pitch one ball at a time to the student, making sure each is in the "strike zone" (i.e., thrown over the plate and between the student's chest and knees). Direct the batter to hit each ball as hard as possible.

Scoring: Count balls hit past the pitcher's mound as "hits"

CAP: Five hits out of six pitched balls (standardized on five members of a junior-high baseball team)

Options

1. If your criterion-referenced tests contained all of the necessary components and were valid and reliable, you may go on to the next chapter.
2. If your criterion-referenced tests lacked one or more components or were not valid or reliable, reread the reading assignment and take the checkpoint again.

9

Treatment-Referenced Evaluation

Unit 9.1: Curriculum-referenced evaluation.

Objective: Given an objective test on the material covered in this chapter, the reader will answer 100% of the items correctly, taking no more than 45 minutes.

Prerequisite: None.

Reading Assignment

In the last three chapters we described a diagnostic model that would enable the average classroom teacher to identify what a student should be taught. The task analytical (TA) model is used to identify all necessary knowledge and/or skills that the child does not presently possess but which are needed to successfully perform a task. Given this information about a child, the teacher would then know what to teach him. The teacher would use the TA model to determine the interaction or relationship between the learner and the task. First, the task to be mastered would be analyzed by isolating and describing the essential subtasks (i.e., skills and/or knowledge) required of an individual to successfully perform that task. Next, the learner would be analyzed (i.e., tested) to determine which of these subtasks he might be lacking. Once this is done the teacher should know what skills and/or knowledge the learner must be taught. Notice we said *what*. Since the TA model yields data regarding what to teach a child, it may be referred to as *curriculum-referenced evaluation* (CRE). However, identifying what to teach a child is only a part of the diagnostic process. Knowing what a child needs to be taught will not guarantee that he will learn it. Equally important is the question of *how* to teach the child what he needs to learn. And this question is best answered through the process of *treatment-referenced evaluation* (TRE).

Personalized Programming

How a child should be taught is more important in the education of the handicapped than it is with normal learners. The latter often learn in spite of poor or inappropriate instruction. Because the handicapped learner has so far to go in so little time, he must have instruction that results in an optimum learning rate—a treatment plan that will take him from point A to point B faster than any other plan.

Research suggests that the two most important variables influencing learning rates are the degree of personalization in programming for the learner and the amount of time he spends interacting with the program (Tannenbaum & Cohen, 1967). Most educators would agree that practice makes perfect; and therefore there is little argument regarding the relationship between time spent on task and academic achievement. However, there does tend to be some confusion regarding the concept of personalization in programming. Many make the mistake of equating personalized programming with individualized instruction. Such educators contend that all one has to do to increase a child's learning rate is to give him one-to-one instruction or let him work at his own rate. Their concept of personalized instruction is a classroom where all of the children are using the same basal reading or math program but each child may be working on a different page in a different book. It may not make any difference that the basal program being used is totally inappropriate for some of the children when one considers their particular learning characteristics. The fact that all of the children are working at their own rate somehow makes this program "personalized." This is not personalized instruction. It is individualized instruction, and they are not the same.

Personalized programming, in the authors' view, is when a child's treatment plan has not been designed solely on the basis of what is comfortable, convenient, or available to the teacher but rather takes into account all of that child's learning attributes. What are some of these attributes? Some children learn best in the presence of other children rather than in isolation or with one-to-one instruction from the teacher. Others learn best with one-to-one instruction from an older peer rather than an adult. Some children are turned on by printed material, for example, workbooks or picture books, while others are turned on by machines. Some children learn best visually while others require material presented in an auditory fashion. Mode of response can be as important as the mode of presentation. While some youngsters enjoy a verbal exchange, others prefer to write or mark their answers. The point is that unless a treatment plan is designed with these learner attributes in mind, we cannot say that we have personalized programming. And without personalized programming it won't make any difference how much time the student spends on task. Practice does not make perfect if the student spends his time on an ineffective treatment plan. We are suggesting here that the most effective treatment plan requires personalized programming and that the latter is based upon data collected through treatment-referenced evaluation.

Treatment-Referenced Evaluation

Although treatment-referenced evaluation (TRE) has been discussed earlier in this text (see Chapter 4), it is important that we deal with it here in a cursory fashion if only to avoid any confusion on the part of the reader regarding the type of testing the term implies. Let's reexamine some contemporary assessment practices that fit under the TRE category.

Auditory vs. Visual

Perhaps the most popular method of TRE in recent years has been that of testing the child to determine strengths and weaknesses in sensory areas. This approach is based upon the assumption that predictable aptitude-treatment interactions, or ATIs, exist. It is the idea that individuals with certain abilities or aptitudes will behave differently in certain programs or treatments than in others. The idea is widely accepted because it is logical, but using the idea has proven to be more difficult than accepting it.

The phrase "auditory learners need phonics programs" is an example of an ATI statement. The method is simple. First, you administer one or more aptitude tests (e.g., the Frostig, Wepman, ITPA) and look for any significant weaknesses and/or strengths. Next you make a prediction about which treatment the child should have. If he is weak (i.e., scores low) in visual perception and strong (i.e., scores high) in the auditory area, the prediction may be made that the child will learn at a faster rate if he is in a phonics program rather than a look-say one. This sounds easy in practice but it doesn't always work. Perhaps one of the reasons it isn't always successful is that the ATI theory has little, if any, empirical credibility. [For a detailed review of the research in ATI the reader is referred to Ysseldyke (1973).]

The excuse often given for the paucity of significant ATIs in the literature is that while most authors agree that correlations of .90 or above are needed to make interpretations necessary for prescriptive programming, the tests used to measure sensory-modality aptitudes do not have reliability coefficients that high.

We suggest that still another reason for the lack of empirical support for ATIs may be its preoccupation with *single* learner attributes. The assumption that you can accurately predict a successful treatment from data on a single learner attribute (e.g., a cognitive or perceptual aptitude) may not be valid. It seems more likely that a combination of factors will influence a child's learning in any given situation. As stated earlier, factors such as the time of day, length of instruction, who does the teaching, and whether instruction is given directly or indirectly, in groups or one-to-one, may be as important *collectively* as the student's sensory-modality preference is by itself. Given all of the above, it is the authors' contention that TRE founded solely upon ATI research is too unreliable to use when such important educational decisions are to be made.

Trial and Error

A second contemporary model of TRE is diagnostic teaching, which has been referred to in the literature as remedial diagnosis (Beery, 1967) and clinical teaching (Lerner, 1971). The Learning Methods Test (Mills, 1955) is an abbreviated version of diagnostic teaching. A child is taught a different group of words by the same instructor who changes teaching methods with each group from look-say to phonics to a kinesthetic ap-

proach to multisensory instruction from day to day over a period of four days. Long-term memory (24-hour latency) for each word list taught is measured, and the results are supposed to indicate which of the different reading techniques was the most effective. In the authors' view, a problem with this evaluative approach may be the influence of prior training which is not controlled for. Shouldn't we expect a child who has had nothing but a visual approach to reading to remember more words taught with look-say, given that he has been trained to attend to visual rather than auditory or kinesthetic-tactile stimuli? Although his performance might suggest that look-say is the best approach, in reality, if you put that child into phonics or a kinesthetic-tactile program (Fernald, 1943) or a multisensory program (Orton, 1966) he might even learn at a faster rate than with look-say.

On a larger scale, the diagnostic teaching process requires that a child spend a longer portion of time interacting with a given treatment plan while the teacher collects data regarding words read or digits written correctly. The hypothesis is simple: if you want to know how a child learns best, teach him until you find the treatment that works. In principle we have no problem with this approach. However, in practice, it may use up valuable time which the learner does not have. It makes more sense to us to incorporate one evaluative phase before diagnostic teaching begins.

Before the teacher attempts to teach the child and collect performance data which will be used to determine the effectiveness of instruction, we suggest that she first collect data regarding the student's learning attributes or characteristics. Such data might then be used to help her design a treatment plan which could still be evaluated through diagnostic teaching. The difference being that having collected data beforehand over a wide range of learner attributes, she is now in a better position to design a plan which time and future scrutiny should prove to be effective. This added dimension simply does away with the trial-and-error characteristic of the diagnostic teaching model.

The One Way

Of course there are those in education who claim that TRE is all a waste of time since there is only one way to teach a child to read, write, and compute, and we must admit that some of them do have statistical data to support their view. Without going into detail regarding the weaknesses of efficacy studies, especially where between- and within-group variances are concerned, let us simply say that in our collective 40 years in special education we have yet to come across one method and/or material that works for every child regardless of his handicapping condition! Despite all of the empirical support for phonics over the years, the authors have found many children who would never have learned to read if they had been dependent solely upon the phonics approach. Likewise (and despite the research) there have been youngsters who would not have learned to read at all if it had not been for such "exotic" reading approaches as i/t/a, Words in Color, or language experience. When it comes to teaching the handicapped, there is no panacea, and educators should not abide by the "majority rules" precept we inherited from the statisticians.

Learner/Treatment Interaction

Considering the issues above, we feel that at the present time the most practical and reliable method of TRE is a process we refer to as *learner-treatment interaction* (LTI). As the name implies, in LTI the teacher seeks to determine the interaction or relationship between the learner and a treatment. There are two basic differences between LTI and aptitude-treatment interaction. One is that ATI tends to focus on single learner attributes, for example, perceptual-motor aptitudes, while in LTI, a wide variety of learner attributes are identified. Secondly, ATI data are always collected through standardized, norm-referenced "aptitude" tests, for example, the Frostig and ITPA, while the LTI data are collected primarily through teacher observations of past and present learner behavior.

The actual process is relatively simple and straightforward. First, the learner's attributes or learning characteristics are identified in writing. This may be accomplished via direct assessment of the learner along with one or more teacher observations of learner behavior in the classroom. For example, do the teacher's past experiences indicate that learning (defined here

as that period of time when the student most consistently makes the desired responses) takes place when the student is in a group or with one-to-one instruction provided by the teacher? Does the child need immediate feedback or can he work independently? How long can he stay on task? Is he primarily a visual or an auditory learner? Neither? Both? Does he have any particular weaknesses and/or strengths in the area of expressive language? How effective are programmed materials? Does he need a behavior-management program, for example, token economy or contract, to keep him on task, or is he self-directed? If the latter is true, what kinds of tasks or activities is he most interested in? These are only a few of the questions about the learner that must be answered before the teacher can hope to make a successful match between learner and treatment.

Once the learner's attributes have been listed, the teacher uses them to develop a learner profile which serves as the basis for all future treatment plans. The only two competencies required of the teacher using the LTI process, then, are the development and completion of (1) a questionnaire regarding learner attributes and (2) a learner profile—a composite of the data from the questionnaire.

Questionnaire

The first step in designing an LTI questionnaire is to identify those variables which are related to achievement. Recent reviews of educational research have identified such variables as time spent on the task, materials used, content covered, size of child work groups, teacher questioning strategies, student responses, and teacher reactions (Brophy & Good, 1974; Rosenshine, 1976). By keying questions to these variables it is possible to construct a questionnaire which may be used to search for past patterns in the student's achievement-related behavior. Although the reliability of teacher-reported data on such a questionnaire may not always be as high as one might wish, it is often as high as that obtained through standardized testing.

Questions may be grouped according to many different formats. Figure 9.1 illustrates a system in which the questions are grouped under three broad categories—antecedents, responses, and consequences. The categories are then subdi-

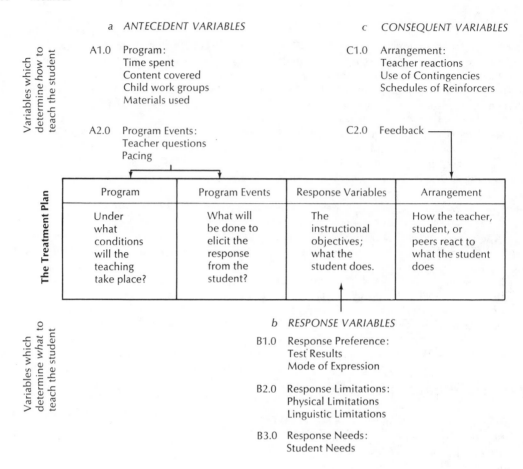

a ANTECEDENT VARIABLES

Variables which determine *how to* teach the student

A1.0   Program:
        Time spent
        Content covered
        Child work groups
        Materials used

A2.0   Program Events:
        Teacher questions
        Pacing

c CONSEQUENT VARIABLES

C1.0   Arrangement:
        Teacher reactions
        Use of Contingencies
        Schedules of Reinforcers

C2.0   Feedback

The Treatment Plan

Program	Program Events	Response Variables	Arrangement
Under what conditions will the teaching take place?	What will be done to elicit the response from the student?	The instructional objectives; what the student does.	How the teacher, student, or peers react to what the student does

b RESPONSE VARIABLES

Variables which determine *what to* teach the student

B1.0   Response Preference:
        Test Results
        Mode of Expression

B2.0   Response Limitations:
        Physical Limitations
        Linguistic Limitations

B3.0   Response Needs:
        Student Needs

Figure 9.1

Categories of questions for the LTI questionnaire and their relationship to the treatment plan.

vided to conform with the components of a treatment plan. In this case the treatment plan is a slight modification of the Is Plan used in precision teaching (White & Haring, 1976), and it answers two questions—what to teach, and how to teach.

While no standard set of questions is used in the LTI questionnaire, the authors invite the reader to use those outlined in Table 9.1. When writing questions, make sure that they are relevant to educational programming. If a question doesn't lead to information that will help in writing the child's program, it should not be included.

Table 9.1

Suggested Questions for an LTI Questionnaire and/or Interview

Directions: Respond to each of the items by rating each antecedent, response, and consequent variable according to its rate of occurrence (i.e., how often it *actually* happens) and its effect (i.e., whether or not it "works"). Circle the appropriate number to the right of the item using the key below. Elaborate when appropriate by describing the variable in as much detail as space and time allow.

Table 9.1 *(cont.)*

KEY:

Occurrence	*Effect*
(2) this actually happens all the time	(2) when this happens "learning" always occurs (i.e., the student consistently makes the desired responses)
(1) this actually happens sometimes	
(0) this never happens	(1) when this happens "learning" sometimes occurs (i.e., the student makes the desired responses but is inconsistent)
	(0) when this happens "learning" never occurs (i.e., the student never makes the desired responses)
	(NA) not applicable (should be circled when an antecedent, response, or consequent variable cannot be rated because it never happens)

Examples:

Occurrence // Effect

Student receives instruction from an adult. Elaborate. "female, certified elementary education, ten years' experience."   0 1 ②   // 0 ① 2 NA

The above ratings indicate that the student *always* receives instruction from an adult and that the desired responses occur *sometimes* but are inconsistent.

Student receives instruction from a peer. Elaborate.   ⓪1 2   // 0 1 2 ⓝⓐ

The above ratings indicate that the student *never* receives instruction from a peer and the effect rating is not applicable since the effect is not known.

Chaining is used to facilitate learning of sequential tasks.   0①2   // ⓪1 2 NA

The above ratings indicate that chaining is sometimes used but is not effective at all.

Incorrect responses are ignored. Elaborate. "incorrect answers with flash cards"   0①2   // 0 1②NA

The above ratings indicate that this technique is sometimes used and is very effective because it always produces the desired result.

Note to Teachers: If you are completing this form without the aid of an interviewer, be sure that you rate each variable according to what *actually* occurs in your classroom and not what you think other people expect to happen. Remember that the information you provide will not be used in any way to evaluate your performance as a teacher. The purpose of this questionnaire is to make judgments about students, not teachers.

Before you begin, be sure you understand what aspect of the student's learning you wish to analyze. You may want to evaluate his overall learning (i.e., what happens in all learning situations in general). Then again, you may wish to confine your analysis to one subject/skill area (e.g., reading). Or you may want to be quite specific and analyze a particular task within a given subject/skill area (e.g., ability to read nonsense trigrams). Whichever you decide, be sure you do not unknowingly change what you intend to analyze halfway through the questionnaire.

Table 9.1 *(cont.)*

Also be certain you understand the terminology used in the questionnaire. It is recommended that you read through the terminology section below before you begin in order to avoid any misunderstandings.

Terminology:

"Programmed instructional materials" refers primarily to such items as workbooks that require responses from the student and provide immediate feedback (answers). In most (but not all) cases the student is provided with a payoff (e.g., proceeding to the next task or skipping it) for correct responses, or a punisher (e.g., recompleting a task) for incorrect responses.

"Highly-structured activities" are part of a learning environment in which the student is given little or no opportunity to respond in any manner other than that prescribed by the teacher. Student responses (both wanted and unwanted) are anticipated and all contingencies are planned for.

"Mnemonic devices" are especially helpful in paired-associate learning activities. A common example is using something the student can remember to trigger the retrieval of something the student has trouble remembering. "You *write* with your *right* hand. Show me the hand you write with. What hand is that? Left? or right?"

"Direct instruction" does not necessarily have to be given one-to-one. It may be provided in a group setting and requires interaction (usually verbal) between the teacher and student(s). Task-specific questions are asked directly of the student who is given immediate feedback regarding his response (or lack of response).

"Task signals" are used here to refer to what the teacher says or does to get the student's attention before she asks a question or gives a directive. Examples are "Ready . . . ," "What are we going to do now?" "Show me you are ready." They can be given in a visual, auditory, kinesthetic-tactile or multisensory manner but should not be confused with prompts.

"Prompts" are used when the teacher models a *portion* of the desired response, e.g., saying the first sound or syllable of a correct answer. Not to be confused with the term "modeling" which implies that the *entire* desired response was performed by the teacher.

"Chaining" consists of modeling steps sequentially in a task leaving out one step (the first or last) which the student performs. In an example of backward chaining, the student would listen to the teacher model the student's telephone number in sequence up to the last digit which he would be required to provide. If he couldn't remember this digit, the teacher might prompt him by pointing to a picture of the digit or saying the sound of the first letter in the word. If he still couldn't remember it the teacher would have to model (i.e., say the word) for him.

"Perseverations" refer to behaviors repeated over and over, e.g., saying the same word(s) or repeatedly touching the same object.

* * * * *

A. Antecedent Variables
   A1.0 Program (General conditions under which instruction takes place)
         A1.1 Time spent (*When* the student works on the task *and* for *how long*)

		Occurrence //	Effect
1.1.1	Student works on the task in the morning.	0 1 2	// 0 1 2 NA
1.1.2	Student works on the task in the afternoon.	0 1 2	// 0 1 2 NA
1.1.3	Student works on the task more than once per day.	0 1 2	// 0 1 2 NA
1.1.4	Student works on the task for less than 10 minutes per day *total time.*	0 1 2	// 0 1 2 NA
1.1.5	Student works on the task for less than 20 minutes per day but more than 10 minutes *total time.*	0 1 2	// 0 1 2 NA

Table 9.1 *(cont.)*

		Occurrence //	Effect
1.1.6	Student works on the task for less than 30 minutes per day but more than 20 minutes *total time.*	0 1 2	// 0 1 2 NA
1.1.7	Student works on the task for less than 60 minutes per day but more than 30 minutes *total time.*	0 1 2	// 0 1 2 NA
1.1.8	Student works on the task for at least 60 minutes per day *total time.* Elaborate.	0 1 2	// 0 1 2 NA
1.1.9	Student works on the task for 1 to 5 minutes *at any one time.*	0 1 2	// 0 1 2 NA
1.1.10	Student works on the task for 5 to 10 minutes *at any one time.*	0 1 2	// 0 1 2 NA
1.1.11	Student works on the task for more than 10 minutes *at any one time.* Elaborate.	0 1 2	// 0 1 2 NA
1.1.12	Student perseveres in the face of failure.	0 1 2	// 0 1 2 NA
1.1.13	Student tires or gives up easily.	0 1 2	// 0 1 2 NA

A1.2 Student work groups

		Occurrence //	Effect
1.2.1	Student works on the task in the classroom.	0 1 2	// 0 1 2 NA
1.2.2	Student works on the task outside of the classroom. Elaborate.	0 1 2	// 0 1 2 NA
1.2.3	Student works on the task while he is at his desk.	0 1 2	// 0 1 2 NA
1.2.4	Student works on the task while he is at the teacher's desk.	0 1 2	// 0 1 2 NA
1.2.5	Student works on the task while he is out of his seat (e.g. sitting or lying on the floor, standing or moving about). Elaborate.	0 1 2	// 0 1 2 NA
1.2.6	Student works on the task among his peers.	0 1 2	// 0 1 2 NA
1.2.7	Student works on the task apart from his peers.	0 1 2	// 0 1 2 NA
1.2.8	Student works on the task isolated from peers (i.e., cannot see and/or hear them). Elaborate.	0 1 2	// 0 1 2 NA
1.2.9	Student works on the task in a manner other than those described above. Elaborate.	0 1 2	// 0 1 2 NA
1.2.10	Student is distracted from the task by extraneous stimuli in the environment (e.g., noise, and/or movement.) Elaborate.	0 1 2	// 0 1 2 NA
1.2.11	Student engages in hyperactive behavior (e.g., continuous and excessive movement that interferes with the task.) Elaborate.	0 1 2	// 0 1 2 NA
1.2.12	Student receives instruction from an adult. Elaborate.	0 1 2	// 0 1 2 NA
1.2.13	Student receives instruction from a peer. Elaborate.	0 1 2	// 0 1 2 NA
1.2.14	Student receives instruction on a one-to-one basis.	0 1 2	// 0 1 2 NA
1.2.15	Student receives instruction in a large groups (over 8).	0 1 2	// 0 1 2 NA
1.2.16	Student receives instruction in a small group (under 8).	0 1 2	// 0 1 2 NA
1.2.17	Student instructs himself. Elaborate.	0 1 2	// 0 1 2 NA
1.2.18	Student receives instruction in a manner other than those described above. Elaborate.	0 1 2	// 0 1 2 NA

A1.3 Materials used

		Occurrence //	Effect
1.3.1	Programmed instructional materials are used. Elaborate.	0 1 2	// 0 1 2 NA
1.3.2	Teaching machines are used (e.g., Language Master, Systems 80). Elaborate.	0 1 2	// 0 1 2 NA
1.3.3	A-V materials are used (e.g., tape, filmstrips). Elaborate.	0 1 2	// 0 1 2 NA

Table 9.1 *(cont.)*

		Occurrence //	Effect
1.3.4	Game-type materials are used. Elaborate.	0 1 2	// 0 1 2 NA
1.3.5	Materials are used that emphasize convergent thinking or rote learning (e.g., flashcards). Elaborate.	0 1 2	// 0 1 2 NA
1.3.6	Highly structured activities are provided.	0 1 2	// 0 1 2 NA
1.3.7	Instructional materials with a visual stress are used. Elaborate.	0 1 2	// 0 1 2 NA
1.3.8	Instructional materials with an auditory stress are used. Elaborate.	0 1 2	// 0 1 2 NA
1.3.9	Instructional materials with a kinesthetic-tactile stress are used. Elaborate.	0 1 2	// 0 1 2 NA
1.3.10	Instructional materials with a multisensory stress are used. Elaborate.	0 1 2	// 0 1 2 NA
1.3.11	Mnemonic devices are used to facilitate recall in paired-associate learning. Elaborate.	0 1 2	// 0 1 2 NA
1.3.12	Student displays sensitivity to timed tasks/activities.	0 1 2	// 0 1 2 NA

A2.0 Program Events (What is done to elicit the response from the student)

A2.1	Directions, commands, questions are repeated.	0 1 2	// 0 1 2 NA
A2.2	Direct instruction is given.	0 1 2	// 0 1 2 NA
A2.3	Instruction is varied (i.e., changed).	0 1 2	// 0 1 2 NA
A2.4	Correct responses are modeled for the student.	0 1 2	// 0 1 2 NA
A2.5	Task signals are used to get the student's attention before questions, commands, or directions are given.	0 1 2	// 0 1 2 NA
A2.6	Visual and/or verbal prompts are used to elicit correct responses.	0 1 2	// 0 1 2 NA
A2.7	Chaining is used to facilitate learning of sequential tasks.	0 1 2	// 0 1 2 NA
A2.8	The student maintains eye contact.	0 1 2	// 0 1 2 NA
A2.9	The student has difficulty recalling instructional information. Elaborate.	0 1 2	// 0 1 2 NA
A2.10	The student is able to use newly acquired information in a variety of circumstances and situations.	0 1 2	// 0 1 2 NA
A2.11	The student is able to recall nonschool related material (e.g., TV shows, family events)	0 1 2	// 0 1 2 NA
A2.12	The student engages in daydreaming or fantasy play during the day. Elaborate.	0 1 2	// 0 1 2 NA

B. Response Variables

B1.0	Verbal responses are required.	0 1 2	// 0 1 2 NA
B2.0	Written responses are required.	0 1 2	// 0 1 2 NA
B3.0	Motor responses (e.g., pointing) are required.	0 1 2	// 0 1 2 NA
B4.0	A combination of responses are required. Elaborate.	0 1 2	// 0 1 2 NA
B5.0	Speech (e.g., articulation, fluency, etc.) and/or expressive language problems are manifested. Elaborate.	0 1 2	// 0 1 2 NA
B6.0	Gross and/or fine-motor problems are manifested. Elaborate.	0 1 2	// 0 1 2 NA
B7.0	The student is able to copy material at far point (i.e., from blackboard).	0 1 2	// 0 1 2 NA
B8.0	The student is able to copy material at near point (i.e., at his desk).	0 1 2	// 0 1 2 NA
B9.0	The student is able to trace.	0 1 2	// 0 1 2 NA
B10.0	The student is able to imitate gross-motor movements.	0 1 2	// 0 1 2 NA
B11.0	The student is able to imitate fine-motor movements.	0 1 2	// 0 1 2 NA
B12.0	Verbal and/or motoric perseverations are manifested. Elaborate.	0 1 2	// 0 1 2 NA
B13.0	Physical abnormalities that interfere with visual and/or motor responses are manifested. Elaborate.	0 1 2	// 0 1 2 NA

Table 9.1 (cont.)

			Occurrence //	Effect
C. Consequent Variables				
C1.0	Arrangement (How the teacher, student, or peers react to the student's response)		0 1 2 //	0 1 2 NA
	C1.1	Correct responses are rewarded. Elaborate.	0 1 2 //	0 1 2 NA
	C1.2	Incorrect responses are ignored. Elaborate.	0 1 2 //	0 1 2 NA
	C1.3	Incorrect responses are punished. Elaborate.	0 1 2 //	0 1 2 NA
	C1.4	The student corrects himself.	0 1 2 //	0 1 2 NA
	C1.5	The teacher corrects the student.	0 1 2 //	0 1 2 NA
	C1.6	The student is provided with immediate feedback regarding his responses.	0 1 2 //	0 1 2 NA
	C1.7	The student's behavior in response to failure is:		
		1.7.1 sits and says nothing.	0 1 2 //	0 1 2 NA
		1.7.2 engages in some type of avoidance or escape behavior.	0 1 2 //	0 1 2 NA
		1.7.3 becomes negative and refuses to work.	0 1 2 //	0 1 2 NA
		1.7.4 becomes hostile (i.e., engages in verbally and/or physically agressive behavior).	0 1 2 //	0 1 2 NA
		1.7.5 guesses.	0 1 2 //	0 1 2 NA
		1.7.6 gives up and says, "I don't know."	0 1 2 //	0 1 2 NA
		1.7.7 makes another response. Elaborate.	0 1 2 //	0 1 2 NA
	C1.8	The student frustrates easily.	0 1 2 //	0 1 2 NA

It should be noted here that, whenever feasible, more than one teacher should participate in the completion of the questionnaire. Let's assume that you are designing the questionnaire to be used on a child who is new to your program. If that child's former teachers are available, it would make sense to include them in the LTI process. Actually it would still make sense to consult with former teachers even if the child is not new to your program. The more data you collect from a wide variety of sources, the more insight you should have regarding the child's learning attributes. Don't be put off by teachers who say they don't know what works for a child. "If I knew what worked for Johnny I wouldn't have referred him to special education in the first place!" Explain to them that they can provide an invaluable service if they only tell you what *hasn't* worked with Johnny. Be careful to explain that just because their program hasn't been effective with Johnny doesn't mean that they are not effective teachers. It simply means that the methods and materials they used with one particular child didn't work, and if we can identify what doesn't work with Johnny, we will save a lot of time in the future by not using them again. If you do involve other teachers in the completion of the LTI questionnaire, we suggest that you interview them rather than simply letting them fill out the questionnaire themselves. This way the responses they might make will not be as open to interpretation. If you have any doubts as to what they mean, all you have to do is paraphrase their response to see if you both understand one another. It is usually a good idea to tape the interview so that you'll have a record of it. Playing it back hours after the interview may reveal some previously missed response made by the interviewee.

Profile

Once the questionnaire has been completed by all involved parties, a profile is written which is nothing more than a compilation of both positive and negative learner attributes. The profile can take many shapes and many formats. It could simply be a list of Do's and Don'ts of programming for the student. Figure 9.2 is an example of a profile constructed on a learner, and Figure 9.3 is an example of a treatment plan that was based entirely upon that profile. Figure 9.4 is a sample of the profile used by the Portland (Oreg.) Public Schools. It is incorporated with other forms which make up each handicapped learner's Individualized Education Plan (IEP) and serves as a basis for all future prescriptive programming.

In conclusion, the reader should remember that the purpose of LTI is to collect information which can be used to make an initial treatment plan. Regardless of how it is devised, a treatment plan is always a "guesstimate" of what works for a given child. If such "guesstimates" are based upon useful information they may be right more often than they are wrong, but they are always *predictions* about future behavior. All treatment plans, therefore, should be monitored closely over time in order to ensure their efficacy and the child's success. It is the monitoring of these plans via the process of precision teaching which comprises the remaining portion of this text.

Learner _____Johnny J._____ Date of Birth ___1/2/69___ CA 8-5 _____

School ___Gray_____ Present Program ___Regular Second Grade___

Party Interviewed ___Ms. Johnson_____ Position ___Second-grade teacher_____

Interviewed by _____J. Kaplan_____ Date _____4-5-78_____

		EFFECTIVE	INEFFECTIVE
PROGRAM		works best at large table; likes room to spread out	working at own desk; feels confined and easily distracted by things inside his desk
PROGRAM		in a one-to-one situation	in a group; easily distracted by peers
PROGRAM		with a peer; likes attention of an older child (preferably a boy)	with teacher or aide
PROGRAM		instruction early in the day	tires markedly late in morning and has difficulty concentrating after lunch
PROGRAM		10 minutes instruction	can't concentrate for more than 10 minutes at a time
PROGRAM		isolated from group; facing wall	at desk or facing peers; too distracting
PROGRAM		drill or rote learning activities keep his interest for longer periods of time (with flash cards)	workbook or textbook materials with involved directions and responses
PROGRAM EVENTS		auditory input	visual input
PROGRAM EVENTS		phonics approach to reading	look-say approach to reading; reverses words (e.g., *was* and *saw*) and letters (e.g., *b* and *d*)
PROGRAM EVENTS		repeating directions and verbal prompts	self-pacing
RESPONSES		verbal responses	activities involving written responses
RESPONSES		needs instruction in blending	
RESPONSES		needs to decrease hesitations	
ARRANGEMENTS		verbal praise on a continuous schedule	tokens or points
		attention from a peer	
		needs feedback from environment; will not correct his own work	self-recording

Figure 9.2

A learner profile based on an LTI interview.

Task	Reads simple CVC words correctly		Student	Johnny J.
Aim	Fluency (80 per minute without errors)		School	Gray
By	End of school (June)		Teacher	Ms. Johnson
Program Began	4-7-78	Program Ended	Advocate	J. Kaplan
			Age 8	Grade 2

INCREASE				DECREASE	
PROGRAM	PROGRAM EVENTS	RESPONSE	ARRANGEMENT	RESPONSE	ARRANGEMENT
9-9:10 Room 5 Table in back of room facing wall one-to-one peer tutor flash cards nonsense trigrams with sustained initial consonants	1. Show cards. 2. Use occluder. 3. Say, "Say these sounds as you see them. Hold each sound until you see the next one." Peer models. 4. Expose each sound L-R. 5. Repeat faster until child says word correctly.	Reads word correctly (i.e., able to blend).	1. Give Johnny card if read correctly. 2. Move to next card. 3. Verbal praise 1:1 for each correct (continuous reinforcement).	Reads word incorrectly (i.e., unable to blend sounds into one unit). Hesitates on sound or word prompt.	1. Ignore. 2. Model correct response. 3. Repeat until correct response is made 1:1 for each error (continuous reinforcement). Same as above.

Figure 9.3

A treatment plan based on a learner profile.

115

LEARNER-TREATMENT INTERACTION (LTI) PROFILE

LEARNER _____ DATE OF BIRTH_____CA_____

PRESENT PROGRAM _____

COMPLETED BY_____ DATE_____

TREATMENT GOAL_____

ASPECT OF LEARNING ENVIRONMENT	EFFECTIVE	INEFFECTIVE	REMARKS
Time of day taught			
Length of lesson			
Teacher			
Material(s)			
Method(s)			
Mode of presentation			
Mode of response			
Sensory modality stressed			
Physical setting			
Peer involvement			
Consequent events for correct responses			
Consequent events for incorrect responses			

Figure 9.4

The LTI profile used in conjunction with the IEP in the Portland (Oreg.) Public Schools.

Checkpoint 9.1

Directions: Write the answers to each of the following items. CAP is 100% accuracy in 45 minutes. You may not use reference aids.

1. Compare personalized programming with individualized instruction. How are they different?

2. State the two most important variables influencing learning rates.

3. Compare treatment-referenced evaluation (TRE) using learner-treatment interaction with TRE based upon aptitude-treatment interaction. How are they different?

4. Compare curriculum-referenced evaluation with treatment-referenced evaluation. How are they different?

5. List at least 10 learner attributes to consider before designing a treatment program for a student.

6. State one criticism of treatment-referenced evaluation based upon ATI research.

Checkpoint 9.1 *(cont.)*

7. State one criticism of treatment-referenced evaluation based upon the diagnostic teaching model.

8. Describe the two steps in learner-treatment interaction.

Acceptable Responses

1. Personalized programming requires that all of the student's learning characteristics or attributes are identified and considered before a treatment plan is developed. Individualized instruction does not take all of the student's learning attributes into account. It usually just means that the student is being given one-to-one instruction and/or is working at his own rate.

2. Personalized programming and time spent on a program or lesson.

3. In TRE using learner-treatment interaction, the data are collected primarily through teacher observations of past and present learner behavior. In TRE using the ATI model, data are collected through standardized norm-referenced testing. In TRE using learner-treatment interaction, data are collected on a wide variety of learner attributes. In TRE using the ATI model, data are usually collected on a single learner attribute, for example, perceptual-motor or sensory-modality aptitudes.

4. The purpose of TRE is to find out *how* to teach a child while the purpose of curriculum-referenced evaluation is to determine *what* to teach him.

5. Refer to the items in Table 9.1, the LTI questionnaire.

6. TRE based upon the ATI model is suspect because usually only one learner attribute is measured. This is usually perceptual- or sensory-modality aptitude and the tests that are commonly used to measure these aptitudes (e.g., the Frostig Developmental Test of Visual Perception and the Illinois Test of Psycholinguistic Abilities) do not have enough reliability for prescriptive programming in academic areas. An example would be which reading (decoding) method to use with a student.

7. TRE based upon diagnostic teaching is usually trial and error, and time becomes a factor.

8. First, the learner's attributes are identified in writing, using an LTI questionnaire developed by the teacher or specialist involved. If more than one teacher is going to complete the questionnaire, it is advisable to use an interview technique. Second, data from the questionnaire/interview should be compiled, and an LTI profile of the student developed from these data. This is no more than a list of what is effective and what is not effective with regard to length of lesson, time of the day instruction is given, physical setting, methods and/or materials used, peer involvement, and teacher involvement, among others.

Options

1. If you scored 100% on the assessment for this unit, you may go on to the next chapter.

2. If you scored less than 100%, go back and reread the reading assignment. Then take the checkpoint again.

10

Introduction to Formative Evaluation

Unit 10.1: Formative evaluation.

Objectives: 1. The learner will be able to define *formative evaluation*.
2. The learner will be able to list problems with norm-referenced tests.
3. The learner will be able to contrast performance and learning.

Prerequisites: Knowledge of test reliability and validity as explained in Appendix A, Unit 4.

Reading Assignment

Two general types of evaluation procedures, *summative* and *formative evaluation*, are available for teachers and psychologists who wish to measure changes in child behavior (Bloom, Hastings, & Madaus, 1971). The traditional measures employed (achievement and aptitude tests) are included in the category of *summative evaluation*, i.e., evaluation which occurs after teaching and learning have taken place. Summative evaluation is designed to measure the end result of instruction and to identify the students who have and have not met the objectives of instruction. Testing which occurs at the end of a unit of teaching is also referred to as summative.

In contrast, *formative evaluation* measures learning as skills are being formed. Whereas summative evaluation is used to describe the outcomes of instruction, formative evaluation is used to measure progress towards objectives.

Educational tests have been used for placement in texts and materials, for description of student abilities and aptitudes, as measures of achievement, and to diagnose deficiencies or learning problems. Most commercial standardized tests are summative in nature. Standardized diagnostic tests such as reading placement tests, unless they are given repeatedly to the individual learner, measure only the performance of the student at one time. This measure of prior achievement is then used to determine the level of initial instruction.

Although standardized tests are often useful when trying to compare a student's performance on a test to the performance of other students, factors related to the actual test construction need to be considered when evaluating test results. The test user needs to judge the reliability and validity of the test for a particular student (see Chapter 1). This is necessary in order to achieve an accurate measure of achievement on previous learning.

One of the major goals of this text is to present evaluation systems which will result in useful data. Accurate evaluation of learning, achievement, or learning potential will lead to better teaching because it assures that instruction begins at the level appropriate for the individual learner. Precise evaluation of child growth (changes in child behavior) is, in fact, the essence of effective teaching.

Formative evaluation should be *direct* and *frequent*. *Direct* evaluation refers to evaluation which measures performance of the student in the materials she is using or is going to use. Indirect evaluation refers to evaluation derived from materials other than the ones the student is currently using or about to use. For example, if a student has been taught math in Greater Cleveland, Book 3, her growth should be measured by evaluating the content she has been taught in the Greater Cleveland series. If an indirect measure of performance was taken (that is, a test such as a standardized achievement test was given), the student's evaluation could contain measures related to concepts that the student had not been taught or exposed to. Is it fair to penalize the student, that is, to say that she is behind the "norm" or average, because we as teachers and publishers of texts have not attempted to teach a skill? Definitely not. Yet this has been the practice for many years.

Test Validity

The validity of a test which measures only those concepts and skills actually taught in a specific class will be much higher than the validity of a test which has been designed to cover content taught a different group of students in a different setting. Test validity must be a crucial consideration when selecting a test. Such critical decisions as educational placement and program decisions are often based on test results. These results need to be valid. Achievement should reflect what has been taught. An accurate measure of achievement should evaluate learning in relation to concepts and skills that have been presented to the learner. If a teacher uses Greater Cleveland math in the classroom and then measures learning with a test designed for the content contained in Greater Cleveland, then the content validity will be high. However, if another measure is used, the correlation between the material presented and the test items may not be as high. Stephens (1977) states, "If test results are not directly related to what is to be taught, it is not instructionally relevant for assessment purposes . . . few standardized or clinical tests meet the requirement of relevance to curriculum" (p. 155).

teach	test	validity
GCB3	GCB3	High
GCB3	NRT	Unknown

In addition to being direct, formative evaluation must also occur frequently. Frequent evaluation refers to ongoing or continuous assessment of the skills being taught. If at all possible, assessment should occur daily.

Norm-referenced tests have been the traditional measures of educational performance. They are neither direct nor frequent measures of performance, yet these same tests continue to be manufactured and used. Each year more and more college students are taught to give these tests which may not be valid for making instructional decisions. Many of these tests are particularly invalid for special students. The battery of tests which compare a student to other students continues to grow and multiply. This is happening despite the fact that for more than 10 years researchers have been stockpiling evidence establishing the inefficiency of such tests (Bateman, 1968; Popham & Husek, 1969; Hammill & Larsen, 1974a).

Norm-referenced tests continue to be used despite the fact that the concept of frequent measurement in the classroom has been in existence since the beginning of education. The concepts of direct and frequent measurement have been formalized within the last 20 years, and the tools of formative evaluation have become readily available within the last 5 years.

When will the widespread usage of the often inaccurate and unreliable norm-referenced tests stop? Perhaps it will slow down as the users of such tests become wiser consumers. Wise con-

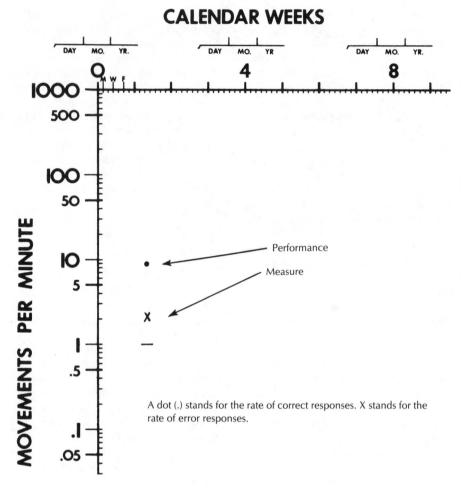

Figure 10.1

A performance measure.

NOTE: The chart used throughout this section is a six-cycle chart. It will be explained in Chapter 11.

sumer use of tests demands that tests be selected according to the criteria of potential usefulness and accuracy of results (validity and reliability). Because most norm-referenced tests are neither direct nor frequent measures of behavior, their usefulness is limited. The most useful types of evaluation are those which measure directly and are administered frequently in order to give the teacher up-to-date results.

Norm-referenced tests provide a measure of how well a child performed on one occasion (Figure 10.1). However, educators should be more concerned with measures of learning or child growth. Learning is measured by evaluating changes in performance over time. In order to

measure learning, more than one performance score must be obtained.

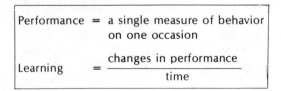

When only one measure of behavior is taken it is difficult to determine where a child is going or what type of growth will occur (Figure 10.2).

When there is more than one performance measure, it becomes possible to see if the child is getting better, staying the same, or getting

CALENDAR WEEKS

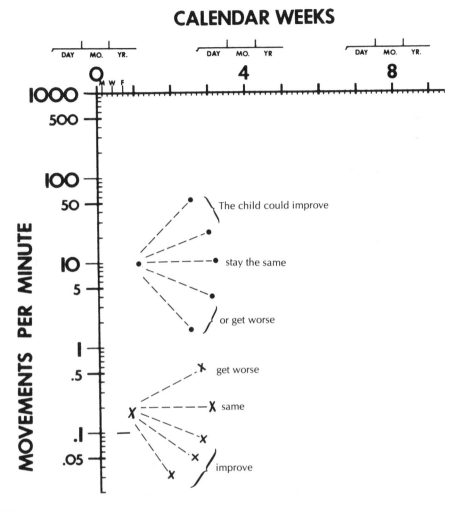

Figure 10.2

Some possible growth patterns which can be obtained from one performance measure.

worse. When two performance measures are gathered, a comparison can be made between the points and a better idea of possible growth can be obtained (Figure 10.3). As more data are collected (Figure 10.4), your perception of growth (learning) becomes more and more accurate (Lindsley, 1976).

Systems of ongoing and direct evaluation are needed to obtain measures of learning. The less frequent the evaluation, the less information the teacher will have to make curriculum and program decisions. It is difficult to judge how much learning is taking place in December, January, or February if the primary measures of performance are given in September and May.

Accountability

Norm-referenced tests which are summative and measure performance or global changes in performance during a school year do not meet the current demands for accountability and effective programming. More frequent measures of performance are needed to properly measure and evaluate child growth.

Advantages of Formative Evaluation

Evaluation that occurs as skills are being developed is well suited to the educational needs of

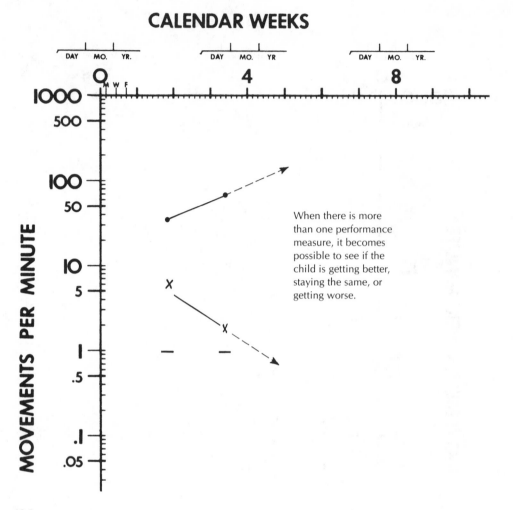

Figure 10.3

Two performance measures.

teachers and learners because it allows for more rapid detection of potential problems. Formative evaluation also gives us a means of evaluating growth as it is *occurring*. Evaluation which takes place as learning occurs provides the teacher and student with frequent and up-to-date feedback. More frequent feedback can result in earlier detection of problems, earlier changes in programs and procedures, and more rapid growth.

Frequent evaluation and feedback

- earlier detection of problems
- earlier changes in programs
- more rapid growth

It has been stated that accelerating the academic performance of students is the educator's primary responsibility (Starlin, 1971). If this premise is accepted, then it logically follows that educators have a responsibility to utilize those evaluational tools which will provide the results needed to accelerate academic growth. With summative tests that result in after-the-fact evaluation, the teacher often realizes too late that certain methods and/or materials were not as effective as they were originally thought to be. Teachers need data that tells them how the learner is doing as learning is occurring. Formative evaluation provides information to aid in making decisions about changing programs, materials, and procedures as learning is occurring—not after the fact.

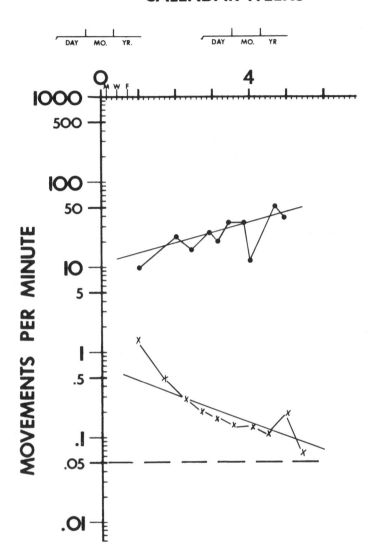

Figure 10.4

Several performance measures.

Teaching vs. Evaluation

When behaviors are measured as learning is occurring, evaluation can become an integral part of the teaching process. Many evaluation systems have been designed, but it seems that some teachers resist becoming involved with them. Often, teachers view their function as only imparting information. They seem to be saying "let someone else do the evaluating." Perhaps this happens because teachers have not been presented with evaluation systems which are designed to guide child growth. Too often, evaluation occurs to satisfy administrators, regulations, and parents. These uses of evaluation ignore the very intent and purpose of educational diagnosis. Evaluation should occur to guide child growth, to give the teacher information to help with the design and delivery of instruction. Formative evaluation can do this if the teacher begins with a positive attitude towards it.

Checkpoint 10.1

Directions: If the statement refers to performance, mark P. Mark L if it refers to learning. CAP is 100% accuracy in 5 minutes. You may not use reference aids.

____1. Tracy wrote 25 letters per minute on Friday.

____2. Sarah wrote 45 numbers correctly on Tuesday, 35 on Wednesday, and 42 on Thursday.

____3. Ann completed her assignment.

____4. Scores on Botel spelling were 19 correct, 1 error.

____5. Frank completed 10 math problems in 2 minutes.

Complete the following statements:

6. Formative evaluation is direct and _____.

7. Most norm-referenced tests are designed to measure behavior _____ . (how often?)

8. One reason for frequent evaluation is that it allows the teacher to _____ .

Acceptable Responses

1. P	4. P	7. infrequently
2. L	5. P	8. detect problems sooner
3. P	6. frequent	

Options

1. If you scored 100% on the assessment for this unit, you may go on to the next chapter.
2. If you scored less than 100%, go back and reread the reading assignment. Then take the checkpoint again.

11

Types of Formative Evaluation

<table>
<tr><td>Unit 11.1:</td><td>Characteristics of formative evaluation systems.</td></tr>
<tr><td>Objective:</td><td>The learner will identify characteristics of each formative system mentioned in the chapter.</td></tr>
<tr><td>Prerequisite:</td><td>Chapter 10.</td></tr>
</table>

Reading Assignment

In recent years, several formative evaluation systems have evolved. The purposes of this chapter are to explore the pros and cons of each system and to provide a model for combining features from two or more systems, as needed, to strengthen the power of formative evaluation. The models to be covered include: diagnostic-prescriptive teaching (Peter, 1965), diagnostic teaching (Kirk, 1972), clinical teaching (Lerner, 1971), narrative log, directive teaching (Stephens, 1970), management by objectives (Mali, 1977), criterion-referenced testing, learning matrices, arithmetic charting, and precision teaching (Kunzelmann, 1970).

Ongoing Data Record

Characteristic of most formative evaluation systems is a provision to record ongoing data in some *systematic* fashion. Table 11.1 provides information on the philosophy, procedures, and data obtained with 10 of the most commonly used formative evaluation systems. Read this table carefully. Encompassed under the guise of formative evaluation is everything from the daily narrative log of teacher opinion and reaction to the formal structure of precision teaching. In between these extremes fall systems such as directive and clinical teaching, which provide formats for lesson planning and data collection. ing the effectiveness of each system in order to

Formative evaluation has become so popular that, like criterion-referenced testing, we must begin to seek not only "formative evaluation" or a "criterion-referenced test" but *good* formative evaluation or *good* criterion-referenced tests. Some systems masquerading as "formative evaluation" have even been misnamed.

Standards for good formative evaluation systems can best be understood by analyzing the components of most systems and then evaluat-

Table 11.1

Common Formative Evaluation Systems

Philosophy	Purpose of Evaluation	Steps	Data Obtained	Proficiency
Diagnostic-Prescriptive Teaching (Peter, 1965)				
Definition: "A method of utilizing diagnostic information for modification of educational programs" (p. 1).				
Adequate education based on child and total dynamics	To modify instruction and environmental variables through an interdisciplinary process	1. Referral to diagnostician	Case study—interdisciplinary	Not specified (for norm-referenced tests according to the norm)
It is important to develop areas of major deficits	To determine the educational relevance of handicaps	2. Report results to teacher	Medical record	
Key to learning is perceptions		3. Teacher implements program	Family history	
Follows a psycho-medical model			Social and psychological data	
			Norm-referenced test scores	
			Standardized test scores	
Diagnostic Teaching (Kirk, 1972)				
Definition: A system of developing educational plans based on diagnostic data obtained.				
Planning should be based on definition of problem	To provide a data base for planning educational interventions	1. Determine child's problem.	Profile from tests such as ITPA	Not specified (for norm-referenced tests according to the norm)
Modality preference must be determined		2. Measure pre-achievement	Standardized test scores	
Standardized tests are accurate evaluative instruments		3. Analyze how child learns	Informal observations	
Follows a psycho-medical model		4. Explore why child is not learning	Norm-referenced test scores	
		5. Formulate a diagnostic hypothesis		

Method	Purpose	Steps	Data Sources	Criteria
Clinical Teaching (Lerner, 1971) *Definition: "An alternating test-teach-test-teach process" (p. 103).* Diagnosis and teaching must be interrelated and continuous Follows a behavioral model	To gather information about child in order to make critical decisions about teaching for that particular child	1. Diagnose 2. Plan 3. Implement 4. Evaluate 5. Modification of the diagnosis 6. Develop teaching plan 7. Modify as necessary	Case history Clinical observations Informal testing Standardized test scores Norm-referenced test scores	Not specified (for norm-referenced tests according to the norm)
Narrative Log *Definition: A written record of comments.* A written record of teacher observations will increase teacher's awareness of child's progress	To provide feedback to teacher and to structure teacher observation	1. Date and write daily comments	Narrative Written account	None
Directive Teaching (Stephens, 1970) *Definition: "A system of instruction that aids those who teach learning and behavioral difficulties to be effective in academic instruction while responding to the student's social behavior" (p. 109).* By changes in simple behavior, complex behaviors are learned; therefore, they can be modified Follows a behavioral model	To allow teacher to provide effective academic instruction and management of social behaviors	1. Gather descriptions of academic functioning, social learning, and reinforcement system 2. Use information for planning and implementing strategies	Academic skills Sensory channels Behavior reinforcement through regulated measures, under different conditions and over time	Established through minimal acceptable performance Criteria should include observable terms and

Table 11.1

Common Formative Evaluation Systems (con't)

Philosophy	Purpose of Evaluation	Steps	Data Obtained	Proficiency
		3. Implement 4. Evaluate while applying treatment (regulated measures)		specific number units to be completed correctly (number of correct trials)

Management by Objectives

(Odiorne, 1965; Mali, 1977)

Definition: "a strategy of planning and getting results in the direction that management wishes and needs to take while meeting goals and satisfaction of its participants" (Mali, p. 1).

Philosophy	Purpose of Evaluation	Steps	Data Obtained	Proficiency
Setting objectives and dates to obtain objectives will increase both accountability and productivity (efficiency of teaching) Assumes that teacher knows how to select appropriate objectives and dates	To determine whether or not objectives have been met	1. Find the objective 2. Set the objective 3. Validate the objective 4. Implement the objective 5. Control and report status of the objectives	Was objective met? Day objectives met	Determined by teacher

Criterion-Referenced Testing

Definition: Evaluation which compares an individual behavior to an objective performance standard or criterion.

Philosophy	Purpose of Evaluation	Steps	Data Obtained	Proficiency
Validity and reliability of test will be greatest if test items are determined by important concepts and not by a ranking procedure	To determine level of instructional placement and mastery of subtasks	1. Select terminal objective 2. Identify essential subtasks 3. Order subtasks	Behavioral data specific to task	Determine by population who can successfully complete task

				Determined by field testing with a group who can successfully complete the task
Child's progress will be best if tasks are taught according to skill hierarchies		4. Field test to determine speed and accuracy needed for proficiency. 5. Administer test		

Learning Matrix

Definition: A system of criterion-referenced testing and recording in a fashion which allows for a visual representation of progress.

Based on a task analytic/behavioral approach	To determine mastery of subtask and direct instructional placement	1. Complete a task analysis 2. Sequence items from easy to difficult 3. Develop grid for coding 4. Develop code 5. Record	Behavioral data collected through direct observation and recorded on grid system which includes a code for mastery of each subtask	Determined by field testing with a group who can successfully complete the task

Arithmetic Charts

Definition: A graphic recording system whose value is related to the type of data collected and the minimization of visual misrepresentation.

A visual picture will be useful to student or teacher	To see if child is making progress	1. Isolate behavior to be charted 2. Construct chart 3. Record	Percent correct; correct and error scores, correct and error rates	Not necessarily identified

Table 11.1

Common Formative Evaluation Systems (con't)

Philosophy	Purpose of Evaluation	Steps	Data Obtained	Proficiency
Precision Teaching (Kunzelmann, 1970)				
Definition: One procedure to plan, monitor, and evaluate changes in performance over time through direct and daily measurement of behaviors.				
To be effective, evaluation must include frequent assessment of learning; this evaluation system can be used with any teaching strategy	To guide child's growth	1. Pinpoint behaviors 2. Record behaviors 3. Evaluate 4. Change as needed and recycle	Daily measures of rate of performance; a linear path of growth	A behavior ratio established through minimal aims for those who can complete the task (sometimes aims are modified according to child's rate on a basic task)
Follows a behavioral model				

guide decision making. A brief description and example of each system follows.

Diagnostic-Prescriptive Teaching

Diagnostic-prescriptive teaching (Peter, 1965) is an example of a psycho-medical approach to evaluation. A diagnostician collects family and medical history, gives the necessary psychological and standardized achievement and aptitude tests, and from these results prepares a prescription for the teacher to follow. Provisions are made for follow-up, and further testing is completed as needed (Figure 11.1).

Diagnostic Teaching

Diagnostic teaching (Kirk, 1972) is very similar to diagnostic-prescriptive teaching. The major difference between the two systems is that diagnostic teaching does not stress the case history approach but instead relies on assessment of modality preference and standardized test results (Figure 11.2). With diagnostic teaching, a psycho-medical approach is utilized in an attempt to pinpoint the nature of breakdowns within internal communication systems or psycholinguistic processes. The intent of the assessment process is to locate the areas of psycholinguistic processes for which remedial treatment needs to be prescribed (Haring & Bateman, 1977).

INDIVIDUAL PRESCRIPTIVE PROGRAM DATA SHEET

Name _____ Age_____ Date_____

Teacher _____ School_____ Grade_____

Referred by_____

Presenting Problem:

Comprehensive History:
  Family:

  Developmental:

  Emotional:

  Educational:

Test Data:

(IQ test, achievement tests, standardized tests and analysis)

Recommendation:
  To the Home:

  To the School:

Figure 11.1

Diagnostic-prescriptive report.

DIAGNOSTIC EVALUATION

Name _____ Age_____ Date_____

Teacher _____ School_____ Grade_____

Referred by _____

Presenting Problem:

<u>INITIAL ASSESSMENT</u>

   Name of Test A:

      Description of Test A
      Test Scores
      Interpretation of Scores

   Name of Test B:

      Description of Test B
      Test Scores
      Interpretation of Scores

   (Continue with tests C, D, etc.)

<u>DIAGNOSTIC HYPOTHESIS</u>

Cognitive: *Perceptual:*

  Strengths: Strengths:

  Weaknesses: Weaknesses:

Recommended materials and teaching techniques:

Figure 11.2

Diagnostic teaching report.

Clinical Teaching

Clinical teaching (Lerner, 1971) incorporates aspects from both the psycho-medical and behavioral evaluation models. Standardized tests, case histories, clinical observations, and informal tests are all utilized in order to make critical decisions about instruction for the individual child. Lerner describes clinical teaching as an alternating test-teach-test-teach process (1971, p. 103). A major part of the clinical teaching system includes establishing a good rapport with the student and maintaining a good clinical teaching environment. Task analysis is incorporated into the clinical teaching system. Procedures are designed for the individual child.

Narrative Logs

Narrative logs have been utilized by teachers, psychologists, and others as long as formalized education has been in existence. It is still the practice to encourage many intern or beginning teachers to keep a log or diary of daily or weekly events.

Example:

2/5/78 Sue was frustrated with reading again today and refused to cooperate—perhaps she should be reassigned to a lower group. Steven S. presented a paper with no legibility errors.

2/6/78 Everything went well.

2/7/78 Began studying the metric system. Children enjoyed measuring with "liters." Gary had another seizure today—will be seeing doctor next week. Today's seizure lasted three minutes.

Directive Teaching

Stephens (1977) has modified and improved the initial directive system he described in 1970. Directive teaching has been expanded to Directive Teaching Instructional Management System (DTIMS). The new system contains a curriculum for assessing and teaching basic academic and social skills. DTIMS is composed of a manual and a computerized delivery system. Assessment tasks include skill statements, items for measuring skills, and criterion scores. Criterion is defined as mastery at 90% to 100% accuracy (Figure 11.3). The DTIMS also contains instructional strategies (Figure 11.4).

Management by Objectives

When combined with good assessment strategies, the management by objectives format becomes the basis for many individualized educational plans as these plans have been designed to meet the requirements of Public Law 94-142 (Figure 11.5).

Criterion-Referenced Testing

Criterion-referenced skill testing, when administered frequently and used with error analysis (as explained earlier in Part 2), becomes a formative evaluation system. Criterion-referenced testing can also be used in conjunction with other evaluation systems and may or may not be considered formative according to the frequency of the evaluation. Combining a criterion-referenced test with a recording system such as management by objectives, learning ma-

SUMMARY OF MODALITY ASSESSMENT

	Sense Skill	Stimulus	Criterion Score	Performance Score	Analysis Score
AUDITORY	Discrimination				
	Immediate Recall				
	Delayed Recall				
VISUAL	Discrimination				
	Immediate Recall				
	Delayed Recall				
HAPTIC	Discrimination				
	Immediate Recall				
	Delayed Recall				
OLFACTORY	Discrimination				
	Immediate Recall				
	Delayed Recall				

0 = at criterion
+ = above
− = below

NOTE: Adapted from *Teaching Skills to Children with Learning and Behavior Disorders* by Thomas Stephens, p. 193. Copyright 1977 by Charles E. Merrill Publishing Co. Reprinted by permission.

Figure 11.3

Directive teaching assessment.

TEACHING STRATEGY

Objective:

Modality:

Individual or Small Group:

Teacher Activity:

Materials:

Student Response:

Evaluation:

Criterion:

Criterion met? _____

If yes:

If no:

Figure 11.4

Teaching strategy (DTIMS).

NOTE: Adapted from *Teaching Skills to Children with Learning and Behavior Disorders* by Thomas Stephens, p. 254. Copyright 1977 by Charles E. Merrill Publishing Co. Reprinted by permission.

trices, or precision teaching can provide a quick visual summary of specific skills. In addition, the F–AC-T (fact-assumed cause-testing) sheet introduced in Chapter 6 is a useful tool in evaluating results of a criterion-referenced test.

Good criterion-referenced tests contain more items than the student can complete in a specified time period. The tests should also be designed to measure a particular response more than one time (Figure 11.6). These tests can mea-sure a specific subskill, or they can measure several subtasks within a task. Criterion-referenced tests can be designed to measure cognitive, affective, or psychomotor skills.

Learning Matrices

A learning matrix is comprised of subtasks of a criterion-referenced test that have been sequenced according to difficulty. The matrix is

OBJECTIVE EVALUATION PLAN

Name_____   Teacher_____

Date _____

Objective	Pretest Score	Criteria	Date Objective To Be Met	Date Met
1.				
2.				
3.				

Figure 11.5
Management by objectives.

Name _____ Criteria_____

Date _____ Score_____

3 +3	5 +3	6 +3	7 +3	6 +3	(5)
8 +3	9 +3	3 +3	4 +3	5 +3	(10)
6 +3	4 +3	5 +3	4 +3	9 +3	(15)
8 +3	7 +3	4 +3	6 +3	5 +3	(20)
6 +3	3 +3	9 +3	5 +3	4 +3	(25)

Figure 11.6
Example of a criterion-referenced test, or probe sheet, for +3 addition facts.

then placed on a grid, which allows for repeated evaluation of skills (Figure 11.7). Codes are then developed to identify mastery and progress towards objectives. Spradlin (cited in Haring & Schiefelbusch, 1976) presents several excellent examples of learning matrices.

Arithmetic Charts

Arithmetic charts may be used to graph data. Raw score, percentage, percentile, rate, or trials to criterion may be charted on the arithmetic chart, although percentage is charted most commonly. Session data are usually plotted consecutively (Figure 11.8).

Precision Teaching

Precision teaching provides a system to chart and evaluate progress by comparing growth to previous learning patterns or proficiency rates which have been established for similar populations. This system includes a six-cycle semi-

logarithmic chart which is designed to predict instructional outcomes. Other components of precision teaching include the lesson plan and data evaluation guidelines. (See Chapters 12 and 13 for details.)

What to Measure

Different evaluation systems will stress measurement of different types of responses. However, for the measurement to be *direct*, it is necessary to measure an observable behavior. When measuring performance, it is often useful to define the behavior so that another person can measure the same behavior and end up with similar data. This is referred to as inter-observer reliability or inter-observer agreement (Repp, Deitz, Boles, Deitz, & Repp, 1976). Measurement of behaviors that concern or puzzle the teacher should be of first priority.

In deciding how to count the behavior, it helps to define the beginning and ending points of the behavior. For example, writing numbers in-

Cutting skills	Date 1	Date 2	Date 3	Date 4	Date 5
12. Cuts outlined figure					
11. Cuts curves					
10. Cuts in straight lines					
9. Cuts 2-inch strip of paper					
8. Cuts 1-inch strip of paper					
7. Cuts ½-inch strip of paper					
6. Cuts ¼-inch strip of paper					
5. Makes one cut					
4. Applies pressure					
3. Pulls thumb and finger apart to release scissors					
2. Brings thumb and finger together					
1. Grasps scissors correctly					

X = mastered
/ = working on skill

Figure 11.7

Learning matrix.

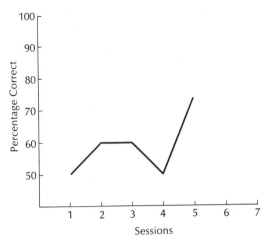

Figure 11.8

Arithmetic charting.

cludes beginning to form the number, writing the number, and completing the number. With this definition, a half-finished number (i.e., 5) would not be counted.

A brief description of common response dimensions follows.

1. A direct measure of the frequency of the behavior can provide information which a teacher can use to compare the behavior to other behaviors (i.e., Jim writes 15 numbers per minute and 12 letters per minute). Frequency tells us how often the behavior occurs. Rate of response is a frequency measure.
2. Sometimes it is helpful to know how long a behavior lasted. Duration is a measure of the length of time the behavior occurred. If a child gets out of his seat frequently, the teacher may gain useful information by timing how long the child stayed in his seat or how long the child was out of his seat.
3. Accuracy informs the data collector of the amount of correct responses. Accuracy is reported by comparing the number of correct responses to the total number of responses. (Accuracy is often summarized as a percentage.)
4. Latency refers to the length of time between the termination of the stimulus and the beginning of the response ($\underset{\text{time}}{S \text{ latency} \rightarrow R}$).
   For example, if the teacher said, "Write the numbers one to ten," and a student started writing 2 minutes later, the latency would be counted as 2 minutes.
5. When measuring such behaviors as yelling or hitting, the magnitude or intensity of the response may help to define the difference between talking and yelling or touching and hitting. An academic response which could include an intensity component is amount of

pen pressure on paper. (This may be helpful when working with a physically handicapped child.) Although intensity can be measured with scientific or bio-feedback instruments (an audiometer to measure decibels, a spigmometer to measure blood pressure) it is difficult to use these instruments in the classroom environment. Other than that, intensity can be estimated in the classroom through inter-judge reliability definitions (i.e., a yell is defined by a pre-agreed-upon volume).

6. Appropriateness of the behavior can be measured by examining situational variables related to the behavior. For example, jumping may be appropriate at recess but not during math. The teacher could count appropriateness by recording "where" or "under what conditions" (stimuli) the behavior occurs. This measure could then be converted to a frequency or duration count.

Although many aspects of a behavior may be measured, the teacher is most concerned about the critical effect of the behavior (White & Haring, 1976). Critical effect refers to how that behavior affects the individual and the individual's relationship to the environment or others. When deciding what aspect of a behavior to count, critical effect and ease of behavior comparisons should be considered. It is often helpful when measuring latency, duration, or magnitude to define a correct and error level (i.e., taking 0–30 seconds to begin to follow a direction is defined as acceptable) and then collecting a frequency count. Frequency is a very useful dimension because most behaviors can be converted to a frequency.

Criteria for Formative Evaluation Data

Formative evaluation has been defined in this chapter as direct and continuous measurement. It follows from this definition that one of the necessary criteria for good formative evaluation is that data must be recorded *frequently*. Clinical teaching (see Table 11.1, p. 127) has included a test-teach-test-teach evaluation model. Following this model, theoretically a teacher could test in September, teach through January, test in February, and still be engaged in *formative evaluation*.

Other evaluation models (clinical teaching, diagnostic-prescriptive teaching, directive teaching) propose that norm-referenced tests be used for evaluation. These tests are often not *direct* measures of performance. Accordingly, the second criterion for formative evaluation, that the assessment be a direct measure of performance, has not been adequately met by some systems. This holds true even if the system has been validated as an effective teaching model. Some of the evaluation systems discussed are primarily *teaching models* and may, in fact, be quite effective as such. These systems, however, may not contain adequate evaluation systems.

Two other considerations which should occur in the selection of a formative evaluation system are (1) the *type of data* obtained by each system and (2) the *standards for proficiency* adopted by each model. The data obtained by each system may, in fact, be quite different and may affect the ease of data interpretation. For example, as more data are gathered with narrative recording, it becomes increasingly difficult to wade through the information and sort out what is really happening.

Another problem with many formative evaluation systems is in the area of proficiency (Figure 11.9). If the child performs the task correctly on one occasion, has he mastered the task? If a child accurately performs 10 instances of a task on one occasion, has he mastered the task? If a child is consistently accurate when adding one-place addition facts, but takes a long time to complete them, has mastery been achieved?

Neither clinical nor directive teaching requires that proficiency be designated in terms of accuracy and speed; these systems concentrate on accuracy alone. Data have been accumulated, however, which show that mastery is related to rate of performance. A relationship exists between performance rate on basic skills such as writing numbers and letters and more complex skills such as writing words and performing mathematical computations (Intermediate School District No. III, 1974; Starlin, 1971).

Proficiency rates can be established for fundamental academic skills by examining child growth with a different level of criteria for prerequisite skills. For instance, if it has been determined that children will master new words more quickly if they first can say the sounds within the words at a particular rate, then the criteria for correct sounds per minute can be established by measuring the subsequent learning of children who achieved higher or lower say sound rates. Records of many children can

be reviewed to determine the level of say–sound rates which results in most rapid acquisition of words containing those sounds. A synopsis of the adequacy with which each system meets the criteria outlined for a good formative evaluation system is presented in Figure 11.10.

Modifying Evaluation Systems

The information presented in Figures 11.9 and 11.10 outlines the strengths and weaknesses of various evaluation systems as they are commonly used. Some systems are presented in a manner which necessitates the use of continuous or daily direct measurement and the identification of desired proficiency rates (precision teaching, criterion-referenced testing). Other systems, however, can be modified to provide a more accurate basis for analyzing learning in classroom situations. Figures 11.11 and 11.12 present two examples of additions or modifications of existing systems.

In Figure 11.11, the narrative log was modified for easier data interpretation and to include a desired behavior rate. Rather than arbitrarily identifying a mastery level, standards for mastery should be identified as in criterion-referenced testing. Field tests should be administered to populations who can perform the task. This modification makes the narrative log much stronger. However, ease of interpretation with the recording system is still questionable. The main problem arises from the narrative recording system, which does not provide a quick visual picture of progress.

The learning matrix system (Figure 11.12) was modified in order to more accurately represent progress. Traditionally only one or two symbols had been used with the matrix: an X or filled-in box ■ to identify mastery, and a slash or half-filled box ◪ to designate an area being worked on. The addition of other symbols allows for more precise information about the progress that is being made. The second major change was the establishment of a uniform interval system for recording progress (in this case, once every 7 days).

An accurate visual picture is crucial to correct interpretation of data. A standard time interval between assessments is necessary in order to present an accurate visual picture. For example,

System	Data	Possible Interpretation
Clinical Teaching	Cat and crayon spelled "k"	Child is a phonetic speller does not know c or k rule.
	3 + 5 = 7 3 + 6 = 8	Child needs to review +3 facts
Directive Teaching	Child spelled 10 words with initial c for k sound correctly.	Child performs task accurately.
	Child added 8 out of 10 addition problems correctly. Child missed 3 + 5 = 7, and 3 + 6 = 8.	Child has achieved 80% mastery.
Precision Teaching		Child initially had many errors, errors were isolated and worked on separately; learning is now occurring, child should master task within 3-4 days.
Learning Matrices		Child has mastered first and second tasks, but not +3 or +4.
Arithmetic Chart		Child's percentage of correct increases.
Narrative Log	John did better today in math and reading. His acting out behavior was under more control.	John actually 1. did better or 2. did more work The teacher was 1. less hassled or 2. in a better mood

Figure 11.9

Examples of data collected in different formative systems.

System	Data Recorded Frequently	Direct Measures	Easy to Interpret	Proficiency Designated
1. Diagnostic- Prescriptive Teaching	No	Minimal	?	According to norm
2. Diagnostic Teaching	No	Minimal	?	According to norm
3. Clinical Teaching	?	Some	?	Not specified
4. Narrative Log	Yes	?	No	No
5. Directive Teaching	Yes	Yes	Yes	Accuracy or trials to cri- terion
6. Management by Objectives	?	Yes	Yes	Often determined by teacher
7. Criterion-Refer- enced Testing	Yes	Yes	Yes	Yes (speed and accuracy)
8. Learning Matrices	Yes	Yes	Yes, if not visually distorted	Yes
9. Arithmetic Charts	Yes	Yes	Yes, If not visually distorted	Varies
10. Precision Teaching	Yes	Yes	With practice	Yes (speed and accuracy)

Figure 11.10

Analysis of formative evaluation systems.

MATH PERFORMANCE

Date	Activity	Rate	Percentage Correct	Comments
5/14	add fractions	39 correct in 10 min	100%	

Figure 11.11

Modified narrative log.

in Figure 11.13, measurement occurred weekly for 3 weeks and then every other week for a time. Leaving weeks 4, 6, and 8 out of the matrix makes it appear that the child was progressing more quickly during the last weeks of the matrix when, in fact, no change in learning occurred. It is not a good idea to change time intervals or to use uneven intervals when recording progress.

Other Modifications

Other examples of modifications which could strengthen systems of evaluation include speci-fying daily or weekly recording of data, standardizing the distances on arithmetic charts (see Chapter 12), designing forms which provide for visual representation of progress, and always designating mastery in terms of "rate" data.

This chapter has not been intended to provide an in-depth presentation of each evaluation system, but rather to introduce a variety of systems along with criteria for evaluating the potential usefulness of each system. For a more thorough understanding of each system, the reader is referred to the sources cited for each.

X = 100% correct at desired speed.
/ = 100% correct, not at desired speed, progress continuing.
— = maintaining previous rate, not much improvement noted.
\ = performance is deteriorating.

WRITE LETTERS	Week 1	Week 2	Week 3	Week 4	Week 5		
j							
a							
e			—	—	/		
o		/		X	X		
c	X	X	X	X	X		
l	X	X	X	X	X		

Objective: To write the identified letter at a rate of 25 correct with 0 errors per minute

Figure 11.12

Modified learning matrix.

NOTE: Mastery is now specified in terms of number of correct and number of errors per minute.

Task	Week 1	Week 2	Week 3	Week 5	Week 7	Week 9
e						X
d					X	
c				X		
b		- - - -	X			
a	X					

Figure 11.13

Nonuniform learning matrix.

NOTE: Visual distortion of progress is caused by changing frequency of recording progress. With this system an evaluator might conclude that the child made more rapid progress with tasks c, d, and e than he did.

Checkpoint 11.1

Directions: Supply the correct answer for each of these questions. CAP is 100% accuracy in 10 minutes.

1. A good formative evaluation system measures behavior directly, frequently, and includes_____.

2. Try to interpret the following data and list interpretation problems:

   a. 9/28—Martha did well in spelling.

Checkpoint 11.1 (cont)

      9/29—Henry read 150 words correctly. Joe is having trouble in subtraction.

      b. 100

      Percentage
       Correct

       50

      c. Mark substituted *look* for *lock* and read *căm* for *cāme*.

   3. What aspects of directive teaching are more direct and frequent than diagnostic-prescriptive teaching?

      Mark T for true or F for false next to each statement.

____4. Accuracy is the best measure of proficiency.

____5. Clinical teaching utilizes task analysis and norm-referenced testing.

____6. Arithmetic charts are proportionate and standardized.

____7. Diagnostic teaching uses repeated measures.

Acceptable Responses

1. Criteria
2. Comparable answers are in Figure 11.9.
3. See discussion of directive teaching, p. 133.
4. F
5. T
6. F
7. F

Options

1. If you scored 100% on the assessment for this unit, you may go on to the next chapter.
2. If you scored less than 100%, go back and reread the reading assignment. Then take the checkpoint again.

12

The Precision
Teaching Essentials

Unit 12.1:	Direct application of precision teaching.
Objectives:	The learner will chart data, ask data questions, apply rate criteria, and evaluate data.
Prerequisite:	Chapter 11.

Introduction to Precision Teaching

As illustrated in Chapter 11, many formative evaluation systems are currently available to classroom teachers and psychologists. Using any of these systems will certainly be better than traditional teaching with only haphazard evaluation. However, of all the formative evaluation systems currently being used, precision teaching offers some unique advantages.

The Precision Teaching Attitude

One of the major differences between precision teaching and other evaluation systems can best be described as a difference in attitude towards evaluation. Precision teaching is first and foremost a tool to help teachers gain information.

It is best used when a teacher wants to gain knowledge and desires to apply technology as an aid to developing a more adequate, individualized program. Figure 12.1 shows some precision teaching data charted on a six-cycle semilogarithmic chart for Henry, age 6. The behaviors recorded are words spelled correctly and incorrectly. The teacher wished to evaluate the effects of limiting the spelling program to words with similar prefixes and suffixes. The effect of the intervention introduced on week 2 is readily apparent. Limiting the spelling vocabulary and systematically introducing new words resulted in an immediate and prolonged reduction of errors. The technology involved in precision teaching allows the user not only to summarize progress but also to *predict* future growth. In Figure 12.1 it is apparent that with continuation of the same program, Henry's errors will most likely remain low.

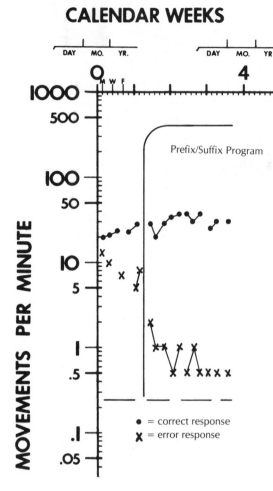

CALENDAR WEEKS

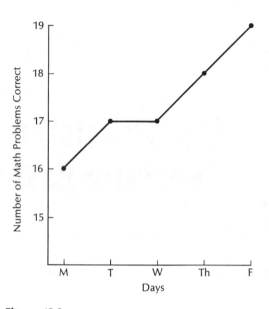

Figure 12.1

The effect of a program change.

Figure 12.3

Data recorded on arithmetic chart.

Most formative evaluation systems follow a test-teach-test-teach model (Lerner, 1971). These evaluation systems can accurately pinpoint where a child is, but really do not involve sufficient technology to measure or predict where a child is going. Precision teaching, a data-gathering system developed by Dr. Ogden Lindsley in the 1960s, utilizes mathematical principles which allow for accurate measurement of child growth and prediction of future growth. Precision teaching provides a means of measuring where a child is, where she is going, and when she will get there (Figure 12.2).

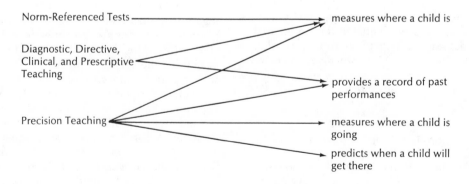

Figure 12.2

Comparison of evaluation systems.

CALENDAR WEEKS

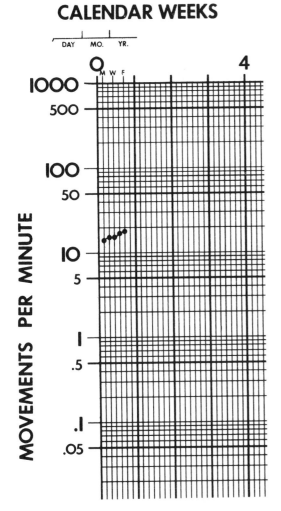

Figure 12.4

Data replotted on a different scale.

Without precision teaching technology, formative evaluation provides a record of current and past performances; however, the total learning picture may be lost or distorted. Traditional record systems (narrative forms, learning matrices, logs, and arithmetic charts) can be complicated to analyze and present an exaggerated picture of changes in child performance (Figure 12.3).

The data recorded on an arithmetic chart in Figure 12.3 visually present a picture of rapid progress. If this data were replotted with different scales, the picture may be quite dissimilar (Figure 12.4).

It follows that one distinct advantage of precision teaching is a standardized scale available in the form of the six-cycle chart. With a standardized scale, the learning picture cannot be distorted. Those using precision teaching will be less likely to make false assumptions about learning, programs, or procedures because they realize that the data is a tool for individualizing programs. The precision teaching approach stresses asking data-based questions. Is Lippincott second-grade reading more difficult for Susan than third-grade Palo Alto? Should multiplication and division be taught simultaneously as inverse processes or consecutively, teaching division only after multiplication has been mastered? Will mainstreaming result in the fastest acquisition of basic academic skills? Each of these questions must initially be approached as an area where more information is needed. Because each learner is unique, these questions should be approached as data-based questions for individual learners.

Isolating Assumptions—Asking Data-Based Questions

Given a limited amount of information on any child's learning, it is important that the data at hand be used wisely and not misinterpreted. This can best be accomplished by first identifying "data traps" or false assumptions and then deciding what additional data the evaluator (or teacher) needs to know. Precision teaching stresses the careful consideration of the meaning of the data provided. Often, the pitfalls involved in overgeneralizing results or in constructing hypotheses for unobservable learning processes can be avoided. The situation described in the following paragraph often occurs in regular classrooms. Can you identify possible "data traps" or false assumptions that might be made from this narrative?

Scott, age 6, resides in the inner city and is in first grade. Scott has trouble identifying the letters of the alphabet and at mid-year is not yet reading more than 10 sight words. The teacher thinks Scott may be retarded and has asked for an evaluation for special class placement.

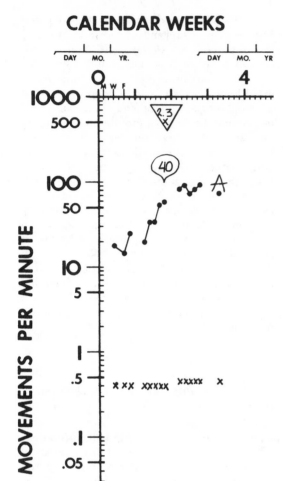

Figure 12.5

Precision teaching data: Ordered multiplication.

Data Traps (False Assumptions)
1. Scott is not ready for reading.
1. Scott learns slowly.
3. Scott has a visual perception problem.

Data-based Questions
1. What specific tasks were presented to Scott?
2. Which letters can Scott point to? . . . name?
3. What methods have been used to teach Scott?
4. What reinforcement systems have been tried?
5. What is Scott's pattern of learning? When was each sight word mastered?
6. How would Scott do with a phonetic approach?
7. What was Scott's "rate" of performance on the tasks presented?

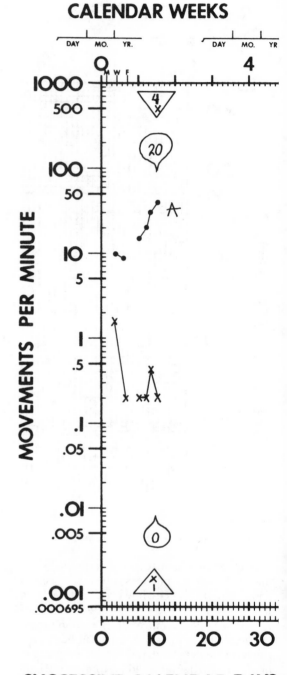

Figure 12.6

Precision teaching data: Multiplication review.

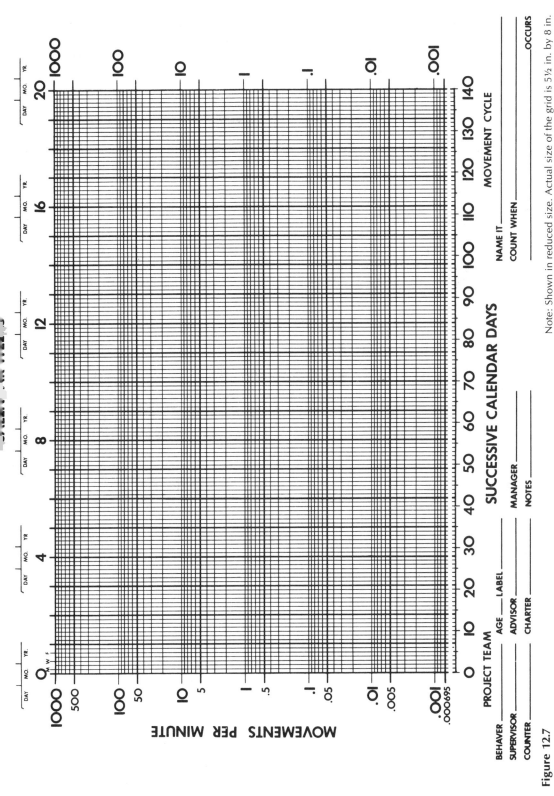

Figure 12.7

The standard behavior, semilogarithmic chart.

147

The intent of precision teaching is to ask specific, data-based questions and seek instructional answers in order to change either programs or reinforcement systems and accelerate learning.

Synthesizing Information

As data are collected for specific programs, techniques, and curricula, this knowledge can be used to form some generalizations. Best guesses can be made about which procedures and programs will most likely work for each child. However, it is never assumed that learning will be the same for all children or that certain techniques will always work.

When precision teaching is used daily to guide learning, child growth can be substantially accelerated. Liberty (1975) has collected data which

indicate that when data decisions rules are consistently and consciously applied, child learning rates can be doubled over a period of weeks.

AN EXAMPLE. One teacher wished to examine data patterns for mastering multiplication facts through a "see-to-write mode." (The student wrote answers to written problems.) The facts were presented one fact family at a time in a sequential order. Newly acquired facts were intermingled in a review sheet. Figures 12.5 and 12.6 present samples of the data collected for two children.

Using the precision teaching system these children who were previously diagnosed as learning disabled mastered multiplication in about 90 days. The data presented in Figures 12.5 and 12.6

Plan Sheet Number _____ of _____   Pinpointed by _____ Date _____

                    Advisor _____   Manager _____

	Correct			Error	
Assessment Rate _____ Date _____ Target Date _____ Prerequisite Skill _____ Objective: Aim Rate _____					
Before (S$_1$)	**R**	**After (S$_2$)**	**R**		**After (S$_1$)**

Figure 12.8

The is-does *plan sheet.*

are "rate data," that is, data recorded in terms of number of responses per minute. Most behaviors can be measured in terms of rate, or frequency of behavior, over a specified time interval.

Characteristics of the Precision Teaching Approach
Asks data-based questions.
Requires direct and continuous measurement.
Considers growth for individual learners.
Measures rate.
Measures learning.

Precision Teaching Components

Integral components of the precision teaching system include the semilogarithmic chart (Figure 12.7) and the *is-does* plan (Figure 12.8). The chart is semilogarithmic because the vertical axis is scaled so that the distances are represented proportionately (Figure 12.9). For example, the distance between 10 and 50 is the same as between one and five, or 100 and 500.

The chart is called semilogarithmic because only the vertical axis is proportionately scaled. The horizontal axis (Figure 12.10) is an equidistant scale. Each heavy line is a Sunday line, and the lines between Sunday lines are day lines.

Precision teaching utilizes a semilogarithmic chart because of the way learning patterns appear on this type of chart. The acquisition of skills or knowledge will follow a pattern. When charted on an arithmetic chart, this pattern most often appears as a curve. However, on a semilogarithmic chart the learning can be drawn as a straight line. This straight line measurement has many advantages. For example, predictions can be made more easily when straight lines represent the learning path (Figure 12.11).

Because the dots on the chart represent repeated measures of the same behavior, they can be used to establish a trend (or pattern) in the student's behavior. The dots can also be used to project a line of progress on the chart. Predictions of future performance can be made from this line. Thus, with the precision teaching evaluation system, the teacher can record not only where a child is, but also where she is going and when she will get there. In Figure 12.12, a line of progress has been projected. The "A"

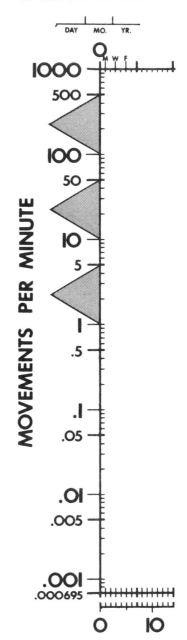

Figure 12.9

The vertical axis is logarithmic.

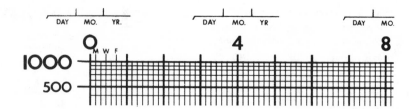

Figure 12.10

The horizontal axis is equidistant.

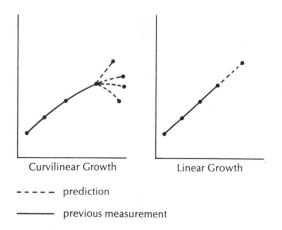

Curvilinear Growth   Linear Growth

- - - - - prediction

———————— previous measurement

Figure 12.11

Predicting from curvilinear vs. linear growth.

placed on the chart stands for aim (the objective). The "A" is placed on the date when the child will be expected to reach the aim. This is the standard procedure for indicating aims and the date the aims should be reached on the six-cycle chart. Such a notation serves both as a quick reference and as an indication of expected growth. The line between the data and the aim serves as a standard for desired progress. The intent is to attempt to establish programs whereby the data will follow that line. When the data starts "falling off course" and the expected progress is not being made (Figure 12.13), changes in program are indicated.

The importance of differentiating performance (a measure of behavior on one occasion) from learning (changes in performance over time) becomes readily apparent in the following ex-

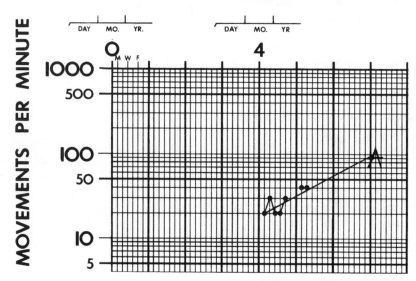

Figure 12.12

Projecting linear progress and recording aims.

CALENDAR WEEKS

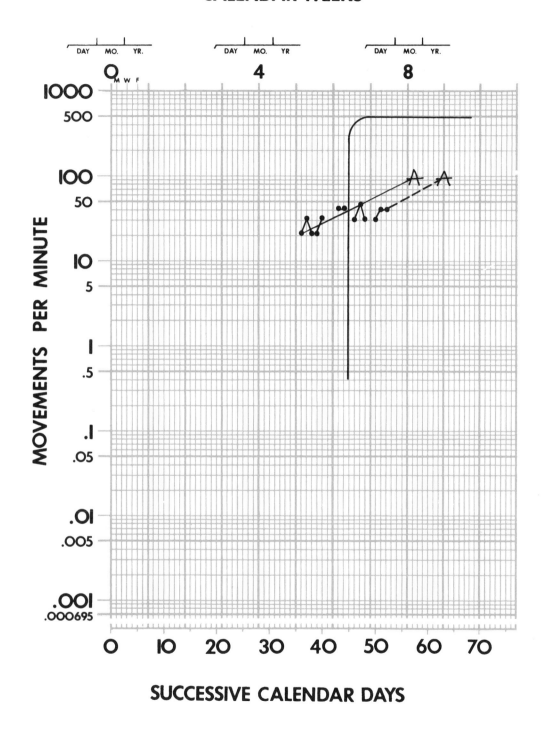

Figure 12.13

Using linear progress to determine program change.

ample. In Figure 12.14, the child is performing at a desirable rate (approximately 20 correct and 4 errors) under condition 1; however, the child is not learning as quickly. If a measure of perfor- mance were the only evaluation used, the child would be placed under condition 1. This would be unfortunate since the child is learning more quickly in condition 2.

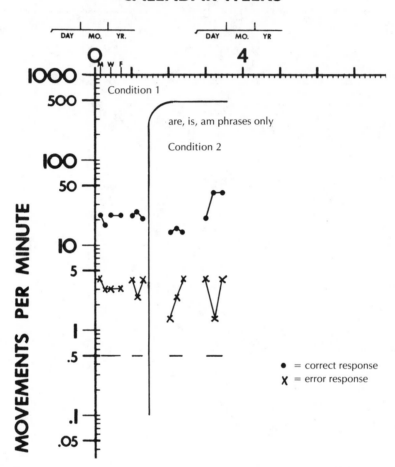

Figure 12.14
Comparing two treatments.

Note to reader: The following material will be covered in a programmed format. Answers will be provided in the lefthand column. It is suggested that you cover the answer column with a piece of paper and uncover the answers as the material is completed.

Introduction to the Six-Cycle Chart

Ideally, data concerning pupil performance should be collected and recorded on a daily basis so that trends may be recognized and predictions about future behavior made. Aside from feeding the data into a computer, the best way to determine if a trend exists is to plot the data on a chart.

Examine the data in Figure 12.15 and then look at the chart in Figure 12.16 which uses the same data.

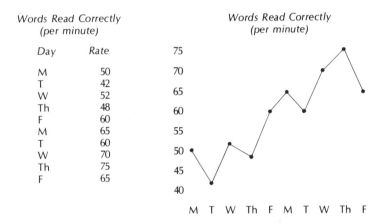

Words Read Correctly
(per minute)

Day	Rate
M	50
T	42
W	52
Th	48
F	60
M	65
T	60
W	70
Th	75
F	65

Words Read Correctly
(per minute)

Figure 12.15

Data presented in numerical form.

Figure 12.16

Data presented on a chart.

It is easier to determine whether the student's rate is accelerating

or decelerating by looking at the data in Figure_____.

12.16

Before deciding which chart to use, it is necessary to discuss which type of data will be recorded. Basically, there are three types of data that may be charted: *(a)* raw score, *(b)* percentage, and, *(c)* rate.

Raw Score reports how many times a student performed a certain behavior. For example, on a Monday, we might give a student a ditto containing 100 addition facts such as, 2 + 3 =   and require her to write the sums to each. If she gets 80 correct we could record the score on conventional, equal-interval graph paper (Figure 12.17).

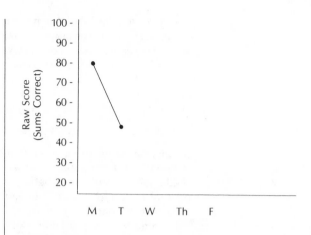

Figure 12.17
Raw scores.

raw

The data recorded in Figure 12.17 are _____ scores.
One problem with recording raw score (or frequency) is that it may not be possible to give the learner the same number of problems each day. Suppose on Tuesday she received 50 problems

raw score

instead of 100 and she got all 50 correct? By charting _____ on the graph it would appear that her performance is getting

50

worse because she went from 80 "down" to _____ (Figure 12.17).

If the number of problems given as well as the number correct is considered, percentage can be computed as well as raw score.

improved, increased

Figure 12.18 shows that the learner's performance has _____ from 80% to 100%.

100 -
90 -
Percentage
(Sums Correct)
80 -
70 -
60 -
50 -
40 -
30 -
20 -

M   T   W   Th   F

Figure 12.18
Percentage.

percentage	The data in Figure 12.18 are recorded in terms of _____ .
	If accuracy alone is used to determine if a student has acquired a skill, then a score of 100% would indicate that the student has
accurate	become_____at the skill.
	Let us assume, however, that it took a student 100 minutes to work 100 problems with 100% accuracy. This would be a *rate* of one correct response per minute.
	Looking only at percentage, it appears that the learner has the skill being measured. However, it has been demonstrated that successful students are able to correctly write addition sums at the rate of 50 per minute, which is 50 times faster than the student in the example. If speed is included along with accuracy as a criterion for possessing this skill, it becomes obvious that the learner
successful	is not a_____student.
raw score, percentage	Three types of data—_____, _____,
rate	and_____—are usually charted.
	These three types of data present different information concerning how well a student is performing a certain task. Skill acquisition can be divided into at least three categories: (a) accuracy, (b) mastery, and (c) automatic.
	Accuracy means that the student gets more problems
correct	_____ than incorrect.
	Percentage correct presents information on a student's
accuracy	_____ .
	Mastery means that the student gets problems correct at a fast
rate, speed	_____ .
	Automatic means that the student gets the problems correct at
fast, high	a_____rate with distractions present.
accurate	A student who is_____at addition can do a sheet of addition facts and get them all correct.
mastered	A student who has_____addition can do the sheet accurately at a rate of 50 problems per minute.
distractions	Accuracy and mastery are determined by testing the student on the skill in isolation. If a student is automatic at addition, then she can add quickly with_____present.
automatic	An example of achievement at the_____level is correct addition and subtraction while balancing a checkbook.

The three levels of achievement can be expressed by the following formulas:

1. Accuracy $= \dfrac{\text{Correct}}{\text{Total}}$

2. Mastery $= \dfrac{\text{Correct}}{\text{Time}}$

3. Automatic $= \left(\dfrac{\text{Correct}}{\text{Time}}\right) + \text{Distractions}$

Raw score alone does not tell if a student is accurate or if the

mastered

student has _____ a skill.

Percentages indicate whether or not a student is accurate, so

raw scores

percentages are better than _____ .

Only rate tells if a student has reached the mastery or automatic

rate

levels of task acquisition. Therefore it is_____that should be collected daily and plotted on a chart in order to determine trend.

What Kind of Chart Should Be Used?

The chart recommended for recording rate data is referred to as the standard six-cycle chart. One reason for using the six-cycle chart is that many different kinds of behavior can be recorded. Supposing you were collecting data on behaviors such as words read correctly for one minute, sums added correctly in 10 minutes, incomplete sentences spoken over one hour, head bangs for the entire school day (300 minutes), runs out of the room for the entire day, or tantrums for the entire day. If a child read 120 words correctly for one minute, her rate would be 120 mpm (movements per minute). If another child added 100 sums correctly in 10 minutes, her rate would be 10 mpm. Another child might speak 100 incomplete sentences in the course of one hour, and her rate would be 1.6 mpm. A fourth child bangs her head 50 times in the course of an entire school day (300 minutes) which is a rate of .16 head bangs per minute. Another youngster runs out of the room 5 times in 300 minutes for a rate of .016 mpm, and still another child has 2 tantrums over the course of an entire school day (.006 mpm).Using the six-cycle chart to record rate data, a teacher could record all of these rates because there is a place (i.e., cycle) for each on the chart.

One reason for using the six-cycle chart is that many different

behavior

kinds of _____ can be recorded on it.

A second advantage of the six-cycle chart is that it is standard. The frequency lines and day lines are always the same on the standard six-cycle chart. (Figure 12.19). This means that the same

the same

set of data will always look _____ on the standard six-cycle chart.

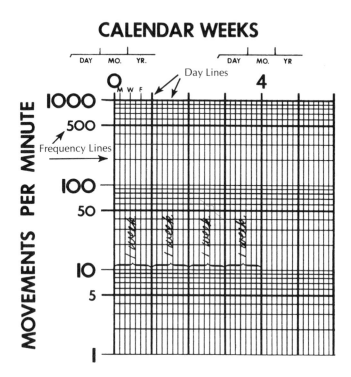

Figure 12.19

Frequency and day lines.

With conventional graph paper, data patterns may appear different according to the scales used. To test this out, complete this simple exercise:

Plot the following data on Chart A (Figure 12.20) and on Chart B (Figure 12.21). Which chart shows the learner making greater improvement?

Day	Rate
M	10
T	11
W	12
Th	13
F	14

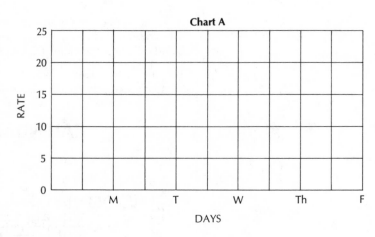

Figure 12.20

Practice chart.

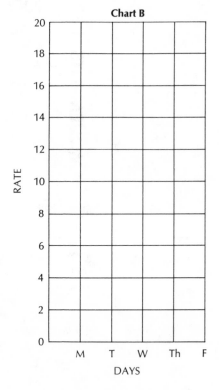

Figure 12.21

Practice chart.

If you have plotted the data correctly on each chart, you will probably see that the data plotted on Chart B seem to indicate

greater, more rapid _____growth than is seen on Chart A.

day	Since the same set of data has been plotted on both charts, there should be no difference between the trends on the charts. Yet, there is a difference! You see that it is possible to make the data appear to show more (or less) improvement by manipulation of intervals on the frequency and _____ axes.
flatter, less steep	On Chart A the days of the week are wide and the frequency lines are in multiples of 5. This spreads the data out and makes the trend line appear to have a_____slope.
steeper	On Chart B, however, the days of the week are narrow and the frequency lines are in multiples of 2. This makes the data closer and makes the trend line appear to have a _____ slope.
standard, six-cycle	When such drastic changes can be made in the intervals on the horizontal and vertical axes, it becomes quite easy to misperceive the actual growth pattern. In contrast, data are not distorted with the _____ chart because the axes are always the same.
predict	Probably the most important feature of the six-cycle chart is that predictions may be made from the rate data plotted on it. With the six-cycle chart, it is possible to estimate how quickly the trend lines are rising or falling. This information makes it possible to _____approximately when the learner will reach a certain rate.
fallen behind	The ability to make such predictions is even more important to special educators than to regular classroom teachers because time is critical with the children who have_____in regular classrooms.
behaviors standardized predictions	So far, three advantages of the six-cycle chart have been mentioned. These advantages are as follows: Many different _____ can be recorded. The chart is _____ . By drawing trend lines, _____ can be made.
a lot of, a half year's	Still another advantage of the six-cycle chart over the conventional graph is that you can fit more data on it. You can record a whole school year's data on just two six-cycle charts. With conventional graph paper, you would have to tape a number of charts together in order to continue the trend lines necessary for easy interpretation of the data. The fourth advantage of the six-cycle chart is that it is possible to record _____ data on one chart.

A fifth advantage of the six-cycle chart is that the scale of the chart is proportionate.

To help you understand this feature, a vertical line has been drawn from the 5 to the 10 and from the 50 to the 100 in Figure

are

12.22. Note the length of the line in each case. The lines _____ the same length.

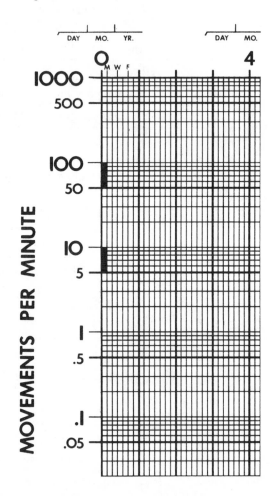

Figure 12.22
The logarithmic chart is proportionate.

The proportion of 5 to 10 is the same as the proportion of 50 to 100. The proportion may be expressed as a ratio of 2 to 1; two

twice

is twice as great as one and 100 is_____ as great as 50.

There are six equidistant intervals on the six-cycle chart (Figure 12.23). Modifications of the six-cycle chart have also been introduced to make charting easier for those who experience difficulty with the six-cycle chart. One modification is the nine-week chart. Because most academic responses occur at a rate of one to five hundred per minute, this chart is useful in recording academic responses. The nine-week chart shown in Figure 12.24 is a one and one-third cycle chart.

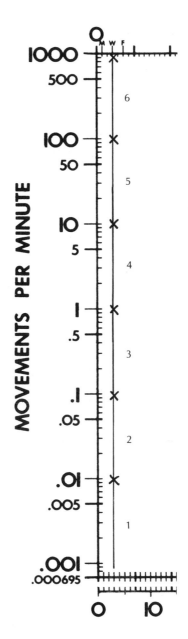

Figure 12.23

Six equidistant intervals.

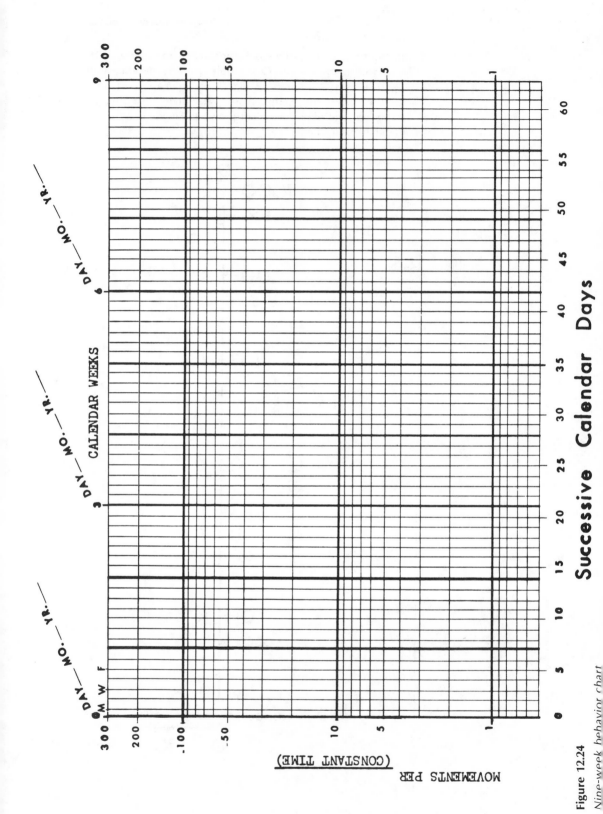

Figure 12.24
Nine-week behavior chart

162

slower	The logarithmic chart reports data in relation to proportions. The usefulness of this information becomes apparent in the following example. A teacher might have two children working on the same material using the same method. Suppose one child increases in one day her performance from 5 words correct per minute to 10, and the other child goes from a rate of 75 to 80 in the same amount of time. If this is charted on conventional graph paper, it may appear that there is no difference between their respective performances or that the second child is doing much better than the first. Neither of these assumptions is necessarily true. Actually, the first child is improving more since the second child is improving at a much _____rate. Rate of improvement (trend) is discussed in Chapter 13.
proportion	The six-cycle chart, because it is logarithmic and drawn in_____ _____, allows us to see immediately that the first child is improving at a greater rate. This allows for more reliable judgments about the effectiveness of the methods and materials used.

Numerous advantages of the six-cycle logarithmic chart have been mentioned in this text and in other texts which cover precision teaching. The six-cycle chart does, however, have its critics. Some of the critics include individuals who resist using the six-cycle chart because it appears to be too complex to be worth the time involved in learning to chart. This group of critics includes those who have never used the chart. Other critics of the chart have used it and have been dissatisfied with the results. Some comments by these two groups and consideration of the problems involved follow:

1. Sometimes it is difficult to get used to reading the chart. Some parents, teachers, and school psychologists, for example, have trouble understanding the chart. This can hinder com-munication during staffings or conferences. The Child Service Demonstration Project (Intermediate School District No. III, 1974) mentions, however, that parts of the chart can be cut off to avoid confusing parents. In these cases, the parents receive only the data as evidence of their child's weekly pro-gress. This is an indication that understanding the chart need not be difficult or confusing.
2. Learning to chart is sometimes viewed as a complex, time-con-suming process. Evidence of the fallacy of this statement was reported by O'Connell and McManman (1977). They collected data with 87 university students which indicated that with as few as 10 practice sessions most students could chart at a rate of 4.5 to 6.0 data pairs (correct and error rates combined) per minute.
3. Rate may not be viewed as a critical measure. Some educators find that rate data are not always worth the time they take to collect. The authors concur and suggest that rate data be collected first and foremost for *priority behaviors* (the most important behaviors). Also *mastery*, as we have defined it,

involves a rate component. Simple percentage describes accuracy only; in some cases, an accuracy measure may be all that is required.

4. The six-cycle chart does not record fine discriminations in specific data rates. It may be difficult to discriminate between a rate of 33 and 34 or 62 and 66, for example. This is true. The purpose of the six-cycle chart is to provide information, however, on *data patterns*. Data patterns can be interpreted readily on the six-cycle chart, and it is these patterns which often lead to instructional decisions.

An examination of the usual criticisms of the precision teaching charting system reveals that many of the negative comments may be related to the fact that those criticizing the system either (1) have not mastered the system (i.e., cannot chart at a proficient rate) or (2) do not have a clear purpose in mind for the evaluation that is occurring (i.e., the evaluation is not meaningful). We have not attempted to present precision teaching as the perfect answer to educational evaluation. We do believe, however, that precision teaching offers some unique advantages and that educators should be familiar enough with the system to consider it as an evaluative option.

How to Use the Six-Cycle Chart

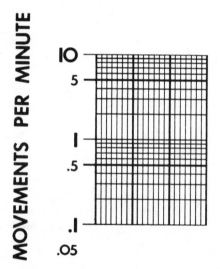

Figure 12.25

The numbers on the left side of the vertical axis indicate the number of movements per minute (responses). The horizontal lines are called frequency lines. The lines which are unnumbered simply represent intermediate numbers (i.e., the line immediately above 1 is 2, and then 3 and 4).

Successive calendar days are located across the bottom of the chart. Note the heavy lines in Figure 12.26.

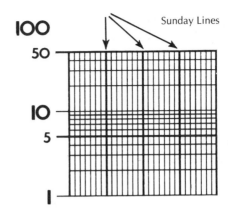

Figure 12.26

Every seventh vertical line is darkened. This is called a Sunday line. The thinner lines between Sunday lines represent the days of the week—Monday, Tuesday, Wednesday, and so forth.

Locate a Sunday line, a Monday line, and a Thursday line in Figure 12.27. Put an S underneath the Sunday line, M under Monday, and T under Thursday on the second week.

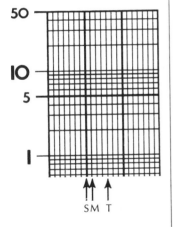

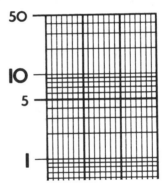

Figure 12.27

If 10 movements per minute (mpm) occurred on a Tuesday, a small dot (.) would be placed at the intersection of the 10 line and a Tuesday line. On Figure 12.28, do the following: Mark 10 mpm on the second Tuesday. Mark 2 mpm on the third Thursday. Mark 20 mpm on the third Friday.

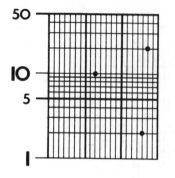

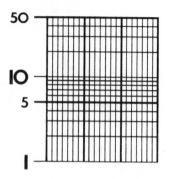

Figure 12.28

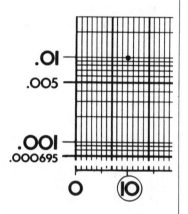

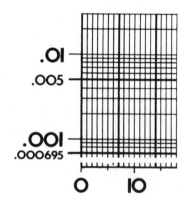

Figure 12.29

The sequence of numbers across the bottom of the chart represents successive calendar days. On Figure 12.29, locate and circle the *numeral* representing the 10th calendar day. Mark .01 mpm on the 10th calendar day.

In Figure 12.30 note that in the upper lefthand corner, above the second vertical line, is an "M" for Monday. Above the fourth line is a "W" for Wednesday and above the sixth line an "F" for Friday. *Draw an arrow to the Monday line of the third week.*

Note also that some weeks are numbered above the chart. The 4 allows the fourth week to be located rapidly. Label the first week Sept. 10, 1979. Notations for the beginning of the week are always charted as *Monday* dates.

On Figure 12.30, plot the following data:

Mon. Sept. 10 30 mpm (movements per minute)
Tues. Sept. 11 35 mpm

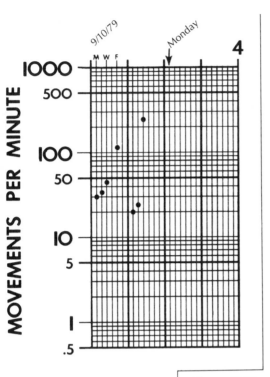

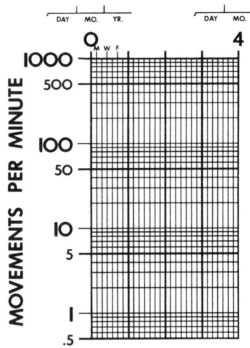

Figure 12.30

Wed. Sept.	12	44 mpm
Fri. Sept.	14	105 mpm
Mon. Sept.	17	10 mpm
Tues. Sept.	18	13 mpm
Wed. Sept.	19	250 mpm

The data you have plotted so far have been expressed in terms of *rate*. Remember

$$rate = \frac{count}{time}$$

To help when plotting large amounts of data, a *rate plotter* has been designed to aid with the division. When used with a six-cycle chart, it functions as a slide rule. Cut out the rate plotter from page 285 and use it in the following frames. (You may wish to make a transparency of the rate plotter.)

Figure 12.31 shows a rate plotter and its correspondence to the six-cycle chart. Place your rate plotter over the one in Figure 12.31. To begin, align the 1 on the chart directly across from the 1 and the arrow notation on the rate plotter.

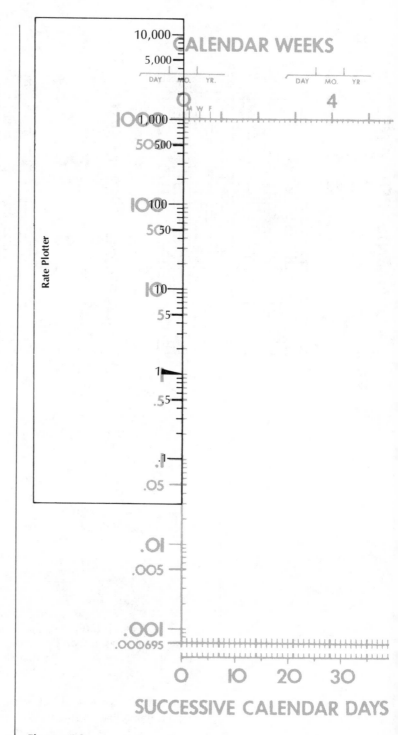

Figure 12.31

Your rate plotter should now be aligned so that the 10 on the

10

plotter is directly across from the _____ on the chart.

The rate plotter can be seen in Figure 12.32. The numbers on the rate plotter are scaled logarithmically just as the numbers on the chart. Two logarithmic scales which slide next to each other comprise a slide rule. Therefore, the rate plotter and the chart can be combined to work multiplication and division problems.

The formula for rate is

$$rate = \frac{count}{time}$$

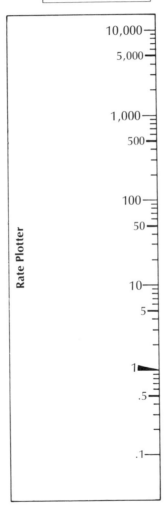

Figure 12.32

Rate plotter.

When using the chart, data are always converted to movements per minute by dividing the count by the number of minutes during which the count took place. It is always possible to do this by division. For example,

time (minutes)	count (movements)	movements per minute (rate)
10	20	2
5	20	4
100	20	.20
150	20	.13
1	20	20

The rate plotter facilitates this division by taking advantage of the logarithmic nature of the chart. The slide rule characteristics of the chart make the conversion of raw data to rate easy.

If the observation time is one minute, the rate plotter is not needed because the raw data are already in movements per minute. If the observation time is longer, you first find the *time* on the rate plotter and place that point over the 1 line of the chart. Then take the number of movements the child actually made during the time you measured her and find that number on the rate plotter. Make a dot on the chart next to that number. Be sure to put your dot on the right day line. This dot represents movements per minute.

Follow these directions for charting 10 movements in 5 minutes.

To chart 10 movements in 5 minutes, these steps were followed:
1. The 5 on the rate plotter was aligned with the 1 on the chart, as shown in Figure 12.33.
2. Movements per minute were found by reading up the rate plotter to the 10 and making a small dot on the horizontal line directly across from the 10 (in this case, the 2 line).

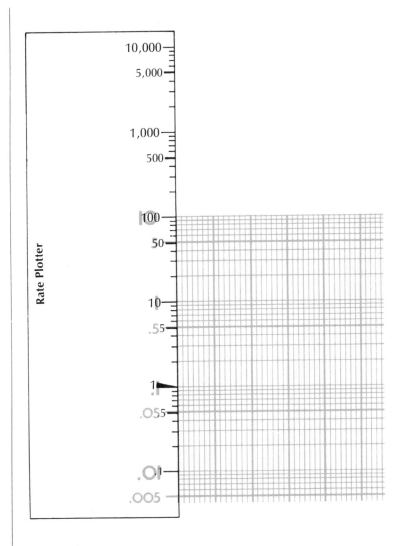

Figure 12.33

Try using the rate plotter to chart 100 movements in 10 minutes. Use the chart in Figure 12.34 to complete the steps below.

1. Place the 10 on the rate plotter next to the 1 on the chart.
2. *Read up* the rate plotter to 100.
3. Place a dot directly across from 100 on the rate plotter. This should be at 10, for 100 movements ÷ 10 minutes = 10 mpm.

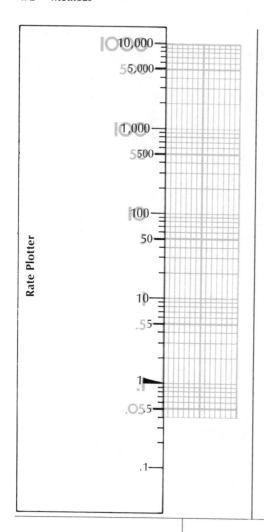

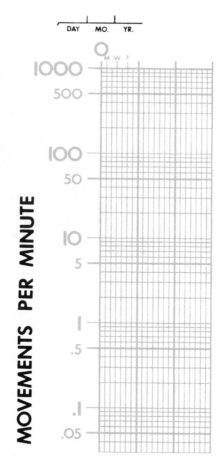

Figure 12.34

minutes

When charting data, it is helpful to know *how long* the session occurred and for how long an interval data were recorded. Length of total session and length of timing may have an effect on response rate. For example, after working for a long time, fatigue or satiation may lower response rate. Similarly, for some students a slight warm-up period may increase response rate. In other words, *response rate* may be related to the length of the recorded session. Response rates should always be reported in terms of the recorded time interval in minutes. If the time interval is not one minute but is always the same, it may be convenient to find the *record floor*. The record floor indicates how many _____ a session was timed or recorded.

Record floors are calculated by dividing the length of the session (in minutes) into the number 1. The least number of times a behavior can occur is once; therefore, 1 is the floor for any behavior.

$$\text{Record floor} = \frac{1}{\text{length of session in minutes}}$$

For example, if a session was recorded for 2 minutes,

Record floor = ½ = .5

It is not necessary, however, to actually calculate record floors by long division. Record floors may be located on the six-cycle chart by using the *rate plotter*. Once a record floor is found, it can be marked on the chart and used to simplify daily charting. Because the same amount of time is used to observe the behavior each day, the rate plotter need only be lined up with the record floor, and raw data charted from it.

For example, to find the record floor for 10 movements in 5 minutes,

1. Align the 5 on the rate plotter with the 1 on the chart.
2. Read down the rate plotter to the 1 with the arrow notation (.2 on the chart).
3. Using Figure 12.35, draw a line along the .2 frequency line for several weeks, skipping over Saturdays and Sundays so the line is a series of dashes 5 days in length.

Using Figure 12.35, record the following data for the first week. Keep the 1 on the rate plotter on .2 (the record floor). Simply move the plotter from day to day and chart from it. When you chart the data below, you will automatically be recording the data in

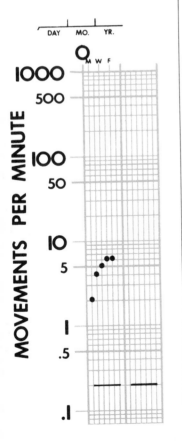

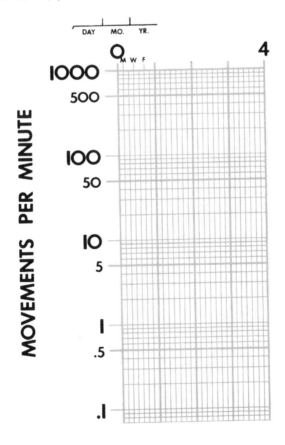

Figure 12.35

movements per minute, that is, the average rate at which the behavior occurred during each minute of the session.

	time	count
Monday	5 min.	10
Tuesday	5 min.	20
Wednesday	5 min.	25
Thursday	5 min.	30
Friday	5 min.	30

The use of the rate plotter makes sense if one thinks in terms of proportions.

100 movements is to 10 minutes as 10 movements is to 1 minute (100:10 as 10:1)

5

5

3

25:5 as _____:1

10:2 as _____:1

9:3 as _____:1

---

record floor

One use of the rate plotter is to calculate the _____ .

---

no need

The record floor is useful when the length of time the behavior is observed is always the same. When the time is always one minute, the record floor isn't needed (it's the 1 line on the chart). When the times are always different, there is _____ to calculate the record floor.

When using the rate plotter, remember to:

1. Locate the record floor by placing the total number of minutes next to the 1 on the chart.
2. Read down the chart to the arrow notation on the rate plotter and draw the record floor.
3. Read up the rate plotter to the total number of movements.
4. Place a dot on the horizontal line next to the total number of movements per minute.

Review: Use of the Rate Plotter

What are the steps in using the rate plotter?

record floor

1. Locate the r _____ f _____ by placing the total number of minutes next to the 1 on the chart.

---

down

2. Read _____ (a direction) the rate plotter and draw the record floor.

---

up

movements (responses)

3. Read _____ (a direction) the rate plotter to the total number of _____ .

---

horizontal (frequency) line

4. Draw a dot on the _____ next to the total number of movements per minute.

Standard notation for the six-cycle chart includes a dot (.) for correct rate, a small triangle or x for errors, and a horizontal line drawn between Monday and Friday for the record floor.

Error rates are plotted in exactly the same manner as correct rates. If correct and error rates are both plotted for a particular response, the procedure is as follows:

record floor

1. Locate the r_____ f_____ by placing the total number of minutes next to the 1 on the chart.

down

2. Read _____ (a direction) the rate plotter and draw the record floor.

up

3. Read _____ (a direction) the rate plotter to the total number of correct responses.

horizontal (frequency) line

4. Draw a dot on the _____ next to the total number of correct movements per minute.

5. Read up or down the rate plotter to locate the total number of error responses on the plotter.

6. Draw an x (or △) on the horizontal frequency line on the chart next to the total number of error responses per minute.

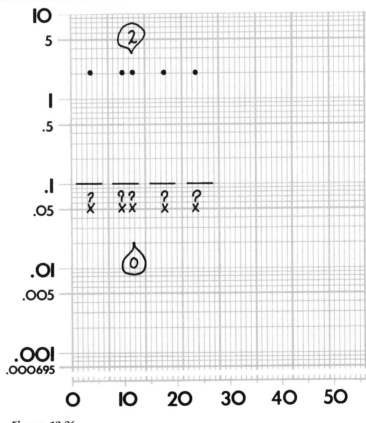

Figure 12.36

one

Using this procedure, correct and error responses and record floor can be plotted with only _____ movement of the rate plotter.

Zero (0) rates are placed at the next major rate line below the record floor, regardless of where the record floor is. Sometimes zero is recorded as a question mark (?), as seen in Figure 12.36.

In plotting daily data, there are two reasons for not placing a score on a day line.

1. An ignored day—the movement cycle *could* have occurred but was ignored—in this case, connect points before and after the ignored day.
2. A *no-chance* day—there was no chance for the movement cycle to occur—in this case, do not connect points before and after the no-chance day.

With practice, the six-cycle chart and rate plotter should become easy to use. Precision teaching practitioners encourage "beginners" to try to reach a plotting rate of 10 (dots, x's, or question marks) per minute.

The only way to become proficient at charting is to practice.

Use the rate plotter and illustrate the following sets of data on the six-cycle chart in Figure 12:37:

Time stopped:_____

Time started:_____

Total time:_____

			Correct	Error	Time
A.	Mon.	Oct. 30	30	2	10 min.
	Tues.	Oct. 31	55	5	10
	Weds.	Nov. 1	102	20	10
	Thurs.	Nov. 2	1	0	10
	Fri.	Nov. 3	3	1	10
	Mon.	Nov. 5	1	10	10
	Tues.	Nov. 6	0	15	10
B.	Wed.	Jan. 5	2	25	23 min.
	Thurs.	Jan. 6	4	30	23
	Fri.	Jan. 7	6	50	23
	Mon.	Jan. 10	12	62	23
	Tues.	Jan. 11	18	65	23
	Wed.	Jan. 12	21	71	23

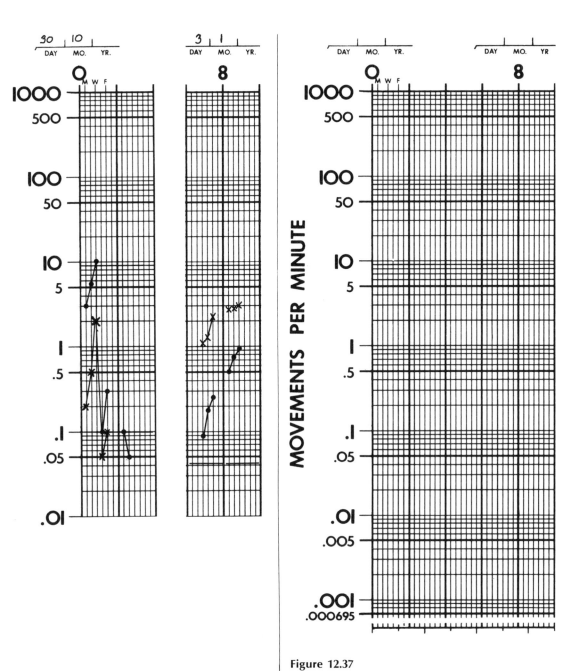

Figure 12.37

Checkpoint 12.1

Directions: Precision teaching is used to measure learning or growth. This series of exercises is designed to help you measure your own growth, or the learning of someone else. For maximum benefit, allow yourself the time indicated in each of the tasks below.

1. On a piece of six-cycle chart paper (Figure 12.38), record the number of letters you can write during a one-minute timing. Do this for five one-minute timings, one timing each day for 5 days. Complete the 5 days of data on the chart. Begin plotting in Week 4 on the chart.
2. On the same chart, record the number of minutes you spend studying each day. Complete the data for 2 full weeks (14 consecutive days). Begin plotting in Week 6 on the chart.
3. On the same chart, record the words read orally from a basal reader during a one-minute timing (either read by you or by a child you know). Complete the data for 4 days of one-minute timings. Begin plotting in Week 8 on the chart.
4. On the same chart, record the number of corrects and errors for each of the days in the following table. Be sure to remember to plot the data in terms of movements per minute. Begin in Week 1 on the chart.

		Correct	Error	Time (in minutes)
Week 1	Monday	100	10	10
	Tuesday	150	5	5
	Wednesday	100	3	2
	Thursday		ignore	
	Friday	150	4	1
	Saturday	210	50	20
	Sunday	340	40	15
	Monday	410	2	5
	Tuesday	50	3	7
	Wednesday	25	0	1
	Thursday	30	0	10
	Friday	50	5	2

Acceptable Responses

1. Check to see if your chart is:
   a. labeled
   b. dated
   c. has record floor drawn
   d. uses a dot for correct responses
2. The record floor for these data should be the average number of waking hours for each day.
3. Make sure the chart is correctly labeled, with a dot for corrects and an x for errors.
4. See Figure 12.39 for the correct plotting of the data.

Options

1. If your chart is correctly filled out, you understand the essentials of precision teaching and can go on to Unit 12.2.
2. If you had difficulty recording data on the six-cycle chart, reread this portion of the chapter and take the checkpoint again.

CALENDAR WEEKS

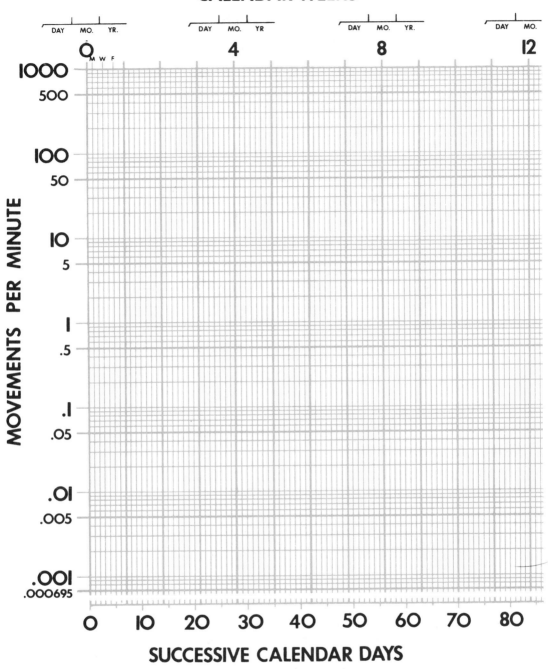

SUCCESSIVE CALENDAR DAYS

MOVEMENT CYCLE

NAME IT _____

COUNT WHEN _____

_____OCCURS

Figure 12.38

179

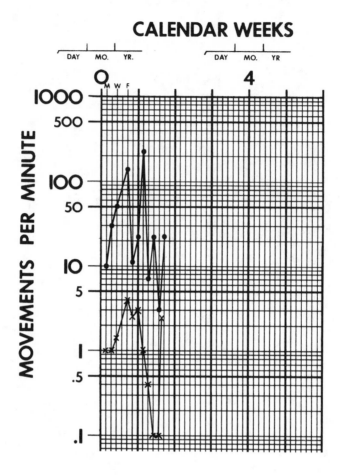

Figure 12.39

> Unit 12.2: The precision teaching plan.
>
> Objective: The learner will complete an is-does plan.
>
> Prerequisite: Unit 12.1.

Treatment Comparison

By looking at the trend of several data points a teacher can tell if a student is progressing toward her aim. In order for this to happen, the data points must reflect information that is related to the objective. In addition, each data point must represent a separate measurement of the same behavior. If each dot on the chart represents the same behavior, trends in the dots represent trends in the behavior.

One excellent use of the chart is treatment comparison. It is possible to compare two treat-

ments (ways of teaching) by making repeated measures of the target behavior when the student is under different treatment plans. In order to make these comparisons it is important to know two things: (1) what exactly does each data point mean and (2) what exactly is the difference between the two treatments?

The data point should be defined by the instructional objective. If the objective is "writes digits," then a dot on the 15 line means the student wrote 15 digits.

The treatments must also be carefully defined in order for comparisons to be made. In precision teaching the treatments are defined through the use of a type of lesson plan called an *is-does* plan.

The Precision Teaching Plan

The two major components of precision teaching are the chart and the lesson plan. The precision teaching plan is called an *is-does* plan to emphasize the differences between the current ongoing events (*is*) and the events which have occurred previously and been proven effective (*does*).

In order to emphasize that data have shown a plan to be effective, one precision teaching trainer has advised users to circle the word "does" over effective plans with red pencil.

The format for the precision teaching plan is basically the same as a S-R-S (stimulus, response, stimulus) model. The items of interest in the precision teaching plan include:

S_1 What happens before the student responds (directions, materials used, explanations).

R The student's response (definition of correct and incorrect).

S_2 What happens after the student responds (consequences, reinforcement, correction procedures for errors).

The following narrative could also be presented in a S-R-S form, as illustrated in Figure 12.40.

Sarah participated in reading from 9:00 a.m. to 10:00 a.m. daily. She read from Ginn Book 2. Each day the teacher would introduce new words and explain to Sarah that she was to read orally and then answer the questions on the board. Sometimes when Sarah was reading the teacher would take a one-minute oral reading sample and count the number of correct and error words per minute. All errors would be corrected through prompting. When the teacher thought Sarah was reading well, he praised her as she read. When she finished reading the story, she was to write the answers to the comprehension questions. Any remaining time before 10:00 a.m. was free time that Sarah could use as she pleased.

In order to make the precision teaching plan easier to read, standard abbreviations have been utilized along with a differentiation for R-S_2 for correct and error behaviors.

Common abbreviations are listed below:

$$
\begin{aligned}
\text{T.} &= \text{teacher} \\
\text{ea.} &= \text{each} \\
\text{vbl.} &= \text{variable} \\
\text{dr} &= \text{desired rate} \\
\text{nec.} &= \text{necessary} \\
\text{e} &= \text{errors} \\
\text{c} &= \text{correct} \\
\text{V.I.} &= \text{variable interval} \\
\text{wpm} &= \text{words per minute} \\
\text{w/} &= \text{with} \\
\text{pts} &= \text{points} \\
< &= \text{less than} \\
> &= \text{greater than} \\
\text{min.} &= \text{minutes}
\end{aligned}
$$

The first initial of a child's name is commonly used to refer to that child. The narrative from Fig. 12.40 is presented in another form in Figure 12.41.

S_1	R	S_2
Reading Ginn Book 2. 9:00 a.m. to 10:00 a.m. daily. Teacher introduces new words and explains that Sarah is to read orally and then answer comprehension questions from book.	Say words aloud while reading. Teacher takes a one-minute sample and counts correct and error words.	When reading well teacher praises intermittently. Errors are corrected through prompting. After reading, comprehension questions are answered. Remaining time until 10:00 a.m. is free time.

Figure 12.40

	Correct			Error	
Before (S1)	**R**	**After (S2)**		**R**	**After (S2)**
Reading, Ginn Book 2, 9:00 a.m. to 10:00 a.m. daily. T. introduces new words and explains that S. should read orally and then answer comprehension questions from board.	Say correct words aloud while reading. T. takes a 1-minute sample and counts correct and error words.	Verbal praise. When finished reading, comprehension questions are answered. Remaining time until 10:00 a.m. is free time.		Say incorrect words.	Each error is corrected through prompting.

Figure 12.41

When initial assessment data is presented along with a target date for projected mastery and an objective, the plan meets the requirements of P.L. 94-142 for an individualized educational plan.

Checkpoint 12.2

Directions: Record the following narrative on an *is-does* plan (Figure 12.42):

Martha participated in math with Mr. Pepper from 10:30 a.m. to 11:30 a.m. daily. The text used was Sullivan Math Book 5. Each day the teacher would introduce the new material and then Martha would work until the end of the period. Correct responses included correct numbers written in the answer. Incorrect numbers written in the answer, or reversed numbers (for 3) were counted as errors. The teacher praised Martha as she worked. At 11:30 the teacher corrected Martha's work in math. Martha charted her correct response rate. If the rate maintained its level from the last rate, or if it increased, Martha was given a star (*) on the chart. Martha corrected her errors with teacher assistance as needed.

The objective of the program was for Martha to be able to add basic addition facts (0–9) at a rate of 30 per minute from Sullivan math with 0 errors. Martha's initial rate on January 9 was 10c, 5e.

Acceptable Responses

Include events such as instructions, program, and materials under the S_1 column (Before S). Include a definition of *correct* and *error* under the R columns. Consequences and feedback should be described in the S_2 columns (After S). See Figure 12.43 for the correct answers.

Options

1. If your is-does plan contains the same information as shown in Figure 12.43, you may go on to the next chapter.
2. If your is-does plan does not resemble Figure 12.43, reread this portion of the chapter and take the checkpoint again.

Tips on Using Precision Teaching

Precision teaching has been discussed by the authors as one formative evaluation system which will offer help to the educator. Precision teaching enables its user not only to evaluate past performance and learning trends but also to predict future behavior. The precision teaching system also provides a lesson planning system which encourages consistency of programming and reinforcement.

IS-DOES PLAN SHEET

Plan sheet number_____of_____

Pupil_____Pinpointed by_____Date_____

Advisor_____Manager_____

Assessment Rate_____Date_____Target Date_____

Objective:

Correct				Error	
Before (S₁)	R	After (S₂)		R	After (S₂)

Figure 12.42

IS-DOES PLAN SHEET

Plan sheet number _____ of _____

Pupil ___ Martha ___ Pinpointed by _____ Date _____

Advisor _____ Manager ___ Mr. Pepper ___

Assessment Rate ___ 10c   5e ___ Date ___ 1/9 ___ Target Date _____

Objective: To be able to add basic addition facts from Sullivan Math Book 5 at a rate of thirty (30) correct and 0 errors per minute.

Before (S_1)	Correct		Error	
	R	After (S_2)	R	After (S_2)
Sullivan, Book 5. 10:30 a.m.- 11:30 a.m. daily. Teacher introduces work. Martha then works until the end of the period.	Correct numbers written in answer.	Teacher praise. 11:30 a.m., T. corrects work. Martha charts response rate. If rate $\geq$ previous day, *put on chart	Incorrect number in answer. Includes *reversed* numbers. (i.e., $\mathcal{E}$ for 3)	Martha corrects errors with teacher's help.

Figure 12.43

184

Precision teaching will be most successful when:

1. The teacher initially counts only priority behaviors.
2. The teacher identifies strategies to make timing and recording behavior easier.
3. The teacher evaluates the recorded data frequently (preferably daily).
4. Probing or criterion-referenced testing is used.
5. The system remains a tool for teaching rather than a "cause." Precision teaching should only be used as long as it helps the student.

Strategies to facilitate timing and recording behaviors include:

1. Take group timings. This works best with written activities. Some teachers, for example, time one-minute handwriting samples, one-minute math fact sheets, one-minute spelling problems.
2. Students can record time stopped and started. This can easily be done with a rubber stamp of a clock on the students' worksheets.
3. A kitchen timer or prerecorded tape can be used to time sessions.
4. Students can work together and time and record data for each other. This has worked well with flashcard drills.
5. Students can read into a tape recorder. Teachers can later record correct and error rates for either samples of behavior or the total session.
6. Use mechanical counters. Single and dual tally counters are available as well as beads and golf score counters.
7. Count for a fixed period of time each day. Counting for different intervals confuses the data pattern since such factors as endurance, boredom, and latency of response may enter into the data analysis.
8. One-minute timings are easy to chart (no rate plotter is necessary).
9. Aids, peers, student teachers, and volunteers can be trained to help develop materials and to count and record behaviors.

Whether you choose to adopt criterion-referenced testing, precision teaching, or another formative evaluation system such as management by objectives, a key to success is to choose behaviors for which you need more data. Once these behaviors have been selected, then choose a time to count when the behaviors are likely to occur and when other distractions will be minimal.

An Example

Three teachers in Arizona evolved a precision teaching program for math facts.[1] This program was used in an open classroom setting. Sev-enty-eight students drilled, timed, and charted math facts by themselves. Many of the students were mainstreamed special education students.

The teachers were concerned that their students were weak in computational mathematics. The pinpoints for the program were addition facts 0–20, subtraction facts 0–20, multiplication facts 0–9, and division facts 0–9. Each student was expected to reach a rate of from 54 to 60 problems (written) per minute in all four areas. Because the program was a drill program, students were not place into it unless (a) they could write digits at a rate of 60–80 per minute and (b) they were somewhat accurate on the facts and already were doing about 15 problems per minute. (Students who are not at least ¼ of the way to capacity probably need direct instruction and not drill.)

DATA COLLECTION. This is how the program worked. Each student was given a file folder. Inside the folder, four charts were stapled to one flap and a sheet of clear plastic was stapled to the other. Every day the teachers would place four probe sheets in the folder (addition, subtraction, multiplication, and division). There were many forms of these probes so the student could not simply memorize them. Every day immediately after the noon recess, when the kids returned to the class, a 10-minute tape of music would play over the room's intercom system. The beginning of the music was a cue for the students to pick up their file folders. A bell would sound on the tape at one-minute intervals, allowing the students to time themselves. Each probe sheet would be placed under the plastic sheet and worked by writing on the plastic with an overhead projector pen. When the student was ready, she would listen for a bell and then work for one minute. When the next bell sounded on the tape, the student would stop working and check what she had done. The answers to each probe sheet were on the back of the sheet, allowing self-checking. Once the rates of corrects and errors were found and the students had recorded the results on the appropriate charts, they would get out their next probe and listen for another bell to start their next timing. The students knew they had 10 minutes to take the four probes, check their own work, and record their own progress.

DATA INTERPRETATION. Students and teachers would review the charts daily. If the students found that their charts were not progressing satisfactorily toward their aim, then they would

---

[1]Special thanks to Ms. Teresa Boyer, Ms. Connie Nygaard, and Ms. Mada Kay Robison.

contract with the teacher for a program change. Many progrems were available for the students to use, including instruction (peer instruction, programmed texts, math fact games, homework) and consequence changes (free time, parent-delivered rewards, class privileges, and redeemable points). The students would select one of these programs and use it for a few days to see if life returned to their charts.

RESULTS. All students in the program (regardless of handicapping condition) reached mastery on the fact probes. It took from 3 to 5 weeks for the average student to reach mastery. Many students progressed at this rate in all four areas at the same time.

It is important to note that by properly designing the program, the teachers were able to collect formative data with minimal daily effort or time. There is no question that such programs take time to develop. But once they are implemented, they can run smoothly and efficiently. When time is saved in the classroom, it should be student time. The teachers spent additional time to design a program which accelerated their students' growth.

13

Advanced Precision Teaching Techniques

Unit 13.1:   Median rates and the semilogarithmic chart.

Objective: The learner will be able to locate and note median rates on the semilogarithmic chart, using conventional notation.

Prerequisites: Chapters 11 and 12.

People who work daily with exceptional learners need to be skilled in analyzing both the performance and progress of their students. *Performance* refers to the behavior of a student in terms of some objective standard. For example, if the objective for the student is to work 40 addition problems a minute and he is currently only working 5, then his performance is 8 times less than expected. *Progress* refers to the student's movement toward an objective. If the student is progressing at a rate which will cause him to go from 5 to 40 in 5 weeks, then he is improving by at least 7 problems a week.

To help you better analyze data on progress and performance, this chapter includes advanced material on precision teaching. The skills presented will be sequenced from the easiest to the most complex. If you wish, pick only those topics that are relevant to you. As in Chapter 12, part of the chapter will be programmed to give you direct application of the skills being taught.

Basic Data Evaluation and Prediction

Charting data in the ways shown in Chapter 12 is a technical skill that provides the educator with a record-keeping system for monitoring student progress through content. Once data have been collected and charted, it is then possible to summarize both the performance of the student relative to the objective and the direction of his progress (data change). Typically, behavior scores are reported in terms of three measures of central tendency: the *mean*, the *mode*, and the *median*. The first section of this chapter includes these measures as techniques for summarizing recorded data. However, the full advantages of precision teaching are realized only through the application of the data evaluation techniques involving the six-cycle chart. The logarithmic nature of the chart allows for both analysis of past performance and prediction of future progress through measuring proportional changes in specific behaviors.

Although the mean, median, and mode provide general frequency values of the data, the scores in and of themselves are not useful in making data decisions about program effectiveness. But these decisions can be made by using 'celeration, which measures *changes* in behaviors. 'Celeration is a term precision teachers use to refer to the *proportion of change in a behavior*. An increase in a behavior can be evaluated by measuring the proportionate *acceleration* of the behavior. Proportionate *deceleration* (decrease) can also be evaluated. 'Celeration can be used to decide when to change programs, materials, or strategies, and it can be examined to determine the effectiveness of treatments. When used in conjunction with an accurate planning system such as the *is-does* plan, the result can be a sophisticated accountability system. Such a system specifies attempts made to change behaviors and the results of these attempts. This can present a picture of child growth for summative, or performance, evaluations. 'Celeration can also be used as a formative, or progress, evaluation tool. These two uses can provide daily insight into behaviors and can result in early program change—to prevent failure before it happens. 'Celeration, then, is the major focus of this chapter.

Data Summary

If we wish to describe a set of data, we could use three measures to describe the most typical results—the mean, the median, and the mode. The *mean* represents the "average" of all the data points. The *mode* is the score most often obtained. The *median* represents the most middle value. These three measures are useful in summarizing correct and error rates. For any group of data, the three measures are calculated by standard procedures.

Figure 13.1 contains seven data points. In order to calculate mean, median, and mode for these data, the following steps should be employed:

Mean $= \dfrac{\text{the sum of the scores}}{\text{number of scores}} =$

$\dfrac{12 + 18 + 12 + 18 + 18 + 8 + 17}{7} =$

$\dfrac{103}{7} = 14$

Mode $=$ the most frequent score $= 18$

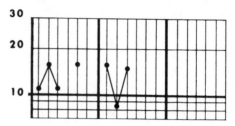

Figure 13.1

Seven data points.

Median $=$ the middle most score, i.e., "the value that falls in the middle when measurements are arranged in order of magnitude" (Mendenhall & Ramey, 1973)

To find the middle score (median):

1. Sequence the scores from lowest to highest.
2. Count the number of scores. (7)
3. For an odd number of scores, count to the middle score. In this example, 17.

$$\left.\begin{array}{c} 18 \\ 18 \\ 18 \end{array}\right.$$
$$17 = 17$$
$$\left.\begin{array}{c} 12 \\ 12 \\ 8 \end{array}\right.$$

4. For an even number of scores, count to the two middle scores and then find the value halfway between these two scores. (Example: for 2, 8, 12, 16, 17, and 19, the median will fall halfway between 12 and 16. To find the halfway point between 12 and 16, add the scores together and divide by 2.)

$$\frac{12 + 16}{2} = \frac{28}{2} = 14$$

Note that for the data in Figure 13.1, the median is 17, the mode is 18, but that the mean is 14. This is because the mean can be affected by one or two scores which are considerably higher or lower than most of the data points (negatively or positively skewed). In the above example, the score of 8 was unusually low, and the mean reflects this factor. For purposes of data evaluation, the median, because it is not affected by skewness, is a more "typical" or representative measure of the data.

Calculating Medians on the Chart

With the chart, medians can be easily calculated. It is not necessary to transfer the scores from the chart to another piece of paper and then sequence the scores. To demonstrate, consider the data in Figures 13.2 and 13.3.

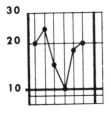

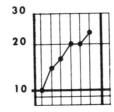

Figure 13.2

Data points.

Figure 13.3

Data points ordered from lowest to highest.

In Figures 13.2 and 13.3, the median is the same for both sets of data, because the scores are the same in both sets. The only difference is that the data from Figure 13.2 have been presented in the order from lowest to highest in Figure 13.3. This leads us to Rule No. 1: the median for scores x, y, and z = the median for y, z, x = the median for y, x, z = the median for x, z, y = the median for z, y, x = the median for z, x, y. In other words, the order of the scores does not change the median or affect its value in any way.

To find the median and note it with standard notation on the chart, follow these steps:

1. Place the teardrop ♀ on the middle day (if there are an odd number of points) or between the two middle days (with an even number of points), as shown in Figures 13.4 and 13.5.

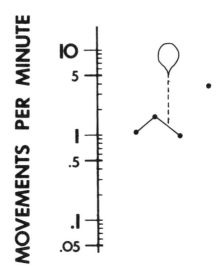

Figure 13.5

Placing the teardrop with an even number of data points.

2. Calculate the median by counting up to the middle rate (Figures 13.6 and 13.7).
3. Write that median rate in the teardrop, as seen in Figures 13.8 and 13.9.

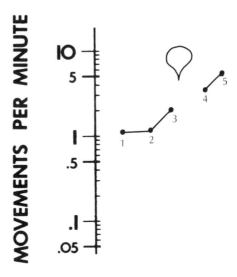

Figure 13.6

Counting an odd number of dots.

It is not necessary to perform the written task of resequencing data points in order to calculate medians on the chart. This task can be performed mentally or by *pointing* to the dots and counting up from the lowest rate to the median rate. For exam-

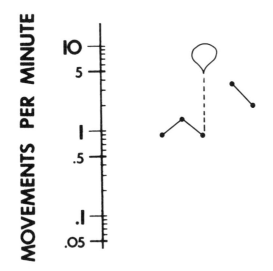

Figure 13.4

Placing the teardrop with an odd number of data points.

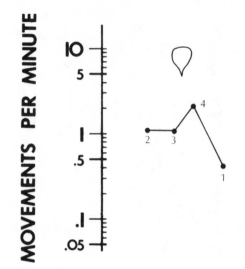

Figure 13.7

Counting an even number of dots.

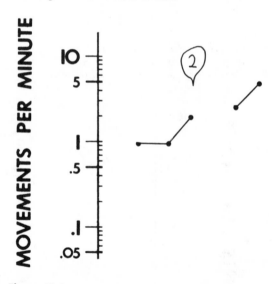

Figure 13.8

A median rate of 2.

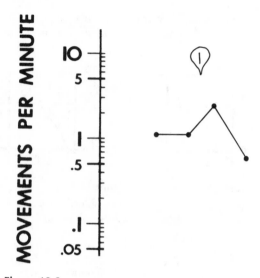

Figure 13.9

A median rate of 1.

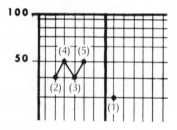

Figure 13.10

Counting up to the median.

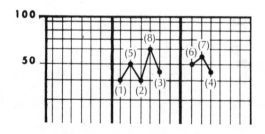

Figure 13.11

An even number of dots.

ple, in Figure 13.10, the points have been labeled in sequential order.

Notice that the data points are numbered from the lowest rate up to the highest. In Figure 13.10, the third score (here it's 40) is the median.

Again, for an odd number of points, the median rate will be the middle score. For an even number of points, the median rate will be halfway between the two middle scores, as shown in Figure 13.11. In that figure, the median is halfway between the fourth and fifth dot and is about 48.

To check the accuracy of this procedure of "counting up" the chart, let's calculate the median for the data in Figure 13.11. Add the two middle scores and divide this sum by 2 (the fourth score + the fifth score ÷ 2) $= \frac{45 + 50}{2} = \frac{95}{2} = 47.5$.

Note the closeness of 47.5 to 48—and how easy "counting up" is.

Checkpoint 13.1

Find and correctly label the medians for the following data. Try to do this by "counting" on the chart in Figure 13.12. Then do it for the correct rates (represented by dots) and again for the error rates (recorded as x's) in Figures 13.13 and 13.14. When finding median error rates, remember to "count down" when you're below the 1-line on the chart. CAP is 100%.

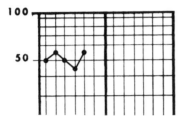

Figure 13.12

Item 1.

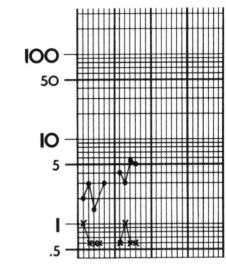

Figure 13.14

Item 3.

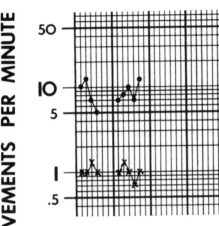

Figure 13.13

Item 2.

Acceptable Responses

Item 1 = 50 correct
Item 2 = 8 correct, 1 error
Item 3 = 3 correct, .6 error

Options

1. If you scored 100% on this checkpoint, you may go on to the next unit in this chapter.
2. If you did not obtain 100% accuracy, reread this section. Then take the checkpoint again.

Unit 13.2:	Standard conventions and the semilogarithmic chart.
Objectives:	1. The learner will be able to determine proficiency rates, performance change, best fit lines, data envelopes, and 'celeration. The learner will have knowledge of the uses of 'celeration slopes and lines of progress. 2. The learner will be able to identify response patterns. 3. The learner will be able to calculate the effects of changes in instructional programs.
Prerequisites:	Chapters 11, 12 and the preceding unit in this chapter.

Need for Early Change

Because time is critical in the lives of exceptional children, it's critical to change ineffective strategies as early as we can. Changes should be made when performance or progress begins to drop off or deteriorate, not after the child falls seriously behind his peers. By applying the 'celeration guidelines listed in this section, teachers have been able to double the weekly growth of students (Liberty, 1975). Accelerating the growth of special education students must be a primary goal for educators who are interested in successful mainstreaming and normalization. Accelerating growth enables special students to begin to catch up with their peers. This formative use of 'celeration has provided opportunities to rid the classroom of much "waste" time. 'Celeration has provided teachers with a tool for early determination of the effectiveness or ineffectiveness of program strategies.

Research on performance levels of students has indicated that students with low performance rates in basic areas (writing numbers, saying sounds, writing letters, simple addition and subtraction) are the students most often referred to special education and are the students most often identified as needing remedial help by teachers (Intermediate School District No. III, 1974).

> All youngsters identified as having problems on the Seattle-Spokane-Tacoma screening instrument also appeared on the teacher's list of students with learning problems compiled before screening. (p. 61). Further information from that screening of 11,000 children indicates that high correct performance (80-100 + / minute) leads to longer skill maintenance without practice (p. 1).

These data further support the critical effect of performance rate and the need to concentrate on accelerating the rates of special education students.

How should we attempt to accelerate growth? First of all, we need to establish some standards for comparison. In other words, we need an idea of where we are going so that we will know when we have gotten there. This is accomplished in teaching through establishing behavioral objectives. A part of the process of formulating behavioral objectives should include specifying a criterion for acceptable performance (CAP). How should this criterion be determined? What are reasonable standards to adopt? CAP is usually determined by finding the median performance rate of a group of the student's peers who are the same age and whom the teacher believes to be masters of the target behavior. These mastery levels can also be determined by taking groups of students functioning at different rates and comparing their subsequent growth. For example, the rate concept can be tested by allowing groups of students working at different rates on basic addition (facts 0-9) to move on to addition with carrying. The progress of these groups can be compared on the second task (addition with carrying) in order to determine which groups learned more efficiently. CAP for facts 0-9 can then be established as that level which enables the student to master the second task more quickly.

A project undertaken by the Child Service Demonstration Project (Intermediate School District No. III, 1974) has set minimal proficiency rates (minimal criteria) by determining the most frequent performance rates found with a screening of 11,000 primary-age children in Washington state (Table 13.1). These minimal proficiency rates become frequency aims (objectives). These aims can be marked on a chart with "aim stars" ($\bigstar$ for accelerate or $\forall$ for deceleration targets) as shown in Figure 13.15.

Under certain conditions, a child may not be ready or able to obtain the minimal aim established for a specific task. For example, a child's rate on complex skills is determined in part by the subskills on which the complex skills depend. Subskills which are basic to many tasks are sometimes called Basic Movement Cycles (BMC). Examples of BMCs for the academic area include: say letters; say sounds; see-to-write letters (copy letters); see-to-write numbers; say numbers; see-to-say numbers (read numbers); hear-to-write numbers (dictation); hear-to-write letters; hear sounds-to-write letters. A child who is slow at "hear sounds-to-write letters" may fall behind on a more complex task like spelling words from dictation.

A formula can be used to determine how fast a remedial student should be able to perform a skill (Figure 13.16). This speed is called the *intermediate aim*. In order to determine it, it is necessary to know the mastery rate for the skill in question. This mastery rate is determined by examining the rate of peers who have mastered the skill. Let's use the example of the skill of doing double-digit addition problems without carrying.

Table 13.1

Minimal Aims

TASK	GRADE					
MOVEMENT CYCLE	Kindgtn.	1st	2nd	3rd	4th	5th
Write Numbers Random (Copy)	25	30	45	60	70	85
Write Letters Cursive (Copy)			20's	30's	40's	50's
Say Letters Random	60	80	80-100	100	100	100
Say Words First Grade			80-100			
Say Words Second Grade				80-100		
Say Words Third Grade					100	
Say Words in Context		100-120	100-150	120-150 & up		

Aims for computation skills are generally set as a ratio of the individual's Write Number rate. 75% of WNR for addition seems to be workable in most cases. Teachers should judge for each child. The aims above are *minimal* and could be higher.

NOTE: From "Progress Report IV of the State of Washington Child Service Demonstration Program" by Intermediate School District No. III, 5601 Sixth Ave., Tacoma, Washington 98406, p. 39. Copyright 1974 by Intermediate School District No. III. Reprinted by permission.

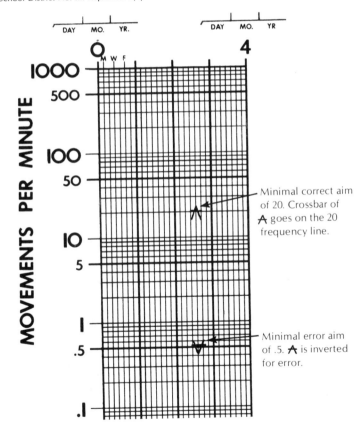

Figure 13.15

Marking objectives on the chart.

$$\text{Intermediate aim} = \frac{\text{Mastery rate (Step 1)}}{\text{BMC rate (Step 2)}} \times \text{Current rate (Step 3)}$$

Figure 13.16

Computing intermediate aim.

Step 1: Determine mastery rate of task. Locate a population of students who are considered masters of the task and give them the addition test. Their score will probably average around 50 digits per minute which means they can work 25 two-digit answers in one minute (White & Haring, 1976).

Step 2: Determine mastery rate on the BMC. In order to do written addition problems the student must be able to write digits. Mastery rate for writing digits is 75 per minute (White & Haring, 1976).

Step 3: Find the child's current rate on the BMC. Administer a "writes digit" probe to the student. For our example, assume the student is writing 50 digits a minute.

Step 4: Use this formula to find the student's intermediate aim, that is, how well the child can be expected to do on the complex skill considering his current performance on the subskill.

In our example, the student's current intermediate aim on double-digit addition is 33 digits a minute.

$$33 \text{ digits} = \frac{50 \text{ digits}}{75 \text{ digits}} \times 50 \text{ digits}$$

Once you have established minimal aims, or proficiency rates, you now know where you are going. The next question is, When do you want to get there? One procedure often used in the public schools to determine when is to "guess a date." If no better information can be utilized, then this procedure, while not highly recommended, is certainly better than not determining a date. Another procedure commonly used is to apply the "next test date" rule. This is what teachers do when they test in September, teach all year, and test again in May. The use of achievement tests in the fall and spring has encouraged teachers to be satisfied with an "I've got till May to teach this" attitude.

A better procedure in determining a date is to first calculate required performance change. Performance change is the proportionate change in behavior rate that is needed to meet basic proficiency requirements. Performance change is calculated by examining the ratio between the child's current level of functioning and the minimal aim. If a child is currently reading 50 words per minute and the minimal aim is 100 wpm, the performance change is calculated by dividing 100 by 50. The perform-

ance change represents the minimum amount of change in a child's performance which will be considered acceptable. It is always calculated by comparing current rate to the minimal aim rate. The steps to determine performance change are as follows:

1. Establish the minimal aim rate for the behavior.
2. Determine current rate by collecting three days of data and finding the middle rate (median) for three days of data. The median is always the middle frequency.
3. Compare the minimal aim rate and current rate by dividing the larger of the two rates by the smaller.
   Example: minimal aim: 50
   current rate: 25
   performance change: $50 \div 25 = 2$
4. The performance change is labeled "$\times$" (times) if the behavior is supposed to increase in frequency and "$\div$" (divide by) if the behavior is supposed to decrease in frequency. For example, here the performance change is $\times 2$.

Performance change is expressed with an "$\times$" or a "$\div$" sign to indicate the desired direction of change. Performance change represents the total amount of change needed for the objective to be met. Examples of calculating performance change follow:

Example 1: Determining performance change for acceleration target. Jan is reading from a third grade basal reader. An acceptable minimal aim can be determined by the minimal aim chart in Table 13.1. The minimal aim is established as 100 correct words per minute. The teacher next needs to determine Jan's current rate. Three days of data are collected (25, 80, 50), and the middle rate is determined (50). Performance change in this instance is $100 \div 50 = \times 2$.

Example 2: Determining performance change for deceleration target. David is working on adding fractions from a fifth grade math test, and the teacher has determined that minimal aim for errors, according to the scores of others who have mastered adding fractions, is 2 per minute. David's current rates are 10, 8, and 8 errors per minute so the middle (median) rate is 8. Performance change in this instance is $8 \div 2 = \div 4$.

Example 3: Determining performance change for a zero component. Scott is matching answers in a third grade comprehension program. The teacher has decided that 0 errors will be the aim, as determined by peers who have already mastered the task. Scott's three-day error rates are 3, 2, and 4 errors per minute. Scott's middle rate is 3. Performance change is computed by dividing 3 by the record floor, since division by zero is impossible. If Scott worked for 10 minutes each session, the record floor is $1/10 \div 1 = .10$. Performance change in this case is $3 \div .10 = \div 30$.

These examples are summarized in Table 13.2.

Table 13.2

Summary of Performance Change Calculation

Calculation *Acceleration* Target (Correct)	$\dfrac{\text{minimal aim}}{\text{median of 3 current sessions}} = \times$ ____	*Example* $\dfrac{100}{50} = \times 2$
Calculation *Deceleration* Target (Error)	$\dfrac{\text{median of 3 current sessions}}{\text{minimal aim}} = \div$ ____	$\dfrac{20}{2} = \div 10$
Calculations involving a "0" component	Change 0 to the record floor since "0" is representative of a "no-count" in relation to the time the behavior is recorded. Any change that is "better" than change to the record floor would represent progress toward a "0" aim. Any change that is greater than change from the record floor would represent change from "0."	$\dfrac{2}{.10} = \div 20$

Performance change is a measure of the total proportionate increase or decrease that is needed in order to bring the behavior to a proficiency level (to meet the minimal aim). Once the total required performance change has been determined, the next step is to consider the time requirements and target dates for completion of the objective. For example, if the goal was to increase behavior from 10 to 50 per minute, the performance change needed would be ×5. However, if the child had 10 weeks in which to accelerate a behavior, the weekly growth needed would be a measure of required progress 'celeration. The next section will present procedures for calculating the weekly progress (progress 'celeration) required to meet the minimal aim within a designated time period.

The following material is in programmed form so that you may have an opportunity to apply the information just presented. You will also be given a chance to practice some additional technical skills as they are introduced.

$\mathcal{A}$ or $\mathcal{V}$	Minimal aims are recorded on the chart with a(n) _____.
mastered the task	Minimal aims are determined by examining performance rates of individuals who have already _____.
$\dfrac{\text{Mastery rate}}{\text{BMC rate}} \times$ Current rate	Minimal aims for skills can also be determined by comparing rates on basic movement cycles. The formula for this comparison is intermediate aim = _____.
when you will get there (the speed, rate)	Minimal aims tell you where you are going. Progress 'celeration determines _____.
minimal aim	Performance change is determined by comparing the median of 3 current sessions to the _____.

Record a minimal aim of 30 on the Friday of Week 2, using Figure 13.17.

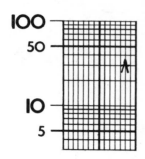

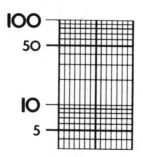

Figure 13.17

Calculate the performance change for a minimal aim of 30 correct compared to a median of 10. (correct 'celeration = minimal aim ÷ median)

$$\frac{30}{10} = \times 3$$

Progress 'Celeration

The student's progress toward an objective can be illustrated on the chart. It is easy to see if the data are moving toward the objective. This movement can be summarized by drawing a line through the data to illustrate the trend which the data points represent. This concept was briefly discussed in Chapter 4 and shown in Figure 4.7. The trend line which is determined from the student's own data is known as the *line of progress* or *best fit line*. Other trend lines which can be drawn on the chart are the *standard 'celeration line* and *minimal 'celeration line*. These lines can be used to represent desired or actual trends in learning.

The rate at which a 'celeration line is accelerating or decelerating can be summarized numerically. This is done by finding any two points on the line which are seven days apart. (It doesn't matter if there are data at these points, so for convenience just use any two Sundays....) Then divide the first point into the second. For example, assume a math student's acceleration line goes through 18 on one Sunday and 22 on the next. The rate at which this line is accelerating is $22 \div 18 = \times 1.2$. This means that the math student is increasing his problems per minute by a function of 1.2 every week. This is a $\times 1.2$ 'celeration slope.

If the data show deceleration of a behavior, the 'celeration line is labeled "÷." Maintenance lines (flat, horizontal 'celeration lines) are labeled "×1." To determine a numerical label for the rate of 'celeration, it is also possible to use a slope finder. Figure 13.18 shows a slope finder, and there is also one located at the back of this book which you can cut out and use. Both contain descriptions of how to use the slope finder. To make the finder you cut out more durable, back it with light cardboard. For more on how to use the slope finder, see White and Haring's text *Exceptional Teaching* (1976, pp. 254-55).

When discussing data with others, using the numerical value of the slope is often a short-cut to help another person visualize your data. For example, a ×2 change could indicate that a child doubled his performance rate within one week. The numerical label also enables the user to judge the statistical "significance" of the change strategy (Helson & Barlow, 1976).

USE THIS EDGE FOR DECELERATION

USE THIS EDGE FOR ACCELERATION

10 — 10
9 — 9
8 — 8
7 — 7
6 — 6
5.5 — 5.5
5 — 5
4.5 — 4.5
4 — 4
3.5 — 3.5
3 — 3
2.5 — 2.5
2 — 2
1.5 — 1.5
1.25 — 1.25
×1 — ×1

HOW TO USE THE SLOPE FINDER

1. Determine if the 'celeration line is moving up the chart (acceleration) or down the chart (deceleration).

2. Place the finder vertically on the chart so that the correct edge is to the right — ACCELERATION for lines moving up, DECELERATION for lines moving down the chart.

3. Place the black arrow on the left-hand edge so that it crosses the 'celeration line in question.

4. Find the point where the 'celeration line crosses the right-hand edge of the finder. That point indicates the slope of the 'celeration line.

5. Remember to keep the left and right edges of the finder parallel to the day lines.

Once a minimal aim and performance change have been determined, the next step is to calculate how long a student has to reach the aim. What is a reasonable amount of time in which to expect the desired change? A ×2 change is a lesser overall change than either a ÷10 or a ×20. It seems reasonable, therefore, to expect that it will usually take less time to 'celerate from 10 to 20 (a ×2 change) than from 10 to 1 (a ÷10 change) or 1 to 20 (a ×20 change). Two procedures for determining minimal weekly 'celeration (progress 'celeration) are *date-determined 'celeration* and *standard 'celeration*.

Date-Determined 'Celeration

If a teacher has established a desired date for mastery of material, then this date can be used as the aim date. A line of minimum 'celeration is drawn as a guide by following these steps:

1. Find the *median*, or middle rate, of the three most recent data points.

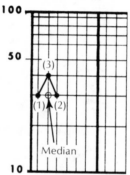

Median = the middle score. Place the little circle O for the middle rate on the middle day line as an indication of the current median rate.

Figure 13.19

Finding the median of three rates.

For the scores 30, 40, and 30, _____ is the median or middle score. In Figure 13.19, the middle score is placed on the middle day.

Mrs. Turnbon has decided, based on Stephanie's previous acquisition of reading skills, to attempt to have Stephanie reading at a rate of 60 words per minute within 12 days. Therefore, the aim rate is 60, and the aim date is 12 days from the last data point.

1. The median, or middle rate, of the three most recent data points is found.

2. An aim star (⋏) is placed in the intersection of the minimal aim rate and the aim date—the cross bar of the star goes on the rate line. Figure 13.20 shows an aim rate of 60 per minute and an aim date of the third Monday.

3. A line is drawn between the median and the aim star, as shown in Figure 13.21.

Figure 13.22 shows the same three steps for a deceleration target.

30

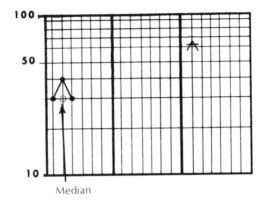

Figure 13.20

Aim star drawn at aim rate and aim date intersection.

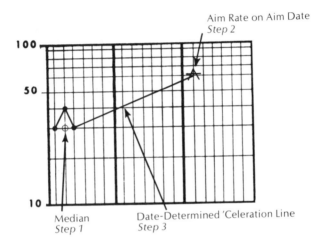

Figure 13.21

Date-determined acceleration.

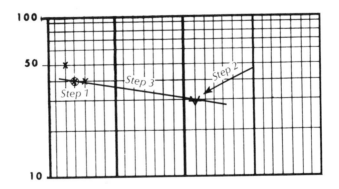

Figure 13.22

Date-determined deceleration.

median

aim date

line

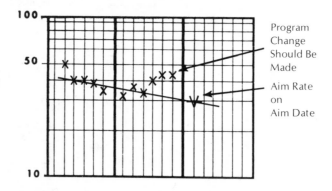

The steps for finding date-determined 'celeration are as follows:

1. Find the _____ of three data points.

2. Place an $\mathcal{A}$ on the chart on the _____ _____.

3. Draw a _____ from the median to the

_____.

Some authors suggest that changes should be made in a program if for any three consecutive days the data are *below* (for acceleration) the date-determined 'celeration line. For deceleration targets, changes should occur if three consecutive days are *above* the date-determined line (White & Haring, 1976). Figure 13.23 shows an example of applying the three-day rule for error rates.

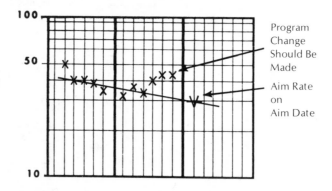

Figure 13.23

Three-day rule for deceleration target.

The date-determined 'celeration line is also known as a minimal 'celeration line because it represents the minimal rate at which the behavior must change if the aim is to be met. This line is interesting for two reasons: first, the line is a kind of floating objective which tells where the student should be on any day; second, the line is formed by connecting the student's actual behavior to the teacher's objective.

Content-Determined 'Celeration

Sometimes the minimal 'celeration line can be determined by considering the amount of content which the teacher wants the child to cover. For example, suppose the student is currently doing 5 multiplication problems a minute when he should be doing 50. This is an actual performance difference of 45 problems, meaning a ×10 performance change is needed. Now suppose the teacher has a procedure which teaches multiplication facts in units of five, and each unit takes one week. In this case, the minimal 'celeration rate can be determined by considering the number of units needed to move the student from 5 to 50 problems. If the difference is 45 problems and each unit teaches 5 problems, the minimal 'celeration can be drawn by placing a dot 5 problems higher than the previous week on each Sunday line for nine weeks. If the student is at 20 one week, he should be at 25 the next. Such a line would not be straight, as seen in Figure 13.24. The line is curved because the weekly growth is not proportional — but absolute. Charting an absolute change on the proportional chart results in a curved line. Unless the student follows the line, he will not complete all of the units in the amount of time for which they were developed.

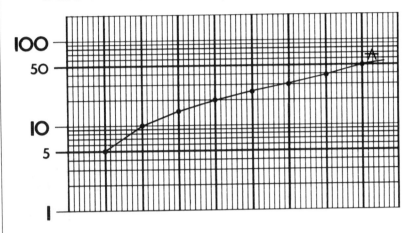

Figure 13.24

A content-determined 'celeration line.

Standard 'Celeration

Students generally are identified for remedial help because they have difficulty keeping up with instruction. Over a period of time, these students fall further and further behind their peers. One way of using 'celeration information is as a preventive tool to identify students who need help before they fall seriously behind their peers. As an example, one project has examined growth which was occurring for 361 precision teaching programs (Liberty, 1975). Each program contained at least 5 data points (with an average of about 11). The results showed that:

1. 50% of the students were able to grow at a 'celeration of ×1.33 or better for acceleration targets.
2. 50% of the students were able to decrease unwanted behavior at a deceleration of ÷1.46.
3. 53% of the students could grow at a rate of ×1.25 or better.
4. 66% of the students made progress in decelerating unwanted behaviors at a rate of ÷1.25.

This information formed the basis for utilizing standard 'celeration to make decisions. A standard 'celeration line is determined by the first three data points of a new program. This line is established by:

1. Determining the median for the data.
2. Placing the median score on the middle day (the second consecutive day for three data points).
3. Projecting a line of ×1.25 (or ÷1.25 for a deceleration target).

Figures 13.25 and 13.26 present examples of standard 'celeration lines for both correct and error targets.

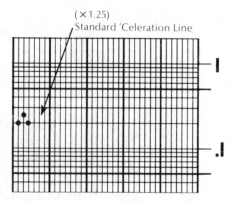

Figure 13.25

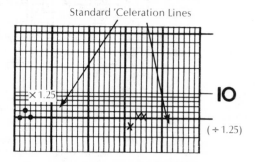

Figure 13.26

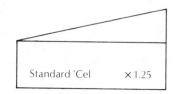

Figure 13.27

Standard 'celeration finder.

To use the standard 'celeration finder:

1. Find the median of three data points in Figure 13.28. Draw a circle at the intersection of the median rate and the middle date.

   This standard 'celeration line of ×1.25 can be drawn on the chart by using the *standard 'celeration finder* (Figure 13.27). Another standard 'celeration finder is located at the back of this book. Cut it out for use in the following frames. To make the finder more durable, back it with light cardboard.

2. Place the standard 'celeration finder on Figure 13.29 so that the point of the left-hand corner is on the median.

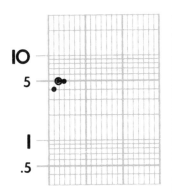

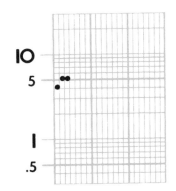

Figure 13.28

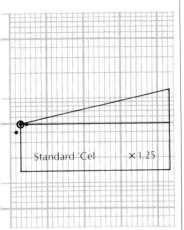

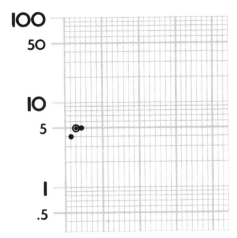

Figure 13.29

3. Align the standard 'cel finder so that the bottom edge is parallel to the horizontal frequency lines in Figure 13.29.
4. Draw a line from the median to the aim rate of 15 in Figure 13.30. This line will be at a slope of ×1.25. Figure 13.31 shows this standard 'cel line.

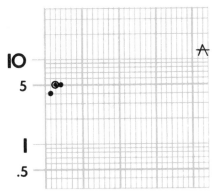

Figure 13.30

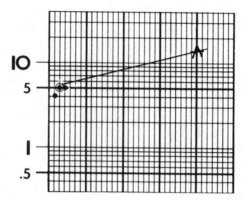

Figure 13.31

Earlier in this chapter we noted guidelines for using the 'celeration line to decide when to change a child's instructional program. We said that changes may be made in any program if on three consecutive days the data fall below the minimum 'celeration line for acceleration targets, or three days above the minimum 'cel line for deceleration targets (Figure 13.32).

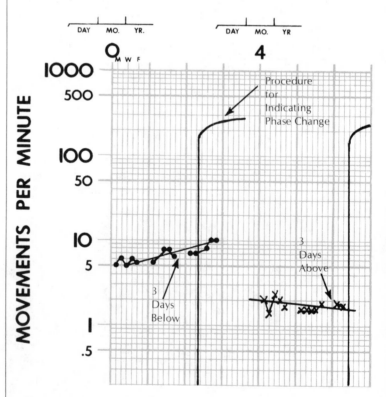

Figure 13.32

It should be cautioned that ×1.25 and ÷1.25 are not magic numbers. For some projects, a rate of growth greater than 1.25 should be the goal — this is only a minimum suggested growth rate.

Draw a standard 'celeration line for the following data. The aim rate is 30.

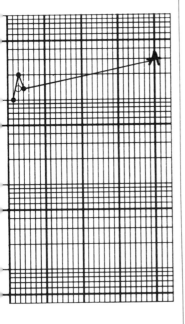

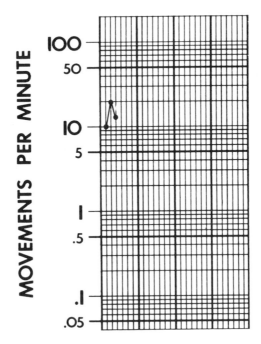

Figure 13.33

For errors or deceleration targets, invert the standard 'celeration finder. The aim rate is .05. Draw the standard 'celeration line and then draw an aim star where your line crosses the .05 line.

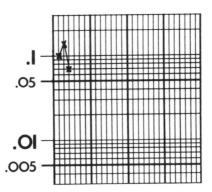

Figure 13.34

Date-determined 'celeration and standard 'celeration are two techniques for drawing a line of prediction to guide future growth. These procedures can help educators to decide when to change programs. The following section is designed to give the reader practice in evaluating data patterns.

Evaluation of Data Patterns

Given a set of data on a particular behavior, the precision teacher should be able to glance at the data (eyeball it) and make decisions concerning the effectiveness of program and intervention techniques. For example, the data in Figure 13.35 indicate that the correct rate is continuing to accelerate and errors are decreasing slightly.

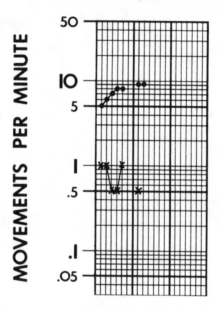

Figure 13.35

Eyeballing the data will generally be a fairly effective procedure for determining if progress is being made. In Figure 13.36, record the pattern of change (acceleration, deceleration, or maintenance) of correct and error rates on the line below each chart.

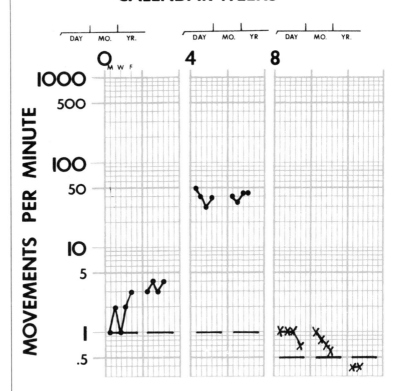

Figure 13.36

(a) acceleration
(b) maintenance
(c) deceleration

(a) _____   (b) _____   (c) _____

Teachers usually wish to decrease errors and increase correct rates. In some cases, maintenance of a previous rate is the desired result, that is, hitting is 0 or reading is 150 words per minute. Try eyeballing the data in Figure 13.37 to observe the effects of the intervention strategy on correct and error rates.

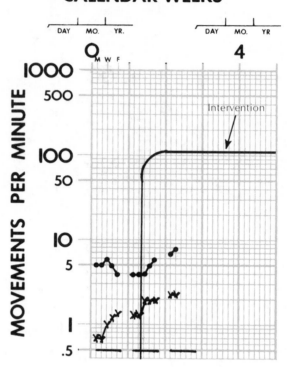

Figure 13.37

Before: correct rate decelerating, errors accelerating

Results before intervention: _____

_____

After: correct rate accelerating, errors accelerating

Results after intervention:_____

_____

_____

The data in Figure 13.38 are much more complex, and eyeballing may not give the necessary information to make a good data-based decision. Record your observations of the correct and error rate patterns before and after intervention.

correct rate decelerating, errors maintaining

Before: _____

_____

correct rate maintaining, errors decelerating

After:_____

_____

Note: These data are fairly complex; you are not expected to be able to evaluate them at this time.

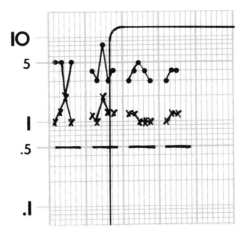

Figure 13.38

precise

More Precise Data Evaluation

When more precise information about data patterns is desired, techniques other than eyeballing the data should be employed to analyze the recorded data. Eyeballing the data is not a good technique to gain

_____ information about data patterns.

As you read other texts on precision teaching, the terms *trend analysis* and *median slope* may be used in addition to *'celeration*. These terms all refer to a procedure for summarizing progress on the six-cycle or any other semilogarithmic chart. The end result of these techniques is a *line of best fit* which may be drawn through the data and extended into future weeks to estimate future performance.

future

Estimating Best Fit Lines

Best fit lines are lines which are drawn through a set of data to represent both the changes in data patterns and the central tendency (mean, median, mode) of the data. Best fit lines may be estimated by trying to draw a straight line through a set of data points. Figures 13.39 and 13.40 represent attempts of three people to determine a best fit line by looking at the data. Perception of best fit lines is one procedure for determining

_____ performance. For example, in Figures 13.39 and 13.40 it appears that there will be an increase in the behaviors. The value in estimating best fit lines is that some conception of the direction of progress may be determined from them.

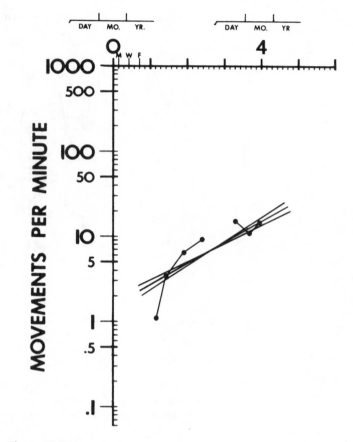

Figure 13.39

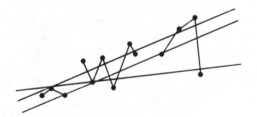

Figure 13.40

Estimate a line of best fit for the following data in Figure 13.41.

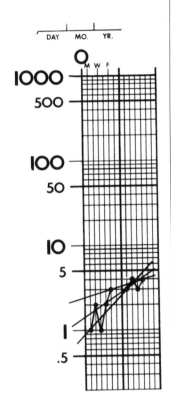

Any line shown is an
acceptable response.

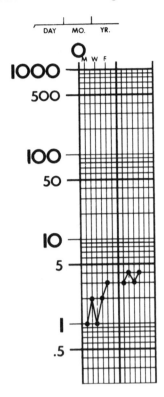

Figure 13.41

Refer again to Figure 13.40. There is much variability (also called bounce) in the data. The estimated best fit lines are further apart than in Figure 13.39. If 100 people (instead of 3) were asked to determine the best fit line, their average line should closely approximate the real

best fit line

The true best fit line is calculated using procedures to be shown later in the chapter. The technique you will read about in the next section ('celeration) is based on statistical procedures (the sum of the least squares) that can predict the future course of growth under the same stimulus and reinforcement conditions.

Estimating the Envelope

The concept of estimating best fit lines can gain more utility with highly variable data (data that bounce around a lot) when provisions for the range of variability are considered. Best fit estimates can incorporate the range of the data through applying the following procedures.

1. A best fit line has been estimated (Figure 13.42).

Figure 13.42

2. The high and low data points are identified (Figure 13.43).

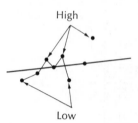

Figure 13.43

3. Two new lines are drawn parallel to the best fit line, even with the high and low points (Figure 13.44). In this way, an envelope is drawn which encloses all of the student's responses.

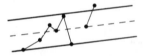

Figure 13.44

4. In cases where one point is much higher or lower than the others, omit that point from the envelope (Figure 13.45).

Figure 13.45

An envelope can be highly accurate in predicting the future

range

_____ of responses.

Estimate the envelope for correct and error rates for the data in Figure 13.46.

When the best fit line intersects an aim rate, that point is the best estimate of when the aim will be met. The top envelope line shows the earliest the criterion will probably be reached and the lower line shows the latest. The wider the envelope, the longer the student's behavior must be monitored after the aim rate has been reached the first time (refer to Unit 8 of survival statistics in Appendix A.) It is not safe to assume a student has mastered a skill until his worst day (the lower envelope line for an acceleration pinpoint) is above the aim rate.

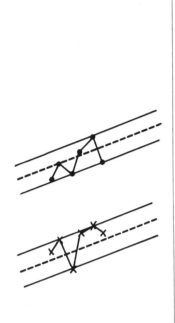

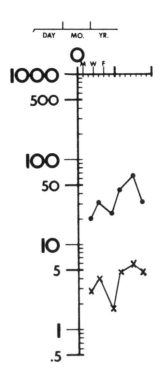

Figure 13.46

Line of Progress

'Celeration has been mentioned earlier as a technique to measure previous growth and predict future growth. It is possible to use the student's data to predict his future performance. This type of 'celeration line doesn't show where the student is supposed to go but where he is going. Lines of progress measure changes in response rates by comparing medians of the first and second halves of the data. For a detailed discussion of lines of progress and how to calculate them, see pages 316-59 in White and Haring (1976).

Changes in Instructional Programs

Changes should be made in programs whenever the desired growth is not occurring and the teacher feels comfortable in planning and introducing another change into the classroom environment. Phase changes should not be made without:

1. Eyeballing the data — Is progress being made?
2. Calculating 'celeration (unless there are an insufficient number of data points and the teacher feels strongly that change is needed).

If 'celeration has been calculated, a phase change should occur if:

1. Three days are *below* the minimum acceleration or three days are *above* the minimum deceleration.
2. The data indicate mastery of material –– it is time to move on.

Review of 'Celeration

When several data points have been collected, a line can be drawn through them. This line may be known as the progress 'celeration, trend, slope, line of progress, 'celeration and/or best fit line. The purpose of the line is threefold: it describes, predicts, and compares.

Description

The line of progress can be used to describe the data. Just as means and standard deviations summarize data collected on several students, the trend line and envelope summarize repeated measurements of the same behavior. A better idea of how a student is progressing can be obtained by looking at his trend line rather than by looking only at his data points. The descriptive power of the line increases as the number of data points increases.

Prediction

The trend line is based on the student's past performance. Because the student's past performance is highly correlated to his future performance, the line can be extended in order to make predictions. This can only be done on logarithmic graph paper, however. Predictions made with the logarithmic chart can be of value in sequencing instruction. They may also be valuable for setting short-term, easily obtainable aims. For example, once a trend line has been established it can be used as a target for each day's growth. The teacher can challenge a student to score above the line of progress on the student's daily probe sheet (test). Because the line was determined from the student's own past behavior, he is competitive only with himself and at a level at which he has already functioned successfully.

Comparison

The progress line illustrates the rate and direction of learning. Changes in a student's program can result in changes in the rate and direction of the trend line. Rate of learning can be determined by finding two points on the line which are one week apart and then dividing these points into each other. For example, if the line crosses 10 on one Sunday and 20 on the next Sunday, the line is moving up at a rate of ×2. ×2 means the student is doubling his behavior every seven days.

The direction of the line refers to acceleration, deceleration, or maintenance. One program may be more effective for maintaining a behavior than for accelerating a behavior.

By indicating program (phase) changes on the chart and looking for differences in direction or rate of learning, it is possible to compare the effectiveness of two programs for a particular student. This kind of comparison between treatments is essential for truly individualized instruction. The best treatment is, of course, the one in which the student learns the most. All methods of initial treatment selection will occasionally be wrong (some more often than others), so it is essential to monitor the student's growth in different treatments.

Checkpoint 13.2

Directions: Fill in the blanks with the correct answers. CAP is 100%.

1. A 'celeration line which is determined from past student data can be used as a

   _____ of performance.

2. A phase change should occur if the data is above the minimum deceleration line

   for _____ days.

3. Trend lines and envelopes can be used to describe data on a single student in the

   same way group data are described by the _____ and

   _____.

4. If Theresa's 'celeration line crosses 32 on one Wednesday and 56 the next Wednesday, then her behavior is _____ _____ at a

   _____ rate.

Acceptable Responses

1. predictor
2. three
3. mean, standard deviation
4. accelerating, 1.75

Options

1. If you scored 100%, you have successfully completed the last checkpoint. Congratulations!
2. If you did not score 100%, reread this section and take the checkpoint again.

Summarizing Data Evaluation

Our knowledge concerning learning continues to grow as more and more data are collected and analyzed for an ever-increasing number of different types of human behavior. At the present time, predictions can be made on the outcomes of program strategies, and comparisons can be made to see if a technique is more or less useful than another for specific students. Generalizations are also beginning to be made about the use of various materials for students in general. Much of this information has been obtained through systematic replication of teaching procedures using individual case studies. Teachers are collecting and analyzing data using standard procedures and arriving at similar conclusions about teaching strategies and materials. Communication is increasing through publications but also through the personal communication of individuals interested in promoting the growth of individualization strategies. For education to be successful this emphasis on the response patterns of individual students must continue. The traditional group studies in which the results are reported as effective for 70% of the students within a class will also continue. However, individual data analysis is beginning to ask about the other 30%. What factors will influence more positive outcomes for the forgotten learners who are capable of learning under the right programming conditions? With the kinds of data evaluation we have examined here, teachers of those learners ae seeking the answers from the learners themselves, from their data.

14

Where We Are Going

This book has attempted to present both a theoretical and practical base for the use of continuous and direct measurement in the classroom. In the past, educators have used many norm-referenced tests which have provided only general and sometimes even invalid information on achievement or academic potential.

Applying Evaluation Procedures

Diagnosis and treatment must be valid for the individual learner. Direct, task analytical evaluation assures that the content of the test is relevant to the learner and to the teaching process. Formative or ongoing evaluation enables the educator to identify problems earlier and thus begin remediation sooner. With exceptional children who already are behind, the need to use new technology to accelerate growth and learning is critical. The techniques are available. Now more teachers need to learn how to apply them.

Adapting Evaluation Systems

Formative evaluation systems can be adapted to your particular environment by analyzing the situation and making priority-based decisions.

The following decision-making models may be helpful. Figure 14.1 presents a model for ordering objectives, assessing, and implementing alternative strategies. It is suggested that the evaluator begin with a comparison of district, school, and classroom needs. Those needs should be used to define the relevancy of the goals. From broad goal statements, specific objectives and criteria need to be determined. Time-cost benefits can be weighed for alternative strategies to meet the predetermined goals. Once strategies have been selected, then program implementation will involve three components: planning, delivery, and evaluation. Using the rules of good formative evaluation systems—frequent and direct monitoring and evaluation—will lead to decisions for either reprogramming or continuation to the next task in the task sequence. This first model presents an overview of the total teaching process.

Once an overall program has been determined, it is often useful to identify the most feasible evaluation system (Figure 14.2).

It is valuable to consider which aspect of the response is most critical. Is it the rate or the duration of the response that is at issue? Once the critical aspect of the response is identified, consider next the ease of counting the behavior and finally the ease and accuracy of interpreta-

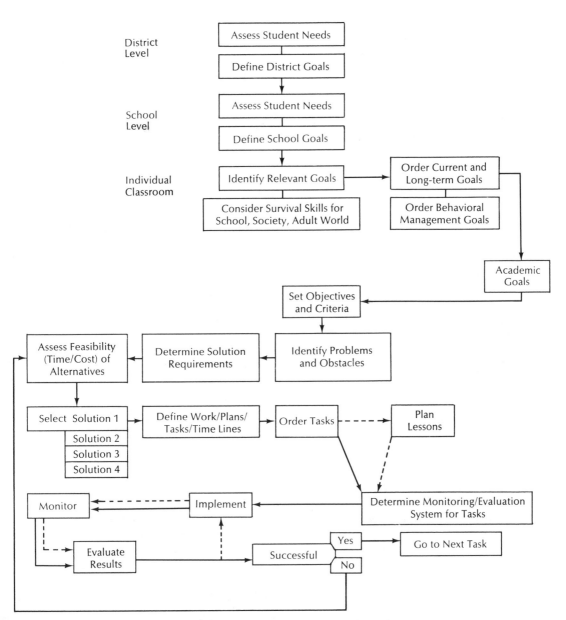

Figure 14.1

Determining and implementing priority programs.

tion. Visual pictures (charts) will allow more rapid review of the data which have been collected. It is important, however, not to be misled by a visual picture which is influenced by the way the chart or table is designed. Standard recording systems should be a component of the evaluation model. When the recording system is standardized, the design of the chart or table will not influence the interpretation of the data. Two examples of the use of a standardized recording system are the scale on the six-cycle chart or the time interval between evaluation sessions on a learning matrix. Predictiveness of the evaluation system will also aid in program planning. For example, short-term predictions concerning teaching outcomes can be made on

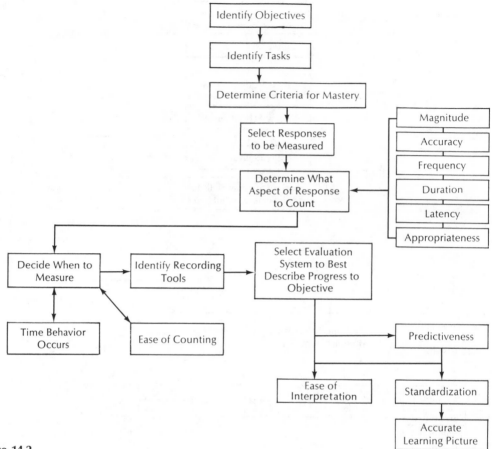

Figure 14.2

Determining evaluation systems.

the six-cycle chart. This allows for earlier program revision.

The Future of Evaluation

Over the past 10 years much data have been collected on formative evaluation (White & Haring, 1976). These data have provided an abundance of information on how children learn and on what factors influence and facilitate learning. Most data were initially collected on the academic and behavioral performance of normal or mildly handicapped students. Researchers and educators are now beginning to study the more severely handicapped child (Haring & Brown, 1976). Task analysis and criterion-referenced procedures are now being extended to severely handicapped populations. Children previously left to lie on hospital wards are being taught to communicate, feed themselves, and interact with their environments.

As education moves into the programming and evaluation of children with severe mental, physical, and emotional problems, our measures and testing will need to be revised. Haring and Brown (1976) suggest that *trials to criterion* may be a more useful measure for recording some responses. Their rationale is that for the severely handicapped a major concern is establishing a response and that rate is not initially a critical factor.

While the best measurement procedures are still being sought, the positive effect of applying criterion-referenced testing and direct instruction is becoming more and more obvious. Across the United States, children in institutions are receiving more than custodial care and are beginning to be placed in public schools. For this growth to continue, many more teachers trained (or retrained) in effective programming and evaluation procedures are needed. These teachers will need to be oriented in the techniques of inter- or trans-disciplinary interaction, since the progress of many of these children involves the close cooperation of teachers, communication therapists, psychologists, audiologists, and occupational and physical therapists.

As the severely handicapped begin to receive appropriate educational planning, children with milder learning impairments will also benefit. The more efficiently we can teach children, the faster they will learn. The procedures offered in this book provide a basis for successful integration of children into normal classroom environments. This will be best facilitated by educating the regular classroom teacher in these techniques. Many children currently in regular classrooms need the success of personalized programs. Many children need to be carefully drilled in the basics of math and reading before proceeding to other tasks. The techniques for evaluating exceptional children can be utilized with all children. When implementing formative evaluation in any classroom, it will be most successful if teachers begin on a small scale with the behaviors which are of highest priority. For some teachers this will mean initially using precise evaluation for the most troublesome problems in their class. Other teachers will feel capable of beginning with one or two specific priority behaviors for each child. The idea is not to overload oneself. This could defeat the purpose of educational evaluation. Direct and frequent evaluation is meaningful when it is used as a tool to assist educators, not when it becomes too cumbersome to be manageable. This means that teachers should start with a system that they feel comfortable with and expand the system according to their needs and personal capabilities.

Many of the techniques mentioned within this book are technical. The results obtained with them have more than validated their usefulness thus far. If teachers continue to share their findings with each other, the pool of knowledge about how children learn will continue to grow.

With this knowledge, teachers of the future should be better prepared to help students learn the skills which are essential for successful living.

A Final Word (Caution)

Evaluation has its basis in comparison. Consequently it tends to accentuate differences within and between individuals. It is wise to remember that every difference is not a meaningful one. In short, just because something can be measured doesn't mean it needs to be measured. In addition, if measurement should reveal a difference, it doesn't follow that the difference must be important.

Current testing techniques have received extensive criticism because of misapplications. The most important of these misapplications centers around significance statements. For example, an IQ score of 69 may be significantly less than the average score of 100. But is it significantly less than an IQ score of 71? No. Yet the result of scoring above or below 70 on an IQ test can have serious ramifications for the student. These ramifications are the result of placing too much significance on a small range of IQ scores.

Many tests are powerful enough to give information about direction. That is, if two students take the test, it will tell which student is performing above the other. But few currently available tests will tell us if the student is performing *significantly* above the other. In spite of this, some educators seem obsessed with making significance statements about children, and they frequently offer test scores to support these statements.

G. V. Glass (1974) has written about an evaluative paradox which can be paraphrased as follows. Learning can be directed most efficiently by evaluating frequently. However, learning flourishes most spontaneously in an environment which is nonjudgmental. If there is any way out of this apparent paradox, it must certainly be to control the way we are judgmental. Special educators, more than any other group of teachers, must constantly remind themselves that it is possible for children to be different without being either good or bad.

Appendix **A**

Survival Statistics

Unit 1: The Normal Curve

Normative evaluation is conceptually linked to the idea of a *normal distribution* or a *normal curve*. Suppose that 10 people were asked to flip a coin 10 times. The number of heads for the group might be summarized as in Figure A. 1.

Hardly anyone would be expected to get all heads or all tails. Most people would be expected to get about 50% heads or tails. As the number of people flipping coins increases, the graph should begin to take on the appearance of Figure A.2.

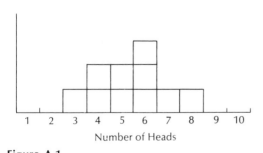

Figure A.1

Ten flips of a coin.

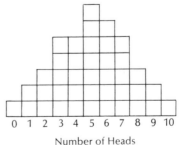

Figure A.2

Forty flips of a coin.

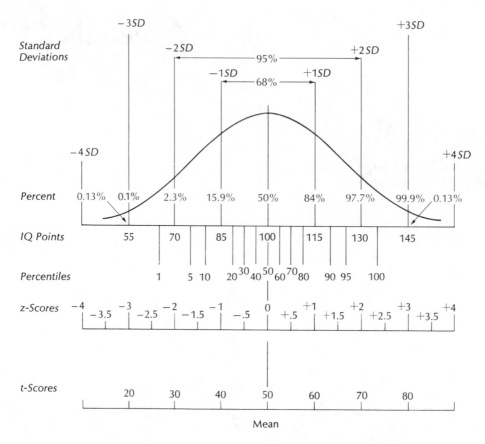

Figure A.3

The normal curve and several types of scores.

Ultimately, if enough people flip enough coins, the graph of the number of heads obtained will approximate what is known as a normal curve. Figure A.3 shows a model of the normal curve, which has been divided to illustrate some of the score concepts discussed later in this appendix.

Many normative tests are constructed in such a way that the scores are forced to normally distribute themselves. Most IQ tests for example, have an arbitrarily designated mean of 100. More people should therefore score 100 on an IQ test than any other score, and as many should score above 100 as below it. The normal distribution makes the assumption that the probability of all responses is equal. That is, a head is as likely as a tail or a high IQ is as likely as a low IQ. However, as it turns out, nature plays with loaded dice. To return to the IQ example—any given person is *not* as likely as any other to have a normal IQ. Even before birth such influences

as diet or traffic accidents may serve to influence the general ability of an individual. Some of these influences may occur more often in one subgroup of society than they will in others. Few of these influences can be expected to raise intelligence. Therefore, a true distribution of intelligence might look more like the bimodal curve in Figure A.4 or like the skewed curve in Figure A.5. A bimodal curve is one which has two peaks, indicating two groups of students within the distribution are scoring differently from each other. The normal curve is not a guaranteed thing. It is a statistical concept that implies a uniform and predictable relationship among the instances of whatever trait is being studied. In reality, however, many traits are not normally distributed. The number of fingers that a group of people have would undoubtably not be randomly distributed; most would have 10 and only a few would have none.

Figure A.4

A bimodal curve.

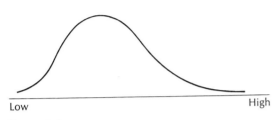

Figure A.5

A skewed (lopsided) curve.

The Center

The *mean* is the center of the normal curve. The mean is known as a measure of central tendency. It is the best predictor of how any individual will behave on the test.

If you are asked to guess the IQ of a stranger, your best bet is to guess 100. The mean is the average of the total of all scores. It is calculated by adding all the scores together and dividing by the number of scores.

The Width

The variability of a distribution of scores refers to the way the scores cluster about the mean. In Figure A.7 distribution A has less variability than distribution B.

When two variables (traits, test scores, etc.) are compared, the comparison is not limited to the difference between the two means. The difference in variability is also compared. The variability of a distribution can be summarized in standard deviations. For a normal curve, 68% of all scores fall within ±1 (one) standard deviation (*SD*) of the mean; 95% fall within ±2 (two). If the definition of mentally retarded were to include individuals with IQ scores lower than -2 standard deviations, then theoretically 2.3% of the population should be retarded (assuming IQ is normally distributed).

Normal IQ		High IQ		Low IQ		Total IQ
95.4%	+	2.3%	+	2.3%	=	100%

Standard deviation is a measure of variability. If all students taking a test make the same score on the test, there would be no variability. The more the scores deviate from the mean, the more the variability of the scores increases. This is the formula for calculating a standard deviation:

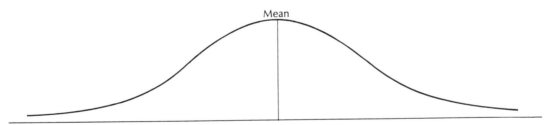

Figure A.6

The mean.

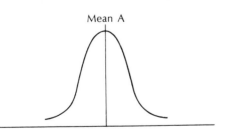

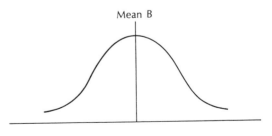

Figure A.7

Two curves with different variability.

$$\text{standard deviation} = \sqrt{\dfrac{\text{the sum of the squared scores} - \dfrac{\text{the square of the sum of the scores divided by the number of scores}}{\text{total number of scores} -1}}{}}$$

or

$$SD = \sqrt{\dfrac{\Sigma x^2 - \dfrac{(\Sigma x)^2}{N}}{N-1}}$$

Unit 2: Test Scores

A test score is the numerical summation of behavior. That testing summarizes behavior is obviously true of pencil and paper tests, but even the scores derived from measurement of heartbeat and brain activity have come to be known as scores of visceral behavior. Scores are useful because they aid our ability to compare people to people, or people to tasks. Inherent in the use of numerical scores is the idea that behavior can be segmented and then represented by a number. In educational testing, however, few scores represent discrete units of behavior. For example, a math test may have two addition problems as in Figure A.8.

If a student gets both these problems right then he would usually get a score of 2 correct, al-

Addition Test

a
1 pt.
$$\begin{array}{r} 3 \\ +2 \\ \hline 5 \end{array}$$

b
1 pt.
$$\begin{array}{r} 838 \\ +282 \\ \hline 1120 \end{array}$$

Score = __2__

Figure A.8

Addition Test

a
1 pt.
$$\begin{array}{r} 3 \\ +2 \\ \hline 5 \end{array}$$

b
1-5 pts.
$$\begin{array}{r} 838 \\ +282 \\ \hline 1120 \end{array}$$

Score = __6__

Figure A.9

though in reality, problem *b* contains five times as much addition behavior as problem *a*.

Whenever designing a test or using a score, the first question one should ask is, What behavior does this number represent? The test designers often select broad behaviors resulting in test scores which don't describe what a student can really do. This is particularly true of the norm-referenced test (NRT) because it is only designed to describe the behavior of kids relative to other kids. In the case of a normative test, the situation shown in Figure A.8 makes some sense because the test isn't trying to find out how well the kid can add but how well he can add compared to others. On a criterion-referenced test (CRT), each point earned should represent the same amount of behavior. In order to do that the test designer must slice the behavior into discrete units. "Addition" is too broad a unit of behavior but "addition facts 0–9" is not. In Figure A.9 the same problems have been scored differently so that a point is given each time the student adds one number to another. The resulting score of 6 describes the kid's addition behavior better than the score of 2 in Figure A.8.

What a score means depends upon whether or not the score is from a NRT or a CRT. If the score is from a CRT, it should be easily translated into a statement of what the kid can do. If the student takes a timed test with the title "Reads Amount of Checks" and gets a score of 30 correct with 1 error in one minute, the score tells how well the kid reads the amount of checks. The raw score (number right and number wrong) is

equal to the behavior so the raw score is all the test user needs. In order to decide if a score of 30/1 is good enough, the test user must compare the score to an established criterion. This comparison can be done without translating the raw score into any other form.

If the test is a NRT, the raw score must be compared to the scores of other people. In order to make this comparison it is frequently necessary to translate the raw score into some other form. By doing so it is possible to compare one kid's score to others.

Summarizing the Distribution

One way to compare a kid's score to others is to make all the scores visible and then to look at them. This can be done in several ways. Suppose that Ed takes a history test that has 25 possible points. He scores 8. Nineteen other kids in the class also take the test. It is possible to compare Ed's score to their scores by way of graphs, histograms (Figure A.10), or frequency distributions (Figure A.11).

Both the graph and frequency distribution are fine for small groups but get cumbersome for large groups. What they both represent is the distribution of the scores and where Ed falls within that distribution. A distribution of scores can be summarized in several ways, some of which have already been covered. For example, the mean score on the history test is 12.9 so Ed's score is below average. The most common procedure for comparing normative scores is to divide up the distribution of scores according

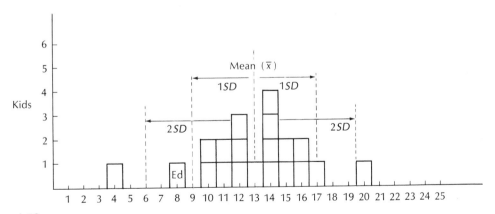

Figure A.10

The histogram.

Score	Frequency	
25		
24		
23		
22		
21		
20	1	
19		
18		
17	1	
16	2	
15	2	Sum of the scores = 258
14	4	N of scores = 20
13	1	Mean ($\bar{x}$) = 12.9
12	3	
11	2	
10	2	
9		
8 (Ed)	1	
7		
6		
5		
4	1	
3		
2		
1		

Figure A.11

The frequency distribution.

to some formula. Calculating the mean is a way of dividing the distribution.

Calculating the *SD* can also be used to divide the distribution into sections (Figure A.12). On the history test, one *SD* is equal to 3.48. So a score which falls within ± 1 *SD* of the mean would be between 9.42 and 16.38. (12.9 + 3.48 = 16.38, and 12.9 − 3.48 = 9.42). Remember that the normal curve has about 68% of its scores between ± 1 *SD* of the mean. In the case of history test, 80% of the scores fall within this boundary, so the scores on the history test are not normally distributed. Two students are more than ± 2 *SD* because one has a score of 5 and the other a score of 20. Ed is more than one *SD* below the mean.

Standard Scores

If the information that a student is ± 1 *SD* from the mean is not sufficiently specific, the raw score can be translated into a standard score. The standard score reports where the student is in the distribution with reference to both the mean and standard deviation. It is more specific because it allows the standard deviation to be divided into fractions. Two common types of standard scores are the *z*-score and *t*-score.

The *z*-score is calculated by subtracting the mean score ($\bar{x}$) from the student's score (*x*) and then dividing the results by the standard deviation. So Ed's *z*-score is −1.41.

	Score	The Score Squared
1.	20	400
2.	17	289
3.	16	256
4.	16	256
5.	15	225
6.	15	225
7.	14	196
8.	14	196
9.	14	196
10.	14	196
11.	13	169
12.	12	144
13.	12	144
14.	12	144
15.	11	121
16.	11	121
17.	10	100
18.	10	100
19.	8 (Ed)	64
20.	4	16
	258	3,558

Sum of scores = 258 (Σx)

Sum of squares = 3,558 ($\Sigma x)^2$

Sum of scores squared = 66,564 (Σx^2)

Number of scores = 20 (N)

Mean = 12.9

$$SD = \sqrt{\frac{\Sigma x^2 - \frac{(\Sigma x)^2}{N}}{N - 1}}$$

$$SD = \sqrt{\frac{3558 - \frac{66564}{20}}{20 - 1}}$$

$$SD = 3.48$$

Figure A.12

Computing the standard deviation.

$$z = \frac{x - \bar{x}}{SD} = \frac{8 - 12.9}{3.48} = -1.41$$

The *t*-score is essentially the same as the *z*-score except steps are taken to get rid of the minus signs and the decimal points. The minus sign is taken care of by adding 50 to the *z*-score, and the decimal is removed by multiplying the *z*-score by 10. The formula for calculating *t*-scores is

$$t = 10\left(\frac{x - \bar{x}}{SD}\right) + 50$$

So Ed's score is

$$t = 10\left(\frac{8 - 12.9}{3.48}\right) + 50 = 36$$

All of the scores on the history test have been translated to standard scores in Figure A.13.

Calculating standard scores may seem like a lot of work but they have some advantages. By converting the scores on two different tests to standard scores it is easier to compare a student's performance on each test. For example, suppose Ed took a biology test the same day he took the history test. And then suppose that for some reason his teacher wished to determine in which course Ed was doing the best (in relation to the other students). On the history test Ed got a raw score of 8 and on the biology test he got a raw score of 15. However, there were 75 problems on the biology test and only 25 on the history test. On which test did he get the best score? By converting the two different test scores to standard scores, it is possible to take into account the mean and standard deviation scores for each test and to compare Ed's scores (Figure A.14). The results indicate that Ed did the best on the history test. But remember that his score on a normative test is related only to the performance of the other students. That Ed got a better standard score on the history test doesn't mean he knows more history than biology.

Percentage and Percentile

Two other ways of reporting scores are percentages and percentiles. The two are different but often confused. *The percentage score is one way to report a student's accuracy.* A percentage is the score obtained, divided by the total possible score. In Ed's case, he scored 8 out of 25 points so he was accurate 32% of the time and wrong 68% of the time (8 ÷ 25 = .32(100) = 32%).

A percentile does not tell if the student was accurate or not. The percentile tells how a student scored in relation to other students.

Raw score (x)	z-score $z = \frac{x - \bar{x}}{SD}$	t-score $t = 10\left(\frac{x - \bar{x}}{SD}\right) + 50$
20	2.04	70
17	1.18	62
16	.89	59
16	.89	59
15	.60	56
15	.60	56
14	.32	53
14	.32	53
14	.32	53
13	.03	50
12	-.26	47
12	-.26	47
11	-.55	45
11	-.55	45
10	-.83	42
10	-.83	42
8	-1.41	36
4	-2.56	24

$$\bar{x} = 12.9$$
$$SD = 3.48$$

Figure A.13

History test scores.

	History Test (25 items)	Biology Test (75 items)
Ed's score (x)	8	15
mean $(\bar{x})$	12.9	52.7
SD	3.48	14.5
z-score	−1.4	−2.6
t-score	36	24

Figure A.14

A comparison of two tests.

Percentiles are determined in two ways. Sometimes, they are determined by rank ordering the scores and finding out what percentage of the total number of scores are the same as or lower than the score you are interested in. In Ed's case, 2 scores are the same as or lower than his score. There are 20 scores so his percentile score would be 2 ÷ 20 = .1(100) = 10 %ile.

Rounded percentiles can be obtained by segmenting the entire range of scores into 100 slices. In the example of the history test, there are 18 scores, meaning that each score covers 1.8 slices (18 ÷ 100 = 1.8). Rounded percentiles are used as a form of the standard score. The procedure for calculating rounded percentiles is supplied in Unit 7.

Grade Equivalency Scores

Anyone who has ever listened to the reading of two students who both scored at the same grade level on a reading test is probably already suspicious of the term *grade level*. Most kids are in the grade they are in because of age, not specific skills. Age may have little or nothing to do with skill acquisition. Therefore, it seems ridiculous to use a term such as grade level to describe a student's academic skills. But it is done all the time.

Grade level is a form of normative comparison based on the average performance of various sample populations. The application of the term is limited by the sample as well as the other limitations inherent in all normative comparisons. If a student scores at the sixth-grade level on a test, then the student is scoring (not functioning) as well as most sixth graders in the original sample. However, those sixth graders and the student may have nothing else in common at all. Perhaps the greatest injustice done to remedial students is to treat them as if they were in the grade that their grade equivalent scores correspond to. A ninth-grade student who reads at the first-grade level undoubtedly doesn't learn like a first grader, care about what first graders care about, or even read in the same way.

Here is an oversimplified example. Suppose the following list of words make up a reading test. Each word is given a score of one point. Ralph and Debbie take the test.

	Ralph	Debbie
ate	✓	✓
they	✓	—
house	—	✓
originally	✓	—
interpretation	—	✓
nevertheless	—	—
	3	3

The average score for a first grader is 1, second grader, 2, and so forth. In this case both Ralph and Debbie would be considered third-grade readers. Armed with this knowledge their teacher might then place them in a book with the following sentence.

"They originally ate at the cafe."

Even with the same test score the students would read the sentence differently because grade level, like any norm-referenced score, does not supply specific information about what a student can or cannot do.

Another problem with grade equivalent scores is the matter of scales. Grade equivalent scores do not represent an equal interval scale, although many people treat them as if they do. The amount of math a student learns between the second grade and the third grade is not the same amount as he learns between the eleventh and twelfth grade. Similarly, the third-grade reading level is not half as difficult as the sixth-grade reading level. In fact, for basic skills the student probably is not exposed to any really new material after about the fourth grade, making the amount of material covered each year progressively less. Saying a student decodes at the tenth-grade level is like applying a grade level equivalency to purely high school content. What would be the value of saying that a student is at the second-grade level in high school economics when high school economics isn't even taught until the ninth grade?

Another problem with grade equivalency scores is the way they are used by test publishers. Many tests which are designed for and normed on students of a limited age-span report grade equivalencies higher and/or lower than the norming sample. In other words, a test which is designed for use on students in grades 6, 7, 8, and 9 may only be normed on students in those grades. Yet, the test manuals may report grade equivalency scores for the test which range from first to twelfth grade. Those equivalency scores that are not based on actual norms are projected.

The frequency with which grade equivalency scores are used to pick programs for students and/or evaluate programming is probably due to their apparent simplicity. But as Tallmadge and Horst (1974) point out, "this apparent simplicity is entirely illusory, and there is ample evidence to contraindicate the use of grade equivalent scores or grade equivalent gains for *any* purpose *whatever* in educational evaluation" (p. 70). This caution does not just pertain to the evaluation of children but also to program and teacher evaluation (Glass, 1974b).

Unit 3: Correlation

Because evaluators are concerned with relationships, they have developed tools for comparison and association. One tool for comparing measurements is the correlation coefficient. A correlation can be obtained by applying two different measurements to the same group of students. It isn't possible to correlate students to students, but it is possible to correlate measures to measures. If two groups of students are measured

with the same test then what is taking place is comparison, not correlation (Diederich, 1967).

The correlation coefficient is usually expressed as a number between –1 and 1. A correlation of –1 is as powerful as a correlation of + 1 but the relationship described is different. A correlation of 0 means that no relationship has been found (Figure A.15).

Look at the example in Figure A.16. Suppose kids W, X, Y, and Z took two tests—A and B. If the two tests were positively correlated then a student scoring high on test A would also score high on Test B. Student W scored low (25 pts.) on both tests, while student Z scored high (100 pts.) on both tests. For these students the correlation between tests A and B would be + 1 (the highest positive correlation).

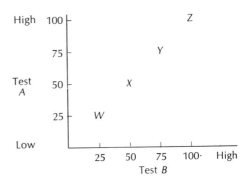

Figure A.16

A positive correlation.

Suppose students M, N, O, and P take tests A and B, as shown in Figure A.17.

In this case, students M and O both scored low on test B, (25 pts.) but student O scored high (75 pts.) on test A. Similarly, students N and P scored high on test B (90 pts.) but student N scored low on test A (25 pts.) while student P scored high (75 pts.). No relationship between tests A and B can be determined or described for this group of students. The correlation is 0.

Suppose students G, H, I, and J also took the tests, as shown in Figure A.18.

-1	-.9	-.8	-.7	-.6	-.5	-.4	-.3	-.2	-.1	0	.1	.2	.3	.4	.5	.6	.7	.8	.9	1
Best				High				Low		None		Low			High					Best

Figure A.15

The range of correlations.

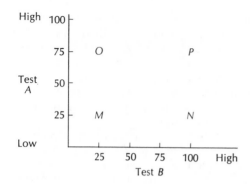

Figure A.17

A 0 correlation.

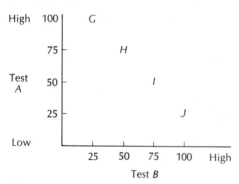

Figure A.18

A negative correlation.

In this case, students scoring high on test *A* have scored low on test *B*. This is a negative correlation (-1). Because a perfect correlation is rare, most correlations are in the form of decimals (.25,-.43,.87). An *r* means correlation coefficient. For example, $r = 1$, $r = .23$, $r = -.48$.

If the test being used is published, then the correlation coefficients pertaining to it should be in the manual. If they aren't, the test should be viewed with some suspicion as it is the professional responsibility of the publisher to supply such information. On the other hand, it is the professional responsibility of the test user to be able to calculate correlation coefficients whenever using a test on kids who differ from the original norming sample. The necessary calculations are simple, given a hand calculator and a clear set of procedures (for example, Bruning & Kintz, 1968).

How Do You Know a Good r If You See One?

The question of how high a correlation coefficient must be to be "high" is a difficult one to

answer. When *r* is used to summarize a test's reliability or validity it is determined by giving the test to students. The test scores are then correlated to something else (other test scores, for example.) The resulting *r* tells something about the test but it also tells something about the students who took it. For example, suppose a reading test is given to 500 adults and their scores correlate with their ability to draw circles at $r = .95$. The same reading test is then given to 500 4-year-olds and the correlation is found to be $r = .25$. The difference in the correlation is due to the different sample populations, not the test.

Because *r* may be affected by many things it should always be viewed as an estimate. Because test reliability and validity coefficients are often expressed as *r* they should also be regarded only as estimates.

The first consideration in deciding how high a correlation coefficient must be is the way it will be used. A teacher might demand higher correlation coefficients for IQ tests than for tests of bowling skill. The second consideration is who it will be used on. It is easier to make predictions about groups of people than about individuals. The correlation coefficients derived from group studies tell us about groups, not individuals. A reading test might be useful for assigning large numbers of students to programs but it could be nearly worthless in planning instruction for an individual student. Experts have indicated that a correlation high enough to be of any use in predicting about groups must be a minimum of from .3 to .5 (Guilford, 1965; Kelley, 1927). But these correlations are not high enough to use when devising an individualized program. Kelley says that correlations of .94 or above are necessary to make predictions about individuals.

If a teacher wanted to predict how an individual student will perform on a test, one thing she could do is guess. With no other information about the student, the smart teacher will always guess that the student is average (because most students are).

Suppose a teacher wanted to predict what a student's IQ score will be. If she has no information on the student she should predict the mean (usually 100). If she predicts the mean she will be correct a certain amount of time and she will be in error a certain amount of time. The percentage of times she is wrong (which in this case would be very high) is called the error of prediction. Any useful information the teacher can find out about the student should lower the error of prediction. This information may include past test scores.

Suppose the teacher wants to predict test score B and she already knows how the student scored on test A. Test A and test B are correlated at .50. Knowing the student's score on A will decrease the teacher's error of prediction of B by 13.4%. If the two tests correlated at .35 the error of prediction would be reduced by 6.3%. Table A.1 shows the error reduction for sample correlations. Using this table, it can be seen that if a teacher predicts from a test which has a correlation coefficient of .45, the size of the error of prediction is only going to be reduced by about 11% (Guilford, 1965). That is 11% less error than a prediction made with no previous test information at all.

In using Table A.1 it is important to remember one thing. If the test doesn't measure anything worthwhile a prediction made from it will be worthless even if A correlates to B at the $r = .95$ level. Also remember that the error of prediction

Table A.1

The Relationship of r to Error of Prediction

r	Percentage of error reduction
.00	.0
.05	.1
.10	.5
.15	1.1
.20	2.0
.25	3.2
.30	4.6
.35	6.3
.40	8.3
.45	10.7
.50	13.4
.55	16.5
.60	20.0
.65	24.0
.70	28.6
.75	33.9
.80	40.0
.85	47.3
.90	56.4
.95	68.8
.98	80.1
.99	85.9
.995	90.0
.999	95.5

will always be very high. Reducing the error of prediction from 95% to 75% may not be an educationally significant reduction.

Cause and Effect

When two variables are positively correlated an observer should be able to predict the student's behavior on one variable by observing the student's behavior on another variable.

Students who are successful in spelling are likely to be successful in math. This does not mean that studying spelling will improve math; it means that math and spelling are correlated due to some other variable (or factor). One variable is that good students may tend to be good students regardless of subject matter. There is no cause and effect relationship between spelling and math.

Most shark attacks take place in shallow warm water. Shallow warm water is more highly correlated to shark attacks than is deep cold water. But lots of sharks live in deep cold water, so why the correlation? A third independent variable, having nothing to do with water or sharks, is the behavior of swimmers. Most people swim in shallow warm water—few swim in the Arctic Ocean. Therefore, most shark attacks take place where the most swimmers are available. Warm shallow water does not cause sharks to be hungry.

Many testing instruments attempt to establish their validity through correlational research. The IQ test, for example, was originally designed to correlate with school success. However, there is an unfortunate tendency among educators to interpret correlations as evidence of cause and effect.

Up to a certain age the best estimate of a child's intelligence is not obtained by giving the child an IQ test. Very young children have trouble exhibiting the behaviors which some IQ tests require. It is possible, however, to estimate what the child's IQ score will be when he is old enough to take the test by giving an adult IQ test to the child's mother. The IQ score of the mother is moderately correlated to the future IQ score of the child. But any direct cause and effect that might have existed between the two theoretically ended after conception and birth. If the mother is run over by a bus and killed, the child's IQ score will not drop to 0.

Many variables correlate with school failure. Low scores on tests such as the Frostig or ITPA may correlate with low IQ or achievement test scores, both of which may correlate with school failure. This does not mean, however, that training a student in the skills necessary to pass the Frostig test will raise the student's IQ score or prevent school failure. The cause and effect relationship between many tests of student ability and academic achievement has not been established.

Teachers and testers should be careful about interpreting correlation coefficients. The coefficient summarizes the relationship between two measures given to a group of individuals. The same relationship may not exist for any single individual or for a different group. And the relationship may not be one of cause and effect.

Unit 4: Reliability, Validity, and Standard Error of Measurement

In order for any evaluative instrument to be of use with human subjects, that instrument must be reliable and valid. *Reliability* is the degree to which an instrument behaves predictably. An automobile which never starts in the morning is reliable. It may not take you anywhere but you can depend on it. *Validity* is the degree to which an instrument predicts reality. A compass which consistently points 10° east of magnetic north is reliable (because of its consistency) but is not valid. If the compass always points to magnetic north it is both reliable and valid.

A test which is not reliable is of no use in evaluating a student. Testing instruments must measure the same thing every time or they are not reliable. If an evaluative instrument is valid, it correctly describes reality. That is, it measures the thing it was designed to measure. An instrument can be reliable without being valid, but an instrument can't be valid without being reliable.

Suppose that a teacher has designed a history test that included the following item:

Circle the correct letter:

1. The first man on the moon was
   a. John Glenn
   b. Glenn Ford

c. Jules Vern
d. Neil Armstrong

This item would seem to measure the student's recall of a fact. However, it also measures the student's ability to read, follow directions, and draw a circle. To the extent that a student cannot do those things, the test is invalid. Does a student need to know how to read in order to know who the first man on the moon was? No. Yet many teachers turn almost any test into a reading test.

When it is not possible to directly measure a concept or behavior, evaluators are forced to make inferences from behaviors they can measure. Intelligence, for example, cannot be seen or weighed. Its presence is inferred from behaviors such as defining words, solving problems, or tracing mazes. Educational instruments predict some percentage of the sought-after trait but not all of it. No testing instrument can be expected to measure exactly a human cognitive trait. For this reason all test scores are made up of two components: true score (X_T) and error score (X_E). Test score = $X_T + X_E$. Similarly, the variability (σ^2) of the scores obtained when groups of students are tested reflects error ($\sigma^2 E$) in this way: $\sigma^2 T + \sigma^2 E$ = test score variability.

Reliability

Reliability is estimated by correlating the test score to itself. This is done by exposing the same student (or group of students) to the same test twice and correlating the results. There are three methods of doing this: test–retest, parallel forms, and internal consistency.

Test–retest reliability is synonymous with the stability of the test score over time. This form of reliability coefficient is of interest in cases where the test is designed to identify "types" of students for differential programming. It makes little sense to place a student into a particular program for the whole year because of a test score which will change in a few months. Differences between the first and second test score may reflect error of measurement or changes in the student. In either case, a low test–retest reliability coefficient limits the use of the test in making decisions over time.

The term *test–retest reliability* means that if a student is evaluated on a test and scores 23, then if the student is reevaluated on the test he should score at or near 23 again. The test–retest reliability of a set of calipers measuring a student's head size is high. The test–retest reliability of an instrument designed to measure a student's "good feelings" might not be as high. Some human traits are more easily measured than others due to their observable nature.

The *alternative* (or *parallel*) *form* method of determining reliability involves the administration of two forms of the same test. The two scores are then correlated. This method has one advantage in that the student does not take the same test items twice. It has a disadvantage in that the two forms may not be equally difficult.

The *internal consistency* method attempts to establish reliability through a single administration of the test. These methods remove the effect of time found in the first two methods. The internal consistency of a test is often derived by correlating the even-numbered items with the odd-numbered items. This procedure is sometimes called the split-half method.

Even if high reliability coefficients are reported in a test manual that still doesn't mean the test is reliable. Remember that the reliability coefficient is a correlation coefficient which is calculated by applying a statistical formula to data obtained on a sample of students. Statistical procedures require that certain assumptions about sample size and selection be met in order to assure the coefficient's accuracy.

Validity

Validity is determined by correlating the test score to reality. The problem, of course, is that reality is not easily defined. In the case of IQ, the validity of a test score is often established by correlating the test score to other IQ test scores. These other IQ scores reflect a certain amount of IQ plus a certain amount of measurement error. In situations where the validity of a test depends upon its correlation to other tests, the resulting validity coefficient is derived by correlating reality to reality plus error to error. The validity coefficients of some tests are determined by correlating them to other tests which were themselves correlated to other tests. This is particularly true of short-form tests. These tests

claim to be valid because their scores correlate to scores on larger tests.

The validity for a test score for brain damage might be determined by correlating it to EEG findings or even to autopsy findings. The validity of a math test could be determined by correlating it to the math grades of the students taking the test. Each of these procedures is limited by the reliability of the other measures used. As a rule, the validity of a test can't exceed the square root of its reliability (Dick & Hagerty, 1971).

Because validity is difficult to establish, there is sometimes no mention of it in test manuals. Authors (or publishers) realize that if they produce a reliable test it will be bought because most teachers know very little about validity. Teachers should be aware of at least five types of validity—content, concurrent, predictive, construct, and cash validity.

Content validity refers to the relationship between the test items and the purpose of the test. A valid spelling test should be made up of items which are similar to the spelling a student will do in the classroom. Content validity is what most classroom teachers are interested in as it is necessary in order to generalize from the test score to classroom practice. In content validity the test score is correlated to the task. Criterion-referenced tests should have high content validity.

Concurrent validity refers to a test's ability to accurately describe the student's current level of functioning on certain tasks. The test score is correlated to other measures of the student's current behavior.

Predictive validity refers to a test's ability to accurately predict the student's future level of functioning. The predictive nature of tests is an area of great concern. Tests such as IQ tests are designed to be prognostic; that is, to predict how the student will do in future academic situations. In order to have predictive validity, IQ tests sample a wide variety of behaviors. Because these tests are intended to predict performance in all school subjects, their global scores (and even their subtest scores) do not reflect the specificity necessary for diagnostic tests. The IQ score does not tell the teacher how or what to teach a kid. Predictive validity should never be confused with the content and concurrent validity necessary for diagnostic tests.

In establishing predictive validity, an effort is made to correlate the test score to the student's future. This can only be accomplished by carrying out long-term studies. IQ tests such as the Weschler and Binet established predictive validity by testing students and then observing the students years later. Other test developers will try to establish predictive validity by correlating the scores on their new test to the scores on one of the already validated tests. This correlation is obtained by giving the same group of students the new test and the older test. The result is then reported as the predictive validity of the new test. This procedure does not establish the predictive validity of the new test at all; instead, it establishes the concurrent validity of the test.

Construct and *cash validity* are of particular interest in special education. Many tests which are routinely given to special students are based on constructs of psychological functioning. The ITPA, for example, is based on a theory of psycholinguistics developed by Osgood (1953). The test items, however, are not noticeably different from those making up most achievement tests. As Waugh (1975) points out, the ITPA is listed in Buros' *Mental Measurements Yearbook* as a test of general achievement, not language. Naming a test after some type of psychological or perceptual functioning does not make it a test of that function.

Tests that sell well may have high cash validity (Dick & Hagerty, 1971). It is possible to have cash validity in the absence of any other type of validity. One cannot assume that because a test sells well, it is useful.

In the absence of validity data (or even in its presence), it is necessary for the teacher to sit down with the test and carefully analyze it. Look at the items and ask yourself, "Do my students engage in tasks similar to these?" "Does the test place emphasis on the same curricular areas I do?" The teacher should also note if the author tells how the test was validated and on whom. In order for a test to be valid, it must be validated on a population of individuals similar to the population on which the test is to be used. If a test is reported to be valid for 8-year-old students, it may not be valid for 16-year-olds. To make sure a test score is valid for use in a class,

school, or district it is necessary to compare the behaviors on the test to the behaviors students must engage in in the schools. If the norms of the test are to be used, it is necessary to ask questions about the characteristics of the norming population and the characteristics of populations to which the norms are to be generalized.

Standard Error of Measurement

Another way to judge the reliability of a score is to look at the test's *standard error of measurement*. If a student (or group) is given the same test several times and if the student tries equally hard each time, he should always get the same score. When there are differences between the scores, these differences must be attributed to either learning or measurement error. Once learning has been subtracted, all that remains to account for the variability among scores is error. The greater the variability, the greater the standard error of measurement.

The standard error of measurement is a better criterion for judging the test's usefulness than is the simple reliability coefficient. There are many sources of error in scores, including fatigue, a broken pencil, bad lighting, passage of time, and others. Different techniques for determining reliability account for different sources of error variability. The standard error of measurement accounts for all sources of variance because it is calculated from both the reliability and the standard deviation of the test score. When reading a test manual it is important to notice if the author reports only the reliability or both the reliability and the standard error of measurement.

Suppose a test were developed for the purpose of measuring creativity. The test authors might correlate scores on the even-numbered test items with scores on the odd-numbered items to determine the split-half reliability. Suppose the reliability is .80 for two populations of individuals ages 15 to 20 and ages 40 to 50. But now suppose that the variability (*SD*) of standard scores for each population was different, as shown in Figure A.19.

In this case, the standard error of measurement would not be the same for each age group because the variability is different. The formula for standard error of measurement reads as follows:

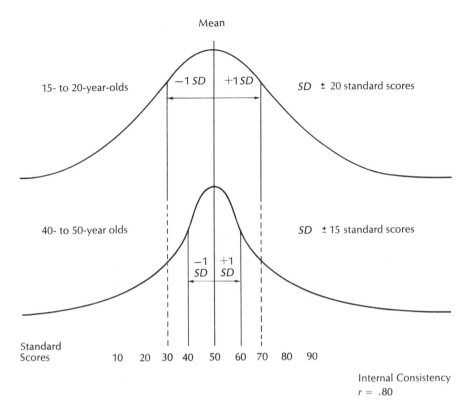

Figure A.19

Two groups with different variability.

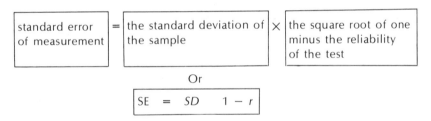

The standard error of measurement for the two groups can be calculated in this way:

15- to 20-year olds $r = .80$

$8.9 = 20 \sqrt{1 - .80}$ $SD = 20$

40- to 50-year olds $SD = 15$

$6.70 = 15 \sqrt{1 - .80}$

In this case, even though the reliability of the test is the same for each age group (.80), the standard error of measurement is not. The standard error of measurement is higher for 15- to 20-year-olds (8.9 standard scores) than for 40- to 50-year-olds (6.7 standard scores). This means that the test scores of the older group can be interpreted with greater confidence than the scores of the younger group. If a 17-year-old individual scored 47 on the creativity test, then his true score is probably between 38.1 and 55.9. If a 45-year-old individual takes the same test and scores 47, his true score would probably fall between 40.3 and 53.7. If it were decided that individuals who score below 40 must be placed in remedial creativity classes, the chances are greater of misplacing a 15- to 20-year-old than a 40- to 50-year-old.

The standard error of measurement must be known if the user of a norm-referenced test is going to place any confidence in the descriptive power of test scores. Obviously, if different populations have different patterns of error variance, then uniform standards should not be used for making decisions from the test scores. For example, suppose the only criterion for placing any student in a classroom for the retarded is that the student's IQ test score is lower than 70. If the standard error of measurement on the IQ test were greater for individuals from a particular cultural background, these individuals would have a greater chance of being accidentally placed in classrooms for the retarded. Any good test manual should supply information about the standard error of measurement, and this information should be broken down according to population variables such as race, sex, socioeconomic status, age, and ethnic background. When this information is not supplied, test users should make efforts to obtain it themselves.

Unit 5: Product Evaluation with Gain Scores

Most standardized achievement testing is done for the purpose of establishing gain. The gain score is nothing more than the difference between two measures of the same kid (or group of kids).

Gain scores may be used in research to establish which program is most effective for teaching a task, or school districts may require teachers to calculate gain in order to justify their programs.

Gain scores are derived by giving a pretest and a posttest and subtracting the difference. (They are sometimes called difference scores.) One should not put too much faith in raw gain scores or in conclusions reached by giving the same individual two separate normative tests and comparing differences in the scores. (See Unit 6.) There are many problems with gain scores. One important problem is measurement error.

All educational measurement has some amount of error (Figure A.20). When a pretest is subtracted from a posttest, the resulting gain is made up of some percentage of true score (how well the kid really can read) and some percentage of error. A rough idea of the amount of measurement error in a test score can be obtained by looking at the reliability coefficients of the test and the standard error of measurement. Characteristically, the reliability of a gain score will be less than the reliability of either the pretest score or the posttest score.

One source of the error in a NRT score is closely linked to content validity. Many NRTs have the student engage in test behaviors which are different from classroom behaviors. For example, some standardized spelling tests require the student to identify misspelled words, whereas most teachers expect their students to

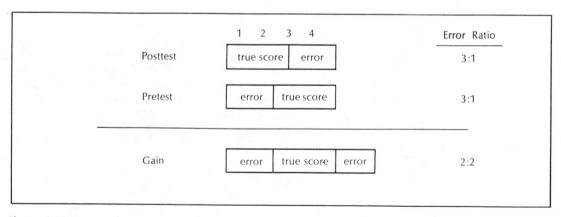

Figure A.20

The cumulative effect of error on gain scores.

produce correctly spelled words. Because of this, the score derived from a NRT may convey little information about what the student really can or cannot do. Therefore, a gain score derived from a NRT score doesn't really describe how much more the student can do now than he could do before.

The solution to the problem of content validity is to use CRTs. The CRT, if properly developed, should supply exact information about what the student can or cannot do. If the pretest says the student cannot spell the Dolch word list and the posttest says the student can, then the gain is obvious. The problem with using CRTs to determine gain is that it is difficult to decide if the gain is significant. In the absence of normative data, it is not possible to use normative procedures for determining statistical significance, and teachers tend to rely upon their judgment as to the educational significance of the gain. If all teachers had the same judgment, this wouldn't be a problem, but obviously they don't. So evaluators use standardized tests which will allow them to analyze the gains and determine statistical significance.

One popular way of deciding if a program has been successful is to compare students' growth to the norms of an achievement test. This isn't the way programs are normally evaluated for research purposes but it is the method often employed in school systems. One danger of using standardized achievement tests for a pretest/posttest comparison is that the norming of the test may not have been done at the same time during the year as the pretesting and post-

testing. Achievement testing is routinely done during the first and last days of school, perhaps in early September and late May. Many achievement tests are normed in October and April which means that the norming population would have had a month more instruction than the students in the fall, and a month less in the spring (Tallmadge & Horst, 1974). This can overinflate the actual gains the students have made. Figure A.21 shows how students in a class may be considered low in the fall but high in the spring simply because they are being compared to inappropriate norms.

In the fall the class scored below the norm and in the spring they scored above the norm, making it look as if they made extraordinary gains. In fact, they gained at exactly the same rate as the norming group.

Pupil gain scores can be used to evaluate teachers. But the use of commercially prepared normative tests to determine gain for this purpose is invalid (Glass, 1974). Unfortunately, the use of teacher-specified objectives and teacher-made CRTs for the same purpose may not be much better (Ebel, 1975).

There are many reasons for an evaluator to calculate gain. But regardless of her reason, she should be aware of the opposite of gain, which is damage. There is a tendency in education to assume that the result of instruction is always either good or neutral. That is not always the case; some instruction is bad and produces damage (Wortman, 1975). Instruction on one objective can be detrimental to the learning of another. For this reason, teachers should check on

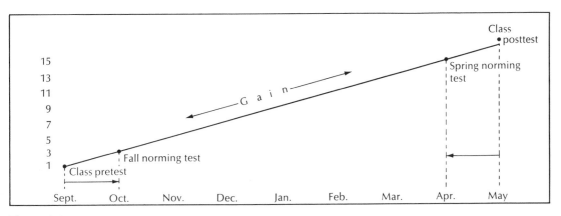

Figure A.21

Average scores of a norming sample and a class.

areas which are beyond the scope of their current instruction. A frequently heard criticism of criterion-referenced testing is that teachers will develop instructional tunnel vision and only teach to one task at a time (Ebel, 1975). The prospect of getting some specificity into instruction may very well outweigh that danger, but in order to protect against both tunnel vision and damage, teachers should look for changes in all areas of student behavior.

Unit 6: Profile Analysis

Charting scores in profile form can be of some use in summarizing data, but profile analysis goes beyond just summarizing scores. It implies the ability to draw conclusions from the patterns revealed when the data are recorded side by side. In profile analysis, the individual test scores are of less importance than the pattern they form. For example, in Figure A.22 the scores of several hypothetical tests are reported under the headings general anxiety, test anxiety, group anxiety, and separation anxiety. After giving all of these tests to Ralph (we'll keep his test anxiety low or it would mess up the hypothetical) the results on each test can be compared to see if there

are any areas of special concern to Ralph. Looking at the profile, and using the general anxiety measure as Ralph's usual level of anxiety, it might be concluded that Ralph will need some extra help learning to deal with groups.

Profile analysis is a popular pastime in special education and usually stems from the search for so called intraindividual (within the individual) differences. The procedure is to administer several tests (or one test composed of several subtests) and then chart the student's high and low scores. Once this is done the high scores are called strengths and the low scores are called weaknesses.

A profile is a system of summarizing information. Profiles are composed of two components: a theoretical framework and an index or scale (Kaplan, 1964). Typically, the theoretical framework will be placed across the horizontal axis of a display and the index down the vertical axis as seen in Figure A.22. The assumptions upon which the validity of a profile hinge are related to these separate axes.

Theoretical Axis

Along the theoretical (horizontal) axis are a series of categories or content areas which are

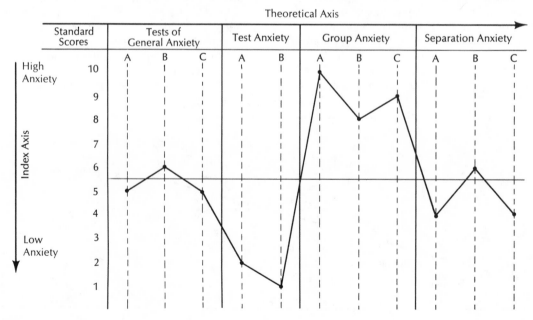

Figure A.22

Anxiety profile.

all conceptually linked. In Figure A.22, the components of the theoretical axis are arranged according to types of anxiety. If, on the other hand, these components were spread along the axis in a random fashion, then the profile wouldn't represent the same theoretical relationships. For example, Figure A.23 shows a profile of hypothetical test scores in the area of ocular control. The components are spread along the horizontal axis in random fashion.

In Figure A.24 the same information is arranged

to conform with the conceptual framework suggested by Kephart (1971). Figures A.23 and A.24 show the same data charted in two fashions. Notice that changing the placement of the components on the horizontal axis can produce any number of different and even contradictory patterns. It is always a good idea to check the placement of members of a profile to see if moving them might change interpretations. Also check the items of each subtest (not the subtest names) to look for similarities. The results in

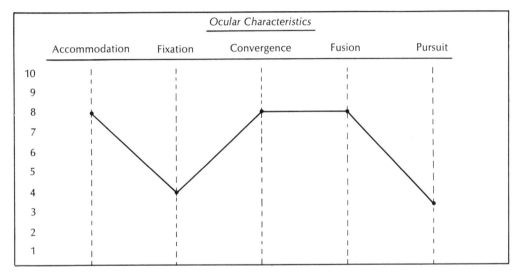

Figure A.23

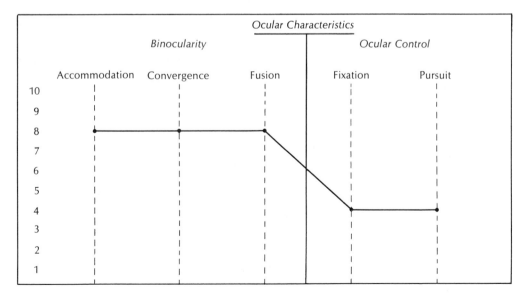

Figure A.24

Figures A.23 and A.24 wouldn't mean much if all the binocularity subtests required the same behaviors and all the ocular control subtests required the same behaviors. If that were the case, the same information could have been obtained by only giving the kid one subtest from each category; for example, fusion and pursuit.

If the arrangement of the components is intended to represent a theoretical relationship, then the profile has construct validity. One way of establishing the degree of construct validity is to correlate the results of the profile to other measures which are based on the same theory. Suppose that a test profile is developed which is intended to recognize individuals who are unable to learn how to read due to mixed dominance. The components along the horizontal axis would probably be things like handedness, eye dominance, and foot dominance. A profile of this kind would sort individuals into the categories of mixed dominance and uniform dominance. Other tests can sort individuals into readers and nonreaders. The question would be How many nonreaders have mixed dominance? If many of them did, one might conclude that there is a relationship between the two. However, there are other questions which should also be asked, such as How many readers have mixed dominance? or Does reading affect dominance?

Kaplan (1964) states that a profile pattern becomes a reference for the application of a term. The ultimate test of profile validity is how often individuals to whom the term is applied have the same pattern as the references. For example, "scatter" on the profiles of the WISC-R and ITPA is frequently sighted as evidence of a learning disability. In order to interpret scatter, it is necessary to shift attention to the index axis of the profile and to examine certain statistical characteristics of profile analysis.

The Index Axis

The index (vertical) axis of the profile provides the common index needed to summarize different measures on the same form. In order for a profile to be of any value, the separate test components must all be scaled in the same way. Usually this is done by translating the scores from a variety of different measures into percentages and/or standard scores which supposedly will allow the separate tasks to be directly compared. Occasionally, profiles of grade equivalent scores will also be seen. It should be pointed out that placing such scores in a profile doesn't make them any more useful. If each of the subtests of the profile is normed on different populations, then the vertical index cannot relate equally to each subtest. Using an index of standard scores does not avoid this issue, as standard scores are also derived from the norming populations and are subject to norming considerations. For example, on the ITPA a variation of $\pm$ 10 scaled scores is considered to be a significant variation in the profile. However, the actual variation needed for statistical significance changes according to the age of the student taking the test. This is because the different subtests have different reliabilities at different ages and do not relate to the profile index in a uniform fashion (Ysseldyke and Sabatino, 1972).

The interpretation and statistical analysis of profile data are very similar to the interpretation and analysis of gain scores. In profile analysis the importance of one subtest depends upon its relative position (along the vertical axis) to other subtests on the profile. Therefore, the reliability of the profile depends upon the reliability of each of its components. The reliability of the total profile also depends upon the correlation between the components because if they are measuring the same thing they can't be contrasted.

A formula for determining the reliability of a decision based on a profile makes use of the sum of the subtests' reliabilities minus the correlation between them (Cronbach, 1960). The formula in expanded notation would read like this:

$$\text{profile reliability} = \frac{\text{the reliability of subtest 1} + \text{the reliability of subtest 2} - \text{2 times the correlation between subtests 1 and 2}}{2 - \text{2 times the correlation between subtests 1 and 2}}$$

As an example, let's apply the formula to just the auditory reception and visual reception subtests of the ITPA. The ITPA manual lists the five-month test-retest reliability of the auditory reception subtest as .44, the visual reception subtest as .30, and the correlation of the two at the .38 level (Kirk, McCarthy, and Kirk, 1971).

$$\text{Profile reliability} = \frac{.44 + .30 - 2 \ (.38)}{2 - 2 \ (.38)} =$$

$$\frac{-.02}{1.24} = .02$$

The five-month test-retest reliability of the comparison between only these two subtests would be .02. Reliability, of course, is a prerequisite for validity.

The relative distance, or scatter, between points on a profile can be analyzed for statistical significance (the probability of similar scatter occurring by accident), or treatment significance (the usefulness of the profile for guiding instruction). Statistical and treatment significance are not always the same. One way to find the statistical significance of scatter is to find the mean standard score and record the degree to which subtests or groups of subtests deviate from it. Take another look at Ralph's anxiety as summarized in Figure A.22. The mean standard score for the profile is 5.5. The subtests vary from this mean in the following fashion:

these two criteria are rewordings of the traditional reliability (time) and validity (usefulness) issues. Waugh (1975) found the means of the visual and auditory subtests of the ITPA and, using the system just applied to Ralph's anxiety profile, classified students as either auditory or visual learners. Her criterion was a scaled score difference between the ITPA auditory and visual subtests of ±10, as required by the ITPA manual. She found that none of the students retained their original classification of auditory or visual learners for longer than two years. One even switched from being a visual learner to being an auditory learner.

A way to determine the treatment significance (how useful the procedure is in guiding instruction) of scatter is to see how often similar scatter occurs in the profiles of individuals who are not members of the population the profile is trying to describe. Psychological reports sometimes comment on scatter between subtests on the WISC-R, particularly when the student is suspected of having learning disabilities. As it turns out, the range of scatter (highest subtest minus lowest subtest) for normal students may be as high as 14 standard scores, indicating that the child who is not learning disabled has considerable profile scatter, too (Kauffman, 1976).

The profile is a valuable tool for summarizing information, but making accurate treatment decisions from normative profiles is a difficult bus-

Mean = 5.5 General Anxiety			Test Anxiety		Group Anxiety			Separation Anxiety		
A	B	C	A	B	A	B	C	A	B	C
−.5	+.5	−.5	−3.5	−4.5	+5.5	+3.5	+4.5	−1.5	+.5	−1.5

In this example, group anxiety test A is the area of anxiety which would seem to be Ralph's biggest problem. However, there is not sufficient information in the profile to tell if ±5 standard scores has the treatment significance to justify treating Ralph's group anxiety.

According to Thorndike and Hagen (1969) profile differences which are significant will stay different over time and be big enough to actually supply some useful information. Essentially,

iness. Such decisions require reliable subtests which do not correlate highly to each other but which are still relevant to the profile. It is possible to have a profile of criterion-referenced measures, however, such profiles are limited to telling what the student can or cannot do. The task specificity of criterion-referenced measures makes the direct comparison of scores difficult. On a normative profile, the mean and standard deviation of the sample population are used to

provide the common index for comparison between different subtests. Because CRTs lack the
normative standard they can only be compared
if the criterion is the same for each test and the
behaviors involved are similar. Of course, if the
two tests are that much alike, then the pattern
is of little interest and the profile form becomes
only a record sheet.

Unit 7: Computational Steps

This unit describes the steps for computing the
mean, standard deviation, z-score, t-score, percentile, and percentage. Two sets of raw data
are supplied in Table A.2. The first set is from
a drama test and will be used to illustrate each
computational procedure. The second set is from
a geology test; you are encouraged to practice
the steps for each computational procedure with
this set of data. If a calculator is used, you should
be able to make all the necessary computations
and translations for the geology data in about

30 minutes. The results of the computations are
summarized in Tables A.3 and A.4.

Table A.2

Raw Data

	Drama Test		Geology Test
1.	25	1.	50
2.	25	2.	45
3.	24	3.	42
4.	23	4.	39
5.	22	5.	38
6.	22	6.	30
7.	22	7.	30
8.	21	8.	29
9.	20	9.	29
10.	18	10.	29
11.	18	11.	28
12.	18	12.	28
13.	15	13.	24
14.	9	14.	23
15.	6	15.	21
		16.	20
		17.	15
		18.	10
		19.	10
		20.	9

Computing the Mean

$$\text{Mean} = \frac{x}{n} = \bar{x}$$

Drama Test (maximum score 30)

	Raw Scores		
1.	25	Step 1.	List the scores in any order, but list each student's score.
2.	25		
3.	24	Step 2.	Add up the scores. Sum = 288.
4.	23	Step 3.	Divide the sum of the scores by the total number of scores. 288 ÷ 15 = 19.2.
5.	22		
6.	22		
7.	22		Conclusion: The mean is 19.2.
8.	21		
9.	20		Now, calculate the mean for the geology test.
10.	18		
11.	18		
12.	18		
13.	15		
14.	9		
15.	6		
	288		

Computing the Standard Deviation

$$SD = \sqrt{\dfrac{\Sigma x^2 - \dfrac{(\Sigma x)^2}{N}}{N-1}}$$

Drama Test (maximum score 30)

	Raw Scores	Scores Squared
1.	25	625
2.	25	625
3.	24	576
4.	23	529
5.	22	484
6.	22	484
7.	22	484
8.	21	441
9.	20	400
10.	18	324
11.	18	324
12.	18	324
13.	15	225
14.	9	81
15.	6	36

$\Sigma x = 288 \quad \Sigma x^2 = 5{,}962$

Step 1. List the scores in any order, but list each student's score.

Step 2. Add up the scores. Sum = 288.

Step 3. Square each score in a list next to the student's score.

Step 4. Add up all the squared scores. Sum of the squares = 5,962.

Step 5. Square the sum of the scores calculated in Step 2. $288^2 = 82{,}944$.

Step 6. Divide the number derived in Step 5 by the number of students. $82{,}944 \div 15 = 5{,}529.6$.

Step 7. Subtract the number derived in Step 6 from the number derived in Step 4. $5{,}962 - 5{,}529.6 = 432.4$.

Step 8. Divide the number derived in Step 7 by the number of students minus one.

$$\frac{432.4}{15-1} = \frac{432.4}{14} = 30.89$$

Step 9. Find the square root of the number derived in Step 8. $\sqrt{30.89} = 5.56$.

Conclusion: The standard deviation is 5.56.

Now calculate the standard deviation for the geology test.

Translating Raw Scores into z-Scores

$$z = \frac{x - \bar{x}}{SD}$$

Drama Test (maximum score 30)

Translating Raw Scores into z-Scores (cont)

	Raw Scores	z-Scores
1.	25	1
2.	25	1
3.	24	.06
4.	23	.7
5.	22	.5
6.	22	.5
7.	22	.5
8.	21	.3
9.	20	.1
10.	18	-.2
11.	18	-.2
12.	18	-.2
13.	15	-.8
14.	9	-1.8
15.	6	-2.4
	288	

Step 1. List the raw scores in any order, but list each score.

Step 2. Compute the mean. $288 \div 15 = 19.2$.

Step 3. Compute the standard deviation.

$$\sqrt{\frac{5962 - \dfrac{82944}{15}}{15 - 1}} = 5.56$$

Step 4. Subtract the mean computed in Step 2 from a raw score. For example, $25 - 19.2 = 5.8$.

Step 5. Divide the number derived in Step 4 by the number computed in Step 3. $5.8 \div 5.56 = 1.04$.

Conclusion: The raw score 25 is equal to z-score 1.04.

Step 6. Repeat the process for each raw score.

Now translate the raw scores on the geology test into z-scores.

Translating z-Scores to t-Scores

$$t = 10 \left(\frac{x - \bar{x}}{SD} \right) + 50$$

Drama Test (maximum score 30)

	Raw Scores	z-Scores	t-Scores
1.	25	1	60
2.	25	1	60
3.	24	.9	59
4.	23	.7	57
5.	22	.5	55
6.	22	.5	55
7.	22	.5	55
8.	21	.3	53
9.	20	.1	51
10.	18	−.2	48
11.	18	−.2	48
12.	18	−.2	48
13.	15	−.8	42
14.	9	−1.8	32
15.	6	−2.4	26

Step 1. List the raw scores in any order, but list each score.

Step 2. Translate the raw scores to z-scores.

Step 3. Multiply the z-score by 10. $(.5)10 = 5$.

Step 4. Add 50 to the score derived in Step 3. $5 + 50 = 55$.

Conclusion: The z-score .5 is equal to the t-score 55.

Step 5. Repeat the process for each z-score.

Now, translate the z-scores on the geology test into t-scores.

Translating the Scores to Percentiles

Drama Test (maximum score 30)

	Raw Scores	Percen-tile	Percentile Score	Rounded Percentile
1.	25	100	96.7	97
2.	25	93.3	96.7	97
3.	24	86.6	86.6	87
4.	23	79.9	79.9	80
5.	22	73.2	66.5	67
6.	22	66.5	66.5	67
7.	22	59.8	66.5	67
8.	21	53.1	53.1	53
9.	20	46.4	46.4	46
10.	18	39.7	33	33
11.	18	33	33	33
12.	18	26.3	33	33
13.	15	19.6	19.6	20
14.	9	12.9	12.9	13
15.	6	6.2	6.2	6

Step 1.   List the scores in order from largest to smallest. List all scores.

Step 2.   Divide 100 by the number of scores. $100 \div 15 = 6.67$.

Step 3.   Round off the number in Step 2 to one decimal. $6.67 = 6.7$.

Step 4.   Assign a value of 100 to the first score on the list. The first 25 score would have a value of 100.

Step 5.   Subtract the number obtained in Step 3 from 100 and assign it to the second number on the list.

Score	Percentile
25	100
25	93.3
24	86.6

Continue subtracting down the entire list.

Step 6.   When several scores are the same, average their percentiles together. The result is rounded to the nearest tenth and becomes the percentile score. For example, since the first two raw scores are 25, their percentiles $(100 + 93.3)$ are averaged to 96.7. This becomes the percentile score.

Translating the Scores to Percentiles (cont)

Score	Percentile	Percentile Score
25	100	96.7
25	93.3	96.7

Step 7. Round off the percentile score from Step 6.

Score	Percen-tile	Percentile Score	Rounded Percentile
25	100	96.7	97
25	93.3	96.7	97

Conclusion: A student who scored 25 on the drama test is at the 97th percentile.

Now translate the raw scores on the geology test into percentiles.

Computing Percentages

Drama Test (maximum score 30)

	Raw Score	Percentage
1.	25	83
2.	25	83
3.	24	80
4.	23	77
5.	22	73
6.	22	73
7.	22	73
8.	21	70
9.	20	67
10.	18	60
11.	18	60
12.	18	60
13.	15	50
14.	9	30
15.	6	20

Step 1.   List the raw scores.

Step 2.   Divide each raw score by the total possible score. For example,
25 ÷ 30 = .83 = 83%.

Conclusion: A student who scores 25 out of 30 has received 83%.

Now, translate the raw scores on the geology test into percentages.

Table A.3

Summary of Drama Test Scores (maximum score 30)

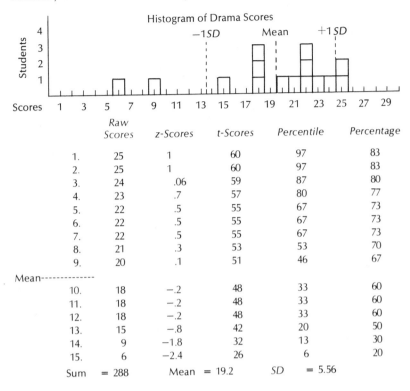

Histogram of Drama Scores

	Raw Scores	z-Scores	t-Scores	Percentile	Percentage
1.	25	1	60	97	83
2.	25	1	60	97	83
3.	24	.06	59	87	80
4.	23	.7	57	80	77
5.	22	.5	55	67	73
6.	22	.5	55	67	73
7.	22	.5	55	67	73
8.	21	.3	53	53	70
9.	20	.1	51	46	67

Mean--------------

	Raw Scores	z-Scores	t-Scores	Percentile	Percentage
10.	18	−.2	48	33	60
11.	18	−.2	48	33	60
12.	18	−.2	48	33	60
13.	15	−.8	42	20	50
14.	9	−1.8	32	13	30
15.	6	−2.4	26	6	20
Sum	= 288	Mean = 19.2	SD = 5.56		

Table A.4

Summary of Geology Test Scores (maximum score 50)

	Raw Scores	z-Scores	t-Scores	Percentile	Percentage
1.	50	2	70	100	100
2.	45	1.5	65	95	90
3.	42	1.3	63	90	84
4.	39	1	60	85	78
5.	38	.9	59	80	76
6.	30	.2	52	72.5	60
7.	30	.2	52	72.5	60
8.	29	.1	51	60	58
9.	29	.1	51	60	58
10.	29	.1	51	60	58
11.	28	0	50	47.5	56
12.	28	0	50	47.5	56
13.	24	−.3	47	40	48
14.	23	−.4	46	35	46
15.	21	−.6	44	30	42
16.	20	−.6	44	25	40
17.	15	−1	40	20	30
18.	10	−1.5	35	12.5	20
19.	10	−1.5	35	12.5	20
20.	9	−1.6	34	5	18
Sum	= 549	Mean = 27.45	SD = 11.53		

Discussion

There are some points to be noted on the drama summary sheet (Table A.3). First, on the graph, note that 9 out of the 15 students scored above the mean. The mean does not cut the data directly in half because the extremely low scores of two students (6,9) pulled the mean to the left. The mean is the average of all scores.

A second point to notice is that 11 out of the 15 students are between ±1 standard deviations of the mean. It is important to note than 11 is 73% of 15. In the normal curve, 68% of the students fall between ±1 standard deviations. Therefore, the drama test scores are not normally distributed (although they are close for such a small number of scores).

A third point is that no student got all of the test items correct. The students who scored at the 97th percentile only got 83% of the items correct. If the teacher had established that 100% of the items needed to be correct in order for a student to be considered competent, then none of the students would have passed the test.

Unit 8: The Reliability and Validity of CRTs

Discussion

The procedures for determining the reliability and validity of CRTs and NRTs are different. The basis of this difference is the reference. The NRT requires calculations which take into account the distribution of scores in a sample group. One way a distribution is obtained is by standardizing the test items on people with varying skills. Another way the distribution is obtained is by varying the difficulty of items. The statistical procedures associated with variability of scores are therefore used in calculations concerning the quality of the test.

A CRT is meant to measure only one objective at a time. Because the score obtained from the CRT can be read as a behavioral statement, there is no need to translate the score into percentiles or standard scores. The test is not standardized on a population of people with varying skills but on a population of people who are already competent at the task being measured. This procedure is combined with the logical analysis of the task and the experimental use of the test to determine its instructional validity. Because the reliability of a CRT is related to the similarity in difficulty between the items, the scores do not vary as on an NRT. Therefore, the statistical methods of determining reliability are different (Popham & Husek, 1969).

Reliability of CRTs

MEASUREMENT ERROR. In dealing with measurement error there are important similarities between NRTs and CRTs. Both are measures of behavior so both have measurement error. If a student takes any test twice, the difference between the two scores is attributed either to learning or measurement error. Charts in the formative evaluation section of this book show data obtained by taking the same measurements over and over again. When there is a change in the total trend of the data, it is thought of as learning. But the variability, or bounce, which is seen in the data from one day to the next is only measurement error. Figure A.25 shows a chart of vowel sounds read per minute. On the chart the student's behavior was different on Tuesday than it was on Monday. This difference of 6 per minute does not mean that the student forgot three-fourths of what he had known the day before. In fact, the trend shows that he is consistently improving. The effect of measurement error can be minimized by giving a CRT several times and determining a trend.

One of the biggest sources of error in many published CRTs is that they don't sample enough student behavior. A test of ruler use for example, may have only four items in which the student compares a line to a ruler. Based upon how the student does on these few items the teacher must conclude if the student can or cannot measure with a ruler.

The confidence that can be placed in a test score is related to the number of items the student completes to get the score. Special education teachers will often say things like "Ed is a really unpredictable learner—one day he has it and the next day he doesn't." However, one explanation for Ed's peculiar learning has nothing to do with Ed. Suppose the teacher gives a four-item test which has a 75% criterion. Ed could pass or fail the test by getting only one additional problem right or wrong.

In Figure A.26, Ed passed the test on Monday and Tuesday but did not pass on Wednesday and Thursday. If the test items are specific

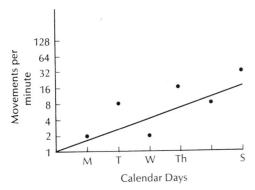

Figure A.25

Minimizing error by determining trend.

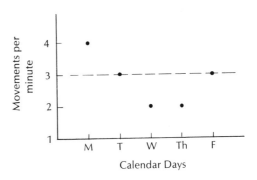

Figure A.26

Ed's scores on the ruler test.

enough to be educationally useful, then four of them are not enough to compensate for the usual daily score variability (measurement error). In other words, to say that Ed had it and lost it is wrong. He never had it at all. With so few items, the measurement error alone was enough to move him from passing to failing. In Figure A.27 a chart of addition facts is shown. If the criterion for addition facts is 50 per minute, then Ed has not really met criterion until the lower envelope line of his data has passed 50. Even though he first passed 50 on the 11th day, he has not really met criterion until the 15th day.

RELIABILITY. Several techniques have been suggested for determining the reliability of CRTs. These suggestions range both in complexity and

utility. Because so many of the CRTs in use today are teacher made, it is likely that two sets of procedures will evolve for determining reliability—one set of procedures to meet the accuracy requirements of researchers, another to meet the time requirements of the classroom.

The most important reliability issue for CRTs is internal consistency. If a CRT has only one objective all items must relate to that objective equally. The reliability of the test is dependent upon the consistency of the items. It has been suggested that variations of the Kuder-Richardson formula used to calculate internal consistency for NRTs be used for determining the reliability of CRTs (Schooley, Shultz, Donovan, & Lehman, 1975). However, the use of techniques which require variability in the test scores is being debated (Chas & Woodson, 1974;

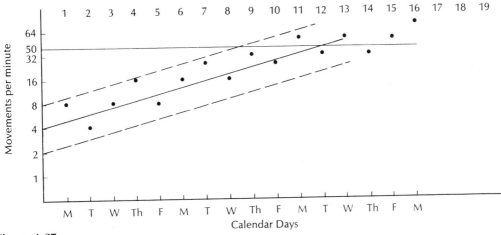

Figure A.27

Ed's addition facts.

Hambleton & Novik, 1973). At the heart of the issue is the fact that the CRT user isn't interested in discriminating between students. CRT items are not selected for the purpose of producing variability in scores. When variability is small (or restricted), reliability coefficients will be low, particularly if the standard statistical procedures are used to calculate them. Therefore, some standard statistical procedures underestimate the reliability of CRTs.

A second problem is that CRTs should be timed, or speeded. Depending upon the procedure used, time may either artificially inflate or deflate internal consistency. For example, when the split-half technique is used to calculate internal consistency the test is either divided by halves or by even and odd questions. If the halves are correlated on a timed test, it is likely that some students will not finish the test and the correlation will be low. If the odd and even items are correlated, the results may be misleadingly high because timing tends to equalize the behavior of test takers, thereby raising the correlation. The requirements for the reliability and validity of tests and test items are as follows:

Below   .50 = Unacceptable (throw it out)
Between   .50 and .90 = Somewhat Acceptable
Above   .90 = OK

Calculating Reliability

Two methods of estimating reliability are described in this section. The methods have been selected primarily for their ease of application.

METHOD 1. One simple technique for estimating the internal consistency of a CRT is to determine the percentage of agreement among the items (Becker & Englemann, 1976). This technique will be broken into three phases—A, B, and C.

The agreement between two items can be determined by following these steps:

Computational Steps, Phase A

Step 1.   Administer the items to a group of students.
Step 2.   Record the responses as seen in Table A.5, indicating for each student if the item is correct (1) or incorrect (0).
Step 3.   Count the number of students who got the same score on both items A and B.
Step 4.   Divide the number of students determined in Step 3 by the total number of students who took the test. $8 \div 10 = 80\%$.

Conclusion: There is 80% agreement between items A and B.

The agreement among all items can be calculated by following these steps.

Computational Steps, Phase B

Step 1.   Administer the items to a group of students.
Step 2.   List all possible item pairs. A-B, A-C, A-D, B-C, B-D, C-D.
Step 3.   Calculate the agreement between each pair.

$$A\text{-}B = \frac{8}{10} = 80\%$$

$$A\text{-}C = \frac{7}{10} = 70\%$$

$$A\text{-}D = \frac{9}{10} = 90\%$$

$$B\text{-}C = \frac{5}{10} = 50\%$$

$$B\text{-}D = \frac{7}{10} = 70\%$$

$$C\text{-}D \quad \frac{8}{10} = 80\%$$

Step 4.   Average together the percentages obtained in Step 3.

$$\frac{80 + 70 + 90 + 50 + 70 + 80}{6} = 73\%$$

Conclusion: There is 73% agreement among the items on the test.

The average agreement of each item can be calculated by following these steps.

Computational Steps, Phase C

Step 1.   Calculate the agreement for every possible combination of items.

A-B = 80%
A-C = 70%
A-D = 90%
B-C = 50%
B-D = 70%
C-D = 80%

Step 2.   List the total percentage of agreement for each item with every other item.

Item 1	Item 2
A-B = .80	A-B = .80
A-C = .70	B-C = .50
A-D = .90	B-D = .70
Total: 2.4	2
Item 3	Item 4
A-C = .70	A-D = .90
B-C = .50	B-D = .70
C-D = .80	C-D = .80
2	2.4

Step 3.   Divide each total in Step 2 by the number of items minus one ($N-1$) to find the average.

Item 1	Item 2
$\frac{2.4}{3} = 80\%$	$\frac{2}{3} = 67\%$
Item 3	Item 4
$\frac{2}{3} = 67\%$	$\frac{2.4}{3} = 80\%$

Conclusion: Items 2 and 3 need revision. If 2 and 3 are revised, items 1 and 4 would probably be raised. Therefore, there is no need to revise them yet.

Table A.5

Method One

		Items		
	A	B	C	D
1	1	1	1	1
2	1	0	1	1
3	1	1	1	1
4	0	0	0	0
5	1	1	0	1
6	0	0	1	1
7	1	1	1	1
8	1	1	0	1
9	1	1	1	1
10	1	0	1	1

Students (row label for students 1–10)

METHOD 2. A second technique is to administer the test to a group of students and then observe the results to see if any items stand out as being too hard or too easy. This technique can be used on NRTs and CRTs (Bloom, 1971).

Observational Steps

1. Administer the test to a group of students.
2. Record the responses as seen in Table A.6.
3. Sum up the number of items correct for each student, and the number of students who got each item correct. For example,
   student 5 got eight items correct.
   Item F was done correctly by nine students.
4. Observe the table for items which stand out as being too hard or too easy.
   Item C was missed by seven students.
   Item H was missed by no students.
5. Observe the table for items which do not seem to discriminate between high and low students.
   Item D was missed by both high-scoring and low-scoring students.

Validity of CRTs

The score on a CRT provides information as to the student's standing in relationship to a task. It tells if the student has received instruction at the task and if the student has mastered the task. The test score is valid to the degree that the information is accurate and usable. For CRTs the most important types of validity are concurrent and content validity. Concurrent validity exists when the test score accurately summarizes what the student can or cannot do at present. In order for a CRT to have instructional utility it also needs content validity. The CRT should be keyed to instruction by way of logically formulated objectives.

If a CRT is used to guide instruction, then a student can improve on the test as a result of instruction. Theoretically, a student won't learn multiplication facts without instruction (of some type) on multiplication facts. Because instruction changes a student's CRT score, the better the instruction, the greater will be the change. A CRT

Table A.6

Method Two

	Items										Student Total Correct
	A	B	C	D	E	F	G	H	I	J	
1	1	1	1	1	0	1	0	1	1	0	7
2	1	1	0	1	1	1	0	1	1	1	8
3	1	0	0	1	1	1	1	1	1	1	8
4	0	1	0	1	1	1	1	1	0	1	7
5	1	0	0	1	1	1	1	1	1	1	8
6	1	1	0	0	0	0	1	1	0	0	4
7	0	0	0	0	0	1	0	1	0	1	3
8	1	1	1	0	1	1	1	1	1	1	9
9	1	1	1	0	1	1	1	1	1	1	9
10	1	0	0	1	1	1	1	1	1	1	8
Item Total Correct	8	6	3	6	7	9	7	10	7	8	

Students (row label for students 1–10)

which is keyed to instruction can be proven valid if the instruction is carried out and if, as a result, the kid improves. For example, one of the subtasks of decoding is blending. One of the subtasks of blending is the ability to combine vowels plus *gh*. Among the teacher's reading objectives there should be one for the ability to combine vowels and *gh*. Once the teacher has a CRT to measure that skill and has identified lessons which teach it, a link has been established between the kid's test behavior and instructional materials. If the CRT is not keyed to appropriate materials, or if the CRT does not reliably measure the student's behavior, little improvement in future tests will take place. A method for determining the predictive validity of a CRT is presented in Chapter 13.

Calculating Validity

For any CRT there are two validity questions to be answered: (1) Does the test discriminate between preinstruction and postinstruction students? and (2) Does the test discriminate between masters and nonmasters of the task? These same two questions can be asked about each test item. Each question can be answered by using one of the methods shown in Figure A.28.

All methods for calculating the validity of CRTs make use of both pre- and posttest data. All four methods for determining validity incorporate an element of instruction. First, the test is given, then instruction takes place, then the test is given again. The effectiveness of the instruction will influence the validity of the test, just as the validity of the test should influence the effectiveness of instruction.

Test Validity Method 1 and Item Validity Method 1 compare pretest and posttest scores in order to contrast masters and nonmasters.

TEST VALIDITY METHOD 1. This method answers the question, How will does the test discriminate between students who have or have not had instruction at the task?

Formula: $1 - \left(\dfrac{\bar{x}_1}{\bar{x}_2}\right) = $ test validity

where $\bar{x}_1$ = mean pretest score
$\bar{x}_2$ = mean posttest score

Test Validity	**Item Validity**
Method 1	*Method 1*
$1 - \left(\dfrac{\bar{x}_1}{\bar{x}_2}\right) =$	A = Number of instructed students who got the item correct
$\bar{x}_1$ = Mean pretest score	B = Number of uninstructed students who got the item correct
$\bar{x}_2$ = Mean posttest score	$(A/N_1) - (B/N_2) =$
	N_1 = Number of instructed students
	N_2 = Number of uninstructed students
Method 2	*Method 2*
$\dfrac{(P_2 + F_1)}{N} =$	$(C/P) - (D/F) =$
F_1 = Uninstructed nonmasters	C = Number of masters who got the item correct
F_2 = Instructed nonmasters	D = Number of nonmasters who got the item correct
P_1 = Uninstructed masters	P = Number of masters
P_2 = Instructed masters	F = Number of nonmasters
$N = F_1 + F_2 + P_1 + P_2$	

Figure A.28
Test and item validity formulas.

Computational Steps (using data in Table A.7)

Step 1. Administer the test to a group of uninstructed students (pretest).

Step 2. Administer the test to a group of instructed students (posttest).

Step 3. Calculate the mean pretest score.

$$\bar{x}_1 = \frac{10}{8} = 1.25$$

Step 4. Calculate the mean posttest score.

$$\bar{x}_2 = \frac{33}{8} = 4.13$$

Step 5. Divide the number in Step 3 by the number in Step 4. $1.25 \div 4.13 = .30$.

Step 6. Subtract the number in Step 5 from the number 1. $1 - .30 = .70$.

Conclusion: Because .70 lies in the acceptable range, the test is sufficiently valid for the purpose of discriminating between uninstructed and instructed groups of students. In fact, if student 3 were excluded from the computation (because that student had met CAP on the pretest and therefore may have actually had instruction) the validity would be even higher.

ITEM VALIDITY METHOD 1. This method answers the question, How well do the individual test items discriminate between students who have or have not had instruction at the task? It is an adaptation of a technique by Brennan (1972) which has been proposed by Crehan (1974).

Formula: $(A/N_1) - (B/N_2)$ = Item validity

where A = Number of instructed students who got the item correct

B = Number of uninstructed students who got the item correct

N_1 = Number of instructed students

N_2 = Number of uninstructed students

Computational Steps (using data in Table A.7)

Step 1. Administer the test to a group of uninstructed students (pretest).

Step 2. Administer the test to a group of instructed students (posttest).

Step 3. Count the number of instructed students. 8.

Step 4. Count the number of uninstructed students. 8.

Step 5. Select an item. In this example use item C.

Step 6. Count how many of the students in the instructed group got item C correct. 8.

Step 7. Count how many students in the uninstructed group got item C correct. 3.

Table A.7

Data for Determining the Validity of a CRT

CAP = +4

		A	B	C	D	E	Student Totals
				Items			
	1	0	0	0	0	1	1
Uninstructed	2	0	0	0	0	0	0
Students	3	1	1	1	0	1	4
(pretest)	4	0	1	0	0	0	1
	5	0	0	0	0	0	0
	6	0	0	1	0	1	2
	7	0	0	0	0	1	1
	8	0	0	1	0	0	1
Item totals		1	2	3	0	4	Total pretest score = 10
							Mean pretest score = 1.25
	1	1	0	1	1	1	4
Instructed	2	1	1	1	1	0	4
Students	3	1	1	1	1	0	4
(posttest)	4	1	1	1	1	0	4
	5	1	0	1	1	0	3
	6	1	0	1	1	1	4
	7	1	1	1	1	1	5
	8	1	1	1	1	1	5
Item totals		8	5	8	8	4	Total posttest score = 33
							Mean posttest score = 4.13
Item validity Method 1		.87	.38	.62	1.00	0	
Item validity Method 2		.87	.62	.62	.75	.25	

Step 8. Divide the number obtained in Step 6 by the number obtained in Step 3. 8 ÷ 8 = 1.

Step 9. Divide the number obtained in Step 7 by the number obtained in Step 4. 3 ÷ 8 = .38.

Step 10. Subtract the number obtained in Step 9 from the number obtained in Step 8. 1 − .38 = .62.

Conclusion: This item is marginally valid for the purpose of discriminating between students who have or have not had instruction. The validity of each item has been calculated and listed in Table A.7. Of the five items, B and E should be omitted.

TEST VALIDITY METHOD 2. Test Validity Method 2 and Item Validity Method 2 both assume that CAP has been set for the test. Remember that CAP is determined by standardizing the test on a population of students who are successful at the task. If CAP has not been meaningfully determined, then these methods are useless. Ideally, the way to set CAP is to establish a cutting score below which the student won't progress successfully to the next task. For example, suppose subtask A is an essential subtask of task B. If CAP for subtask A is 80%, then a student who scores 70% on subtask A should not succeed at task B. (Because CAP is often situation and task specific the test maker is reminded to always report its source.)

Once CAP has been established, then those who score above it are said to have mastered the task. The validity of a CRT depends upon its ability to classify students as masters or nonmasters of the task (Hambleton & Novik, 1973). One way to summarize the test validity is by looking at the proportion of students which the test classifies as nonmasters before instruction and masters after instruction.

Test Validity Method 2 answers the question, How well does the test discriminate between instructed students who have or have not mastered the task? A procedure for answering this question has been described by Crehan (1974).

Formula: $\dfrac{(P_2 + F_1)}{N}$ = Test validity

where F_1 = Uninstructed nonmasters
F_2 = Instructed nonmasters
P_1 = Uninstructed masters
P_2 = Instructed masters
$N = F_1 + F_2 + P_1 + P_2$

Computational Steps (using data in Table A.7)

Step 1. Administer the test to a group of instructed students. Determine how many students are in the group. 8.

Step 2. Administer the test to a group of uninstructed students. Determine how many students are in the group. 8.

Step 3. Determine the number of uninstructed students who did not meet CAP. 7.

Step 4. Determine the number of instructed students who did meet CAP. 7.

Step 5. Add the numbers obtained in Steps 3 and 4. 7 + 7 = 14.

Step 6. Add the number in Step 1 to the number in Step 2. 8 + 8 = 16.

Step 7. Divide the number obtained in Step 5 by the number obtained in Step 6. 14 ÷ 16 = .88.

Conclusion: The validity of the test (its ability to discriminate masters from nonmasters) is acceptable.

One problem with all the procedures described here is that they do not tell how often similar results might be obtained by chance. (For a discussion of this issue the reader is referred to Swaminathan, Hambleton, and Algina, 1974).

ITEM VALIDITY METHOD 2. This method answers the question, How well do the individual test items discriminate between masters and nonmasters of the task?" This technique also assumes that a CAP level has been established for the test. The method described by Johnson (1951) and Brennan (1972) compares the proportion of students above CAP and below CAP to the number passing the item.

Formula: $(C/P) − (D/F)$ = Item validity

where C = Number of masters who get the item correct
D = Number of nonmasters who get the item correct
P = Number of masters
F = Number of nonmasters

Computational steps (using data in Table A.7)

Step 1. Administer the test to a group of students (this group can include both instructed and uninstructed students).

Step 2. Determine the number of students who have met CAP. 8.

Step 3. Determine how many students are below CAP. 8.

Step 4. Select an item. In this example use item C.

Step 5. Count how many of the students who met CAP got item C correct. 8.

Step 6. Count how many of the students who did not meet CAP got item C correct. 3.

Step 7. Divide the number in Step 5 by the number in Step 2. 8 ÷ 8 = 1.

Step 8. Divide the number in Step 6 by the number in Step 3. 3 ÷ 8 = .38.

Step 9. Subtract the number in Step 8 from the number in Step 7. 1 − .38 = .62.

Conclusion: Item C is acceptable but needs revision.

Practice Exercise

This exercise is for practice in calculating the reliability and validity of CRTs. Try following each of the procedures outlined previously. The list provided below should help you to recall each of the methods used to determine the reliability and validity of CRTs. Refer back to the appropriate pages to review the sequential order of computational steps to do each of the procedures. The raw data are supplied in Table A.8. All of the calculations will be done with both the pre- and posttest scores, therefore, $N = 20$.

Answers to the exercise follow Table A.8, and the results of the calculations are summarized in Table A.9.

Reliability: Method 1
     Computational Steps, Phases *A, B,* and *C*
Reliability: Method 2
     Observational Steps
Test Validity: Method 1
     Computational Steps
Item Validity: Method 1
     Computational Steps
Test Validity: Method 2
     Computational Steps
Item Validity: Method 2
     Computational Steps

Table A.8

Student Scores for Practice Computation

| | | Items | | | | | | | Total |
		A	B	C	D	E	F	G	Scores
Pretest									
	Blake	0	0	0	1	1	0	0	2
	Debbie	0	0	0	0	0	0	0	0
	Joe	0	0	1	0	0	0	0	1
	Marybeth	0	0	0	0	0	0	0	0
Students	Connie	0	0	1	0	0	0	0	1
	Kathi	0	0	0	0	0	0	0	0
	Mada Kay	1	1	0	1	1	1	1	6
	Ken	0	0	0	0	0	1	0	1
	Karna	0	0	0	0	0	0	0	0
	Win	0	0	0	0	0	0	0	0

Total pretest score = _____
Mean pretest score = _____

		A	B	C	D	E	F	G	
Posttest									
	Blake	1	1	0	1	1	1	1	6
	Debbie	1	1	1	1	1	0	1	6
	Joe	1	1	0	1	1	1	1	6
	Marybeth	1	1	1	1	1	1	1	7
Students	Connie	1	1	0	1	1	1	1	6
	Kathi	1	1	1	1	1	1	1	7
	Mada Kay	1	1	1	1	1	1	1	7
	Ken	1	1	0	1	1	1	1	6
	Karna	1	0	1	1	1	0	1	5
	Win	1	1	1	0	1	0	0	4

Total posttest score = _____
Mean posttest score = _____

Answers to Practice Exercise

Reliability
Method 2: Observing the data. It can be seen that item C is not a good item as many pretest students got it correct and many posttest students got it wrong. It can also be seen that student 7 scored well above the others on the pretest.

Test Validity Method 1
Step 3 = 1.1
Step 4 = 6
Step 5 = .18
Step 6 = .82
Conclusion = .82

Test Validity Method 2
Step 1 = 10
Step 2 = 10
Step 3 = 9
Step 4 = 8
Step 5 = 17
Step 6 = 20
Step 7 = .85
Conclusion = .85

Item Validity Method 1
(Only item F will be discussed here as an example.)
Step 3 = 10
Step 4 = 10
Step 5 = Item F
Step 6 = 9
Step 7 = 2
Step 8 = .9
Step 9 = .2
Step 10 = .7
Conclusion: = .70

Item Validity Method 2
(Item F only)
Step 2 = 9
Step 3 = 11
Step 4 = Item F
Step 5 = 9
Step 6 = 2
Step 7 = 1
Step 8 = .18
Step 9 = .82
Conclusion: = .82

Reliability
Method 1: Internal consistency (agreement among items)

Phase A

A–B $\frac{19}{20}$ = 95%	B–D $\frac{17}{20}$ = 85%	C–G $\frac{12}{20}$ = 60%
A–C $\frac{13}{20}$ = 65%	B–E $\frac{18}{20}$ = 90%	D–E $\frac{19}{20}$ = 95%
A–D $\frac{18}{20}$ = 90%	B–F $\frac{17}{20}$ = 85%	D–F $\frac{15}{20}$ = 75%
A–E $\frac{19}{20}$ = 95%	B–G $\frac{18}{20}$ = 90%	D–G $\frac{19}{20}$ = 95%
A–F $\frac{16}{20}$ = 80%	C–D $\frac{11}{20}$ = 55%	E–F $\frac{15}{20}$ = 75%
A–G $\frac{19}{20}$ = 95%	C–E $\frac{12}{20}$ = 60%	E–G $\frac{18}{20}$ = 90%
B–C $\frac{12}{20}$ = 60%	C–F $\frac{9}{20}$ = 45%	F–G $\frac{17}{20}$ = 85%

	Phase B
Percentage	Frequency

$95 \times 5 = 4.75$
$90 \times 4 = 3.6$
$85 \times 3 = 2.55$
$80 \times 1 = .80$
$75 \times 2 = 1.50$
$70 \times 0 = 0$
$65 \times 1 = .65$
$60 \times 3 = 1.80$
$55 \times 1 = .55$
Total 20   16.2

$$\frac{16.2}{20} = 81$$

Average Agreement = 81%

Phase C

Average Agreement of Item

A	= .87	E	= .84
B	= .84	F	= .74
C	= .58	G	= .86
D	= .83		

Table A.9

Summary of Computational Exercise

CAP = 6

Pretest		A	B	C	D	E	F	G	Total Scores
	1	0	0	0	1	1	0	0	2
	2	0	0	0	0	0	0	0	0
	3	0	0	1	0	0	0	0	1
Students	4	0	0	0	0	0	0	0	0
	5	0	0	1	0	0	0	0	1
	6	0	0	0	0	0	0	0	0
	7	1	1	0	1	1	1	1	6
	8	0	0	0	0	0	1	0	1
	9	0	0	0	0	0	0	0	0
	10	0	0	0	0	0	0	0	0
Item Totals		1	1	2	2	2	2	1	Mean pretest score = 1.1
Posttest	1	1	1	0	1	1	1	1	6
	2	1	1	1	1	0	1	1	6
	3	1	1	0	1	1	1	1	6
Students	4	1	1	1	1	1	1	1	7
	5	1	1	0	1	1	1	1	6
	6	1	1	1	1	1	1	1	7
	7	1	1	1	1	1	1	1	7
	8	1	1	0	1	1	1	1	6
	9	1	0	1	1	0	1	1	5
	10	1	1	1	0	1	0	0	4
Item Totals	10	9	6	9	8	9	9		Mean posttest score = 6

Table A.9 (cont)

Test Validity Method 1	.82						
Item Validity Method 2	.82	.91	.08	.82	.71	.82	.91
Test Validity Method 2	.85						
Item Validity Method 1	.90	.80	.40	.70	.60	.70	.80
Reliability (Average Agreement)	.87	.84	.58	.83	.84	.74	.86

Appendix B

Writing Performance Objectives

Subtask 1: able to name the three criteria for completeness.

Prerequisite: none.

According to Mager (1962), an instructional objective must include three components to be considered complete. These are listed below:

1. what the learner must do to demonstrate mastery of the task (e.g., "say the alphabet")
2. the conditions under which that behavior is expected to occur (e.g., "Given the directions, say the alphabet from memory")
3. the criteria for acceptable performance (e.g., "in 30 seconds with 100% accuracy")

Put together, the examples given above would read as follows: "Given the directions, 'Say the alphabet,' the learner will say the alphabet from memory in 30 seconds with 100% accuracy." This instructional objective is complete because it includes each of the three components described by Mager. The checkpoint for Subtask 1 follows.

Checkpoint

Subtask 1

List the three criteria for completeness in an instructional objective as cited by Mager (1962). You have 5 minutes in which to complete this checkpoint.

1.

2.

3.

To check your answers, review Subtask 1.

Subtask 2: identifies in writing the three criteria for completeness in an instructional objective.

Prerequisite: meets CAP for Subtask 1.

To be complete, an instructional objective must have three components (Mager, 1962). Read the following objective and the three components.

"The child will be asked to bounce a ball standing still without losing it for 30 seconds."

Behavior: "bounce a ball"
Conditions: "standing still"
                 "The child will be asked"
                 "for 30 seconds"
CAP: "without losing it"

Try the next objective by yourself without looking at the answers that follow.

"Given an objective test on task analysis, the student will write the correct answers to 80% of the questions in 30 minutes without the aid of reference material."

Behavior:

Conditions:

CAP:

Acceptable Responses

Behavior: "write the correct answers"
Conditions: "Given an objective test on task analysis"
                 "in 30 minutes"
                 "without the aid of reference material"
CAP: 80% of the questions"

The checkpoint for Subtask 2 follows.

Checkpoint

Subtask 2

Read each of the following instructional objectives and write the behavior, conditions, and CAP underneath each. You have 30 minutes to complete this checkpoint.

1. "The student shall be able to name the letters of the alphabet from memory when they are presented one at a time on flash cards with 100% accuracy in 2 minutes."

   Behavior:

   Conditions:

   CAP:

2. "The student will be given two lists of 10 words each, the second list will contain words opposite in meaning to the first list. The student will draw a line between the opposite words in the two lists with no more than two mistakes."

   Behavior:

   Conditions:

   CAP:

3. The student will be given a list of three-letter words, each containing the ā sound. The student will say the words correctly 10 out of 10 times in one minute.

Behavior:

Conditions:

CAP:

4. "Given five different colored scraps of paper, the student will paste each onto the correct spot over the written name of the color on a large sheet of paper with 100% accuracy."

Behavior:

Conditions:

CAP:

5. "A student will write the digits 1 to 10 from memory on a standard lined paper in no more than 5 minutes with 100% accuracy."

Behavior:

Conditions:

CAP:

6. "The student will, when presented with 20 pictures of the clock showing different times, correctly tell the time on 19 out of the 20 presented pictures."

Behavior:

Conditions:

CAP:

7. "Without the aid of a dictionary, each student will be able to arrange 25 words in alphabetical order with 100% accuracy."

Behavior:

Conditions:

CAP:

8. "Without a ruler, the learner can cut a strip of paper within ½-inch of 1 foot."

Behavior:

Conditions:

CAP:

9. "Given the names of 10 capital cities, the learner can identify with 90% accuracy the corresponding states."

    Behavior:

    Conditions:

    CAP:

10. "Given 10 written assignments with specific due dates, the student will put at least 8 of them on the teacher's desk on or before the stated deadline."

    Behavior:

    Conditions:

    CAP:

Acceptable Responses

1. *Behavior:* "name the letters of the alphabet"
   Conditions: "from memory when presented one at a time on flash cards"
   CAP: "with 100% accuracy in 2 minutes"

2. *Behavior:* "draw a line between the opposite words in the two lists"
   Conditions: "given two lists of 10 words each, the second list will contain words opposite in meaning to the first list"
   CAP: "with no more than two mistakes"

3. *Behavior:* "say the words correctly"
   Conditions: "given a list of three-letter words each containing the ă sound.
   CAP: "10 out of 10 times within one minute"

4. *Behavior:* "the student will paste each onto the correct spot over the written name of the color on a large sheet of paper"
   Conditions: "given five different colored scraps of paper"
   CAP: "with 100% accuracy"

5. *Behavior:* "will write digits 1 to 10"
   Conditions: "from memory"
   CAP: "in no more than 5 minutes with 100% accuracy"

6. *Behavior:* "tell the time"
   Conditions: "when presented with 20 pictures of the clock showing different times"
   CAP: "19 out of the 20"

7. *Behavior:* "arrange 25 words in alphabetical order"
   Conditions: "without the aid of a dictionary"
   CAP: "with 100% accuracy"

8. *Behavior:* "cut a strip of paper"
   Conditions: "without a ruler"
   CAP: "within ½-inch of 1 foot"

9. *Behavior:* "identify . . . the corresponding state"
   Conditions: "given the names of 10 capital cities"
   CAP: "with 100% accuracy"

10. *Behavior:* "put . . . them on the teacher's desk"
    Conditions: "given 10 written assignments with specific due dates"
    CAP: "at least 8 of them . . . on or before the stated deadline"

Subtask 3: recognizes instructional objectives that meet criteria for completeness.

Prerequisite: meets CAP for Subtasks 1 and 2.

To be complete, an instructional objective must include the three components cited by Mager. An example of a complete objective follows:

"Given a pencil and a piece of lined paper, the student will write his first name without help in 60 seconds. Each letter will be written correctly and appear in proper sequence."

This objective is complete because it contains the behavior, conditions, and CAP described by Mager. An example of an incomplete objective follows:

"The student will pronounce the names of the letters of the alphabet."

This objective is not complete because it only contains one of Mager's components—the behavior. It does not tell you how well the student will pronounce the letters of the alphabet (i.e., the CAP) or under what conditions. The checkpoint for Subtask 3 follows.

Checkpoint

Subtask 3

Read each of the following instructional objectives. Write "C" for complete if the objective includes all three of Mager's components and "I" for incomplete if it does not.

_____ 1. The pupil can spell 50 of the 60 words correctly.

_____ 2. Given a 12-inch ruler, the learner can draw lines at various lengths up to 12 inches—with exact inch and ½-inch intervals—at 90% accuracy.

_____ 3. Given a set of objects or pictures, the pupil knows the number of objects or pictures in the set.

_____ 4. Given no references, the learner will spell 18 of the 22 words correctly.

_____ 5. During a stated six-week period, the child will be seated at his desk when the A.M. tardy bell rings 95% of the school days.

_____ 6. When asked, the student will hop 10 times on one foot without having to touch the floor with the other foot.

_____ 7. Given a basketball, the learner will bounce it.

_____ 8. The learner will know the names of all 50 states.

_____ 9. Given a pair of scissors, the student will hold them properly.

_____ 10. Students will respect members of other races.

Acceptable Responses

1. I (no conditions)
2. C
3. I (no specified behavior; what is the pupil supposed to do?)
4. C
5. C
6. C

7. I (no CAP)
8. I (no conditions; no specified behavior)
9. I (no CAP; what does "properly" mean?)
10. I (no CAP; no conditions; no specified behavior)

Subtask 4: writes instructional objectives that meet criteria for completeness.

Prerequisite: meets CAP for Subtasks 1 through 3.

To write a complete objective, you must include:

1. the behavior you expect of the learner (i.e., what he must do to demonstrate mastery of the task).
2. the conditions under which that behavior is expected to occur.
3. the criterion for acceptable performance (CAP) or how well he must do what you want him to.

Looking at each of these separately may help in learning to write complete objectives.

1. *Behavior:* Try to use words that describe behavior, e.g., verbs like the ones listed below.

to write	to list
to point to	to answer
to recite	to construct
to mark	to trace
to identify	to label
to say	to draw
to solve	to cut
to repeat	

Do not use words that are open to many interpretations (e.g., to know, to understand, to appreciate, to enjoy, to grasp the significance of, to believe, to have faith in).

2. *Conditions:* These should give you more information regarding the actual operation. They should also describe what happens to the learner before he behaves in the prescribed manner. Two examples are "Given the directions" and "Provided with (name the materials)." Conditions should also describe what is happening while the learner behaves in the prescribed manner. Examples of this are "as the teacher shows him one flash card at a time," "performed while standing still," "as the teacher points to each," "from memory," and "without use of reference materials." Try to include as much information regarding conditions so that the reader will know more about how the behavior will occur.

3. *CAP:* Criterion for acceptable performance can be *time* and/or *accuracy.* That is, how many examples does the learner have to do correctly (e.g., 90% accuracy) and how much time is allowed. A third criterion might be frequency of responses (e.g., "bounces a ball 10 times"). CAP can be written in more descriptive terms (e.g., "without touching the floor with his raised foot" or "making all letters the same size").

The checkpoint for Subtask 4 follows.

Checkpoint

Subtask 4

Write a complete instructional objective for each of the following tasks and/or abilities. You have 30 minutes in which to complete the checkpoint.

1. bounces a ball

2. knows the alphabet

3. tells time

4. is on time for school

5. writes his name

6. understands concept of "opposite"

7. hops on one foot

8. completes assignments

9. is not afraid of animals

Acceptable Responses

These are merely suggestions. The reader should not consider her objectives wrong if they do not match word for word.

1. Given a 16-inch playground ball, the child will bounce it without moving his feet or losing contact with the ball for more than one bounce.
2. The student shall be able to name the letters of the alphabet when they are presented out of order and one at a time on flash cards with 100% accuracy in 2 minutes.
3. Given five faces of a clock with different times, the student will state orally the correct time with 100% accuracy in 2 minutes.
4. During a stated six-week period, the child will be seated at his desk when the A.M. tardy bell rings 95% of the school days.
5. Given a pencil and a sheet of lined paper, the student will write his name with no spelling mistakes and all letters properly formed within 5 minutes.
6. Given two lists of opposite words (10 words each), the student will draw a line between the opposite words in the two lists with no more than two mistakes.
7. The learner will hop on one foot (either left or right) keeping hands on hips and standing in an upright position for a distance of 20 feet without falling and without any balance aids.
8. Given a math assignment of 10 problems each for 5 consecutive days, the student will turn in each assignment completed each day without missing a day.
9. Given a class pet (e.g., hamster or guinea pig), the student will hold it without squeezing the animal for at least 60 seconds.

Subtask 5: able to describe the two criteria for relevancy.

Prerequisite: meets CAP for Subtasks 1 through 4.

To be relevant, an instructional objective must meet two criteria. First, the question, "If the learner emits the behavior described in the instructional objective, will I know if he has mastered the task?" should be answered with a Yes.

After reading the objective, the teacher should look at the task and see if the behavior described in the objective will tell her if the learner has mastered the task. An example of an irrelevant objective follows:

Task: skipping

Objective: "When directed, the learner will hop on alternate feet for a distance of 15 feet without losing his balance."

Question: "If the learner emits the behavior described in the instructional objective, will I know if he has mastered the task?"

Answer: No

This is not a relevant objective because the behavior described would not tell you if the learner could skip but whether or not he could hop on alternate feet. The behaviors are not the same. A second criterion for relevancy requires asking another question: "Am I requiring the learner to emit behavior(s) more complex than those required to demonstrate mastery of the task?" This should be answered with a No. An example of such an irrelevant objective follows:

Task: locating words in a dictionary

Objective: "Given 10 words, the student will look up each in the dictionary and use (i.e., write correctly) in a sentence. He will do this with 100% accuracy in 30 minutes."

Question: "Am I requiring the learner to emit behavior(s) more complex than those required to demonstrate mastery of the task?"

Answer: Yes

This is not a relevant objective because the behavior described requires skills you may not have taught the learner. The skills go beyond the task of locating words in the dictionary. The checkpoint for Subtask 5 follows.

Checkpoint
Subtask 5

Describe the two criteria for relevancy in an instructional objective. You have 5 minutes in which to complete this checkpoint.

1.

2.

To check your answers, review Subtask 5.

Subtask 6: recognizes instructional objectives that meet criteria for relevancy.

Prerequisite: met CAP for Subtasks 1 through 5.

For an objective to be relevant, it must meet two criteria. First the question, "If the learner emits the behavior described in the instructional objective, will I know if he has mastered the task?" must be answered with a yes. Second, the question "Am I requiring the learner to emit behavior(s) more complex than those required to demonstrate mastery of the task?" should be answered with a no.

   The following is an example of an objective that does not meet either of the two criteria for relevancy.

Task: locating words in the dictionary

Objective: "Given 10 words, the learner will correctly use (i.e., write) each in a sentence in 20 minutes with 100% accuracy."

Question 1: "If the learner emits the behavior described in the instructional objective, will I know if he has mastered the task?"

Answer: No. Even if the kid writes 10 beautiful sentences, the teacher would still not know if the learner was proficient at looking up words in the dictionary.

Question 2: "Am I requiring the learner to emit behavior(s) more complex than those required to demonstrate mastery of the task?"

Answer: Yes. Writing words in a sentence which indicates you know the meaning of that word requires skills above and beyond those involved in locating those words in a dictionary.

The following is an example of an objective that meets one of the criteria for relevancy.

Task: locating words in the dictionary

Objective: "Given 10 words, the learner will write them in alphabetical order in 5 minutes with 100% accuracy."

Question 1: "If the learner emits the behavior described in the instructional objective will I know if he has mastered the task?"

Answer: No. Even if the kid lists the cards in alphabetical order (meeting the CAP in the objective), the teacher will still not know if he is proficient at looking up words in the dictionary.

Question 2: "Am I requiring the learner to emit behavior(s) more complex than those required to demonstrate mastery of the task?"

Answer: No. Writing words in alphabetical order is a prerequisite to locating them in the dictionary.

The following is an example of an objective that meets both of the criteria for relevancy.

Task: locating words in the dictionary

Objective: "Given 10 words, the learner will write the number of the page each word appears on in the dictionary. He will write the page number next to the word completing the assignment in 20 minutes with 100% accuracy."

Question 1: "If the learner emits the behavior described in the instructional objective, will I know if he has mastered the task?"

Answer: Yes.

Question 2: "Am I requiring the learner to emit behavior(s) more complex than those required to demonstrate mastery of the task?"

Answer: No.

The checkpoint for Subtask 6 follows.

Checkpoint

Subtask 6

Label each of the following objectives "R" for relevant or "IR" for irrelevant. You have 10 minutes to complete this checkpoint.

1. *Task:* bounces a ball
   _____ *Objective:* "Given a 16-inch playground ball, the learner will throw it against a wall and catch it 10 times without dropping the ball."

2. *Task:* using (i.e., typing on) a typewriter
   _____ *Objective:* "Given a manual portable typewriter, the learner will disassemble it in 60 minutes without aid."

3. *Task:* knows concept "red"
   _____ *Objective:* "Given 25 assorted colors of cards (red, blue, green) on a table, the learner will correctly point to the red cards with 100% accuracy in 30 seconds."

4. *Task:* ties shoes
   _____ *Objective:* "The learner will tie his shoes every morning without aid for one week. He will take no more than 5 minutes to do this and the tie will be done correctly (i.e., double bow, single knot)."

5. *Task:* rides a bike
   _____ *Objective:* "Given a two-wheel bicycle, the learner will ride it a distance of 100 yards without touching the handlebars. He will not fall or stop the bicycle until he has covered the specified distance."

6. *Task:* knows concepts "right and left"
   _____ *Objective:* "Given a page with the letters *b* and *d* the learner will say the sound each letter makes with 80% accuracy in 1 minute."

7. *Task:* writes his name
_____ *Objective:* "Given alphabet cards in random order, the learner will sequence the cards so that they correctly spell his name. He will do this
in 60 seconds."

8. *Task:* tells time
_____ *Objective:* "Given the faces of 10 clocks showing different times, the
student will point to each and say the time with 80% accuracy in 60
seconds."

9. *Task:* knows the concept "opposite"
_____ *Objective:* "Given the word, the learner will locate its opposite in the
dictionary. He will do this for 10 words in 20 minutes with 100% accuracy."

Acceptable Responses

1. IR   6. IR
2. IR   7. IR
3. R   8. R
4. R   9. IR
5. IR

Subtask 7: writes instructional objectives that meet criteria for relevancy.

Prerequisite: meets CAP for Subtasks 1 through 6.

For an objective to be relevant, it must meet two criteria. First the question, "If the learner emits the behavior described in the instructional objective, will I know if he has mastered the task?" must be answered with a yes. Second, the question, "Am I requiring the learner to emit behavior(s) more complex than those required to demonstrate mastery of the task?" should be answered with a no.

Checkpoint

Subtask 7

Write instructional objectives for each of the following tasks and/or abilities. Make sure that they are relevant by asking (and answering) the two questions after you have written each objective.

1. *Task:* skips

   Objective:

2. *Task:* is polite

   Objective:

3. *Task:* knows number facts (addition)

   Objective:

4. *Task:* is responsible with the property of others

   Objective:

5. *Task:* can do long division

   Objective:

6. *Task:* knows concepts of directionality (e.g., up, down, right, left, etc.)

   Objective:

7. *Task:* is punctual

   Objective:

8. *Task:* brushes teeth

   Objective:

9. *Task:* hops on one foot

   Objective:

10. *Task:* makes change

    Objective:

Check your answers with your instructor after you have completed this check-point.

Glossary

Ability Training. Treatment which attempts to change cognitive or perceptual characteristics of the student.

Aim. An objective expressed in terms of proficiency rate and a target date.

Aptitude Treatment Interaction (ATI). The belief that individuals with certain abilities will behave differently in certain treatments than individuals who lack the abilities.

Arithmetic Charts. A graphic recording system whose value is related to the type of data collected and the minimization of visual misrepresentation.

Automatic Response. Response performed at a high rate with distractions present.

Best Fit Line. A line drawn through a set of data that best represents both the central tendency of the data and changes in data patterns.

Catch-up Slope. 'Celeration that is greater than the previous average.

'Celeration. A line drawn through data to represent changes in responding.

'Celeration Change. Comparison of 'celeration between two phases of instruction.

Classification. The evaluative process of labeling or naming things in order to facilitate communication and understanding.

Clinical Teaching. "An alternating test–teach–test–teach process" (Lerner, 1971, p. 103).

Correlation. The relationship between two measures of student behavior (not necessarily a causative relationship).

Correlation Coefficient. A fraction falling between + 1 and − 1, usually labeled *r*.

Criterion-Referenced Testing. Evaluation that compares an individual's behavior to an objective performance standard or criterion.

Date-Determined 'Celeration. 'Celeration calculated by a line drawn from the data median to the minimal aim.

Day Lines. Vertical lines on the semilogarithmic chart.

Desired Rate. Equals mastery rate on task divided by mastery rate on basic movement cycle times the child's rate on basic movement cycle.

Diagnosis (educational diagnosis). A form of evaluation that collects data—causally related to the future performance of a specific individual on a specific task. Diagnosis guides instruction.

Diagnostic-Prescriptive Teaching. A method utilizing diagnostic information for the modification of educational programs (Peter, 1965, p. 1).

Diagnostic Teaching. A system of developing educational plans based on diagnostic data obtained.

Direct Evaluation. Evaluation that measures the performance of students in the materials that they are using.

Directive Teaching. "A system of instruction that aids those who teach...to be effective in academic instruction while simultaneously responding to the student's social behavior" (Stephens, 1970, p. 109).

Dynamic Data. Data that describe performance over a period of time.

Envelope. Best fit lines drawn to incorporate the range of responding.

Errorless Acquisition. Learning a skill with a minimum number of errors.

Evaluation. The process by which investigators come to understand things and by which they attach relative value to things; including comparison.

F-AC-T (sheet). Used to summarize a task analytical evaluation.

Fair Pair Criteria. The practice of including an equal number of acceleration and deceleration targets.

Fluency Building. Correct responses continue to increase, but not as sharply as in acquisition.

Formative Evaluation. Evaluation that occurs as skills are being developed.

Frequency Data. The number of times a behavior occurs.

Frequency Lines. Horizontal lines on the semilogarithmic chart.

Frequent Evaluation. Ongoing or continuous assessment (daily if at all possible).

Generalization. A skill learned in one environment or under one condition is used under new conditions or in a new environment.

Intermediate Aim. Established by placing a small "A" on the 'celeration line one to two weeks from the initial date.

Is-Does Plan. The precision teaching lesson plan that indicates events before responding, the behavior recorded, and events after responding.

Labeling. A classification process. Not useful in diagnosis.

Learning. Changes in performance over time.

Learning Matrices. A system of criterion-referenced testing and recording in a fashion that allows for visual representation of progress.

Maintenance. Continued mastery of a skill.

Management by Objectives. A strategy of planning and getting results in the direction that management wishes and needs to take while meeting goals and satisfaction of its participants (Mali, 1977, p. 1).

Mastery. The student has reached his aim.

Mean. The average score; a measure of central tendency.

Measurement. The assignment of numerals to objects or events according to rules (Campbell, 1940).

Median. The middle-most score; a measure of central tendency.

Median Slope. A 'celeration line that is drawn by connecting median intersections of both halves of the data (White, 1972).

Minimal Aim. Proficiency rate, minimal criterion for mastery.

Minimal Criterion for Acceptable Performance. The lowest score of individuals who possess the skill being measured.

Minimum 'Celeration. The minimal amount of change considered acceptable; calculated by comparing current rate to the minimal aim rate.

Mode. The most frequent score; a measure of central tendency.

Narrative Log. A written record of comments.

Net Effect. A comparison of rate on the last data day to the extended 'celeration line from the previous phase.

No-Effect Point. The intersection of a projected 'celeration line from the previous phase with the celeration line of the intervention phase. Identifies the point at which the intervention is causing zero effect.

Norm-Referenced Test. An evaluation that compares an individual's behavior to the behavior of others.

Percentage. Number correct divided by the total possible correct.

Performance. A measure of behavior taken on one occasion.

Precision Teaching. An evaluative system that summarizes changes in performance over time through direct and daily measurement of behaviors.

Precision Teaching Attitude. Evaluation is best used when the teacher wants to gain information and desires to apply technology as an aid to decision making.

Probe. A criterion-referenced test.

Proficiency. Criterion level necessary for student to satisfactorily perform next skill in skill sequence.

Prognosis. Prediction.

Proportionate Scale. A scale that measures growth in a multiplicative fashion and more accurately indicates rate of improvement.

Psychoeducational Evaluation. Assessment of processing abilities (also referred to as psychomedical evaluation).

Psychoeducational Evaluation Philosophy. If the pupil hasn't learned, there must be something wrong with him.

Rate. The number of responses divided by the time the behavior was observed.

Raw Score. The number of responses.

Reliability. How consistently a test measures the same thing.

Six-Cycle Chart. A semilogarithmic chart that is standardized and can record 20 weeks of data; used with precision teaching.

Standard 'Celeration. 'Celeration of ×1.25.

Standard Error of Measurement. A boundary of confidence that can be placed around a test score. Standard error is calculated from the standard deviation and reliability of the test.

Standardization of Criterion-Referenced Tests. Process of testing age-mates who possess the skill to establish criteria.

Static Data. Data that describe performance at only one time.

Step Change. The immediate effects of a phase change.

Subtask. An essential component of a task which, when mastered, enables the learner to successfully perform the task.

Summative Evaluation. Evaluation that takes place at the end of a unit or section of instruction.

Task. Any behavior or set of behaviors.

Task Analysis. The process of isolating, sequencing, and describing the essential components of a task.

Task Analytical Model. Diagnosing a child's learning problem by applying the cycle of fact finding, task analyzing, hypothesizing, and validating.

Task Analytical Philosophy. If the child hasn't learned, there must be something wrong with the way he was taught.

Terminal Objective. A performance objective that describes the behavior required of the learner at the end of a period of instruction.

Testing. A process to determine how a child functions in reality by asking him to perform a selected sample of behaviors.

Traditional Acquisition. Learning a skill through reduction in the number of errors.

Validity. How well a test describes reality. Does the test measure what it's supposed to measure?

Bibliography

Adams, J.L. *Conceptual blockbusting.* San Francisco: W.H. Freeman & Co., 1974.

American Psychological Association. *Standards for educational and psychological tests.* Washington, D.C.: Author, 1974.

Bateman, B.D. Educational implications of minimal brain dysfunction. Paper presented at conference on Minimal Brain Dysfunction, New York Academy of Sciences, N.Y. March 20-22, 1972.

Bateman, B.D. The efficacy of an auditory and visual method of first grade reading instruction with auditory and visual learners. In H. Smith (Ed.), *Perception and reading.* Newark, Del.: International Reading Association, 1968.

Bateman, B.D. *Essentials of teaching.* Sioux Falls, S. Dak.: Dimension Publishing, a division of Adapt Press, 1971. (a)

Bateman, B.D. *Learning disorders* (Vol. 2). Seattle, Wash.: Special Child Publications, 1971. (b)

Baumeister, A.A., & Muma, J.R. On defining mental retardation. *The Journal of Special Education,* 1975, **9,** 293–306.

Becker, W.C., & Engelmann, S. Achievement gains of disadvantaged children with IQs under 80 in Follow Through. Technical Report, 74-2. Eugene, Oreg.: University of Oregon Follow Through Project, October, 1974.

Becker, W.C., & Engelmann, S. *Teaching 3: Evaluation of Instruction.* Chicago: Science Research Associates, 1976.

Beery, K. *Developmental test of visual-motor integration.* Chicago: Follett, 1967.

Berliner, D.C., & Cahen, L.S. Trait treatment interaction and learning. In F.N. Kerlinger (Ed.), *Review of research in education* (Vol. 1). Ithaca, N.Y.: Peacock, 1973.

Berlyne, D.E. *Conflict, arousal, and curiosity.* New York: McGraw-Hill, 1960.

Blanton, R.L. Historical perspectives on classification of mental retardation. In N. Hobbs (Ed.), *Issues in the classification of children.* San Francisco: Jossey-Bass Publishers, 1975.

Bloom, B.S., Hastings, J.T., & Madaus, G.F. *Handbook of formative and summative evaluation of student learning.* New York: McGraw-Hill, 1971.

Boulding, K. The schooling industry as a possible pathological section of the American economy. *Review of Educational Research,* 1972, **42,** 129–143.

Bracht, G.H. Experimental factors relating to aptitude treatment interactions. *Review of Educational Research,* 1970, **40,** 627–645.

Bracht, G.H. *The relationship of treatment tasks, personological variables, and dependent variables to aptitude treatment interactions* (Doctoral dissertation, University of Colorado, 1969). *Dissertation Abstracts International,* 1970, **30 A,** 4268. (University Microfilms No. 70-5820, 215)

Brennan, R.L. A generalized upper-lower item discrimination index. *Educational and Psychological Measurement,* 1972, **32,** 280–303.

Broadbent, D.E. The hidden preattentive process. *American Psychologist,* 1977, **32,** 109-118.

Brophy, J.E., & Good, T.L. *Teacher-student relationships.* New York: Holt, Rinehart & Winston, 1974.

Bruning, J.L., & Kintz, B.L. *Computational handbook of statistics*. Glenview, Ill.: Scott Foresman & Co., 1968.

Buros, K. (Ed.). *The seventh mental measurements yearbook* (Vol. 1). Highland Park, N.J.: Gryphon Press, 1972.

Campbell, N.R. *Final report, Committee of the British Association for Advancement of Science on the problem of measurement*. London: British Association, 1940.

Carnine, D.W. Effects of two teacher presentation rates on off-task behavior, answering correctly, and participation. *Journal of Applied Behavioral Analysis*, 1976, **9**, 199–206.

Chall, J.S. *Learning to read: The great debate*. New York: McGraw-Hill, 1967.

Chas, M.I., & Woodson, E. The issue of item and test variance for criterion-referenced tests. *Journal of Educational Measurement*, 1974, **11**, 63–64.

Crehan, K.D. Item analysis for teacher-made mastery tests. *Journal of Educational Measurement*, 1974, **4**, 255–262.

Cromwell, R.L., Blashfield, R.K., & Strauss, J.S. Criteria for classification systems. In N. Hobbs (Ed.), *Issues in the classification of children*. San Francisco: Jossey-Bass Publishers, 1975.

Cronbach, L.J. *Essentials of psychological testing*. New York: Harper & Row, 1960.

Cronbach, L.J. How can instruction be adapted to individual differences? In R. M. Gagne (Ed.), *Learning and individual differences*. Columbus, Ohio: Charles E. Merrill Publishing Co., 1967.

Cronbach, L.J. The two disciplines of scientific psychology. *American Psychologist*, 1957, **12**, 671–684.

Cronbach, L.J., & Furby, L. How we should measure 'change'—or should we? *Psychological Bulletin*, 1970, **74**, 68–80.

Cronbach, L.J., & Snow, R.E. Final report: Individual differences in learning ability as a function of instructional variables. Stanford, Calif.: Stanford University, March 1969.

Davis, I.K. *Competency based learning: Technology, management and design*. New York: McGraw-Hill, 1973.

Deno, E. Some reflections on the use and interpretation of tests for teachers. *Focus of Exceptional Children*, 1971, **2**(8), 1–11.

Diana v. State Board of Education. Civil Action No. C–70 37RFP (N.D. Cal. January 7, 1970 and June 18, 1973).

Dick, W., & Hagerty, N. *Topics in measurement: Reliability and validity*. New York: McGraw-Hill, 1971.

Diederich, P.B. Pinhead statistics. In F.T. Wilhelms (Ed.), *Evaluation as feedback and guide*. Washington, D.C.: National Education Association, 1967.

Dolch, E.W., & Bloomster, M. Phonic readiness. *The Elementary School Journal*, 1937, **38**, 201–205.

Doll, E.A. *Measurement of social competence*. Circle Pines, Minn.: American Guidance Service, 1953.

Dunn, L.M. Special education for the mildly retarded: Is much of it justified? *Exceptional Children*, 1968, **35**, 5–22.

Dunn, R., & Dunn, K. Learning style as a criterion for placement in alternative programs. *Phi Delta Kappan*, December 1974, 275–278.

Eaton, M.D., & Lovitt, T.C. Achievement tests vs. direct and daily measurement. In G. Semb (Ed.), *Behavior analysis and education – 1972*. Lawrence, Kans.: University of Kansas Press, 1972.

Ebel, R.L. Educational tests: Valid? biased? useful? *Phi Delta Kappan*, October 1975, 83–88.

Fernald, G.M. *Remedial techniques in basic school subjects*. New York: McGraw-Hill, 1943.

Filler, J.W., Robinson, C.C., Smith, R.A., Vincent-Smith, L.J., Bricker, D.D., & Bricker, W.A. Mental retardation. In N. Hobbs (Ed.), *Issues in the classification of children*. San Francisco: Jossey-Bass Publishers, 1975.

Freeman, R.D. Special education and the electroencephalogram: Marriage of convenience. *The Journal of Special Education*, 1967, **2**, 61–73.

Galton, F. *Inquiries into human faculty and its development*. London: J.M. Dent & Co., 1883.

Glaser, R. Individuals and learning: The new aptitudes. *Educational Researcher*, 1972, **1**, 5–12.

Glass, G.V. Excellence: A paradox. Speech presented at the second annual meeting of the Pacific Northwest Research and Evaluation Conference sponsored by the Washington Educational Research Association, May 24, 1974. (a)

Glass, G.V. Teacher effectiveness. In H.J. Walberg (Ed.), *Evaluating educational performance.* Berkeley: McCutchan Publishing Corp., 1974. (b)

Goldstein, K. *After effects of brain injuries in war.* New York: Grune & Stratton, 1942.

Guilford, J.P. *Fundamental statistics in psychology and education.* New York: McGraw-Hill, 1965.

Hambleton, R.K., & Novik, M. Toward an integration of theory and method for criterion-referenced tests. *Journal of Educational Measurement,* 1973, **10,** 159–170.

Hammill, D.D. Paper presented at 2nd annual conference on Humanistic Behavior Modification, Las Vegas, March 1976.

Hammill, D.D., & Larsen, S.C. The effectiveness of psycholinguistic training. *Exceptional Children,* 1974, **41**(9), 455–459. (a)

Hammill, D.D., & Larsen, S.C. The relationship of selected auditory perceptual skills and reading ability. *Journal of Learning Disabilities,* 1974, **7,** 429–435. (b)

Hammill, D.D., & Wiederholt, J.L. *The resource room: Rationale and implementation.* Philadelphia: Buttonwood Farms, 1972.

Haring, N.G., & Bateman, B.D. *Teaching the learning disabled child.* Englewood Cliffs, N.J.: Prentice-Hall, 1977.

Haring, N.G., & Brown, L. *Teaching the severely handicapped* (Vol. 1). New York: Grune & Stratton, 1976.

Haring, N.G., & Schiefelbusch, R.L. (Eds.). *Teaching special children.* New York: McGraw-Hill, 1976.

Heber, R., Garber, H., Harrington, S., Hoffman, C., & Falender, C. *Rehabilitation of families at high risk for mental retardation.* Progress report. Rehabilitation Research and Training Center in Mental Retardation. Madison: University of Wisconsin, 1972.

Heidbreder, E. *Seven psychologies.* New York: Appleton-Century-Crofts, 1961.

Hobson v. Hanson, 269F, Supp. 401, 1967.

Hoephner, R. Published tests and the needs of educational accountability. *Educational and Psylogical Measurement,* 1974, **34,** 103–109.

Holland, J., Solomon, C., Doran, J., & Frezza, D. *The analysis of behavior in planning instruc-*tion. Menlo Park, Calif.: Addison-Wesley, 1976.

Hunt, E., & Lansman, M. Cognitive theory applied to individual differences. In W.K. Estes (Ed.), *Handbook of learning and cognitive processes* (Vol. 1). New York: Lawrence Erlbaum Associates, Publishers, 1975.

Intermediate School District No. III, 5601 Sixth Ave., Tacoma, Washington 98406. Progress Report IV of the State of Washington Child Service Demonstration Program. Tacoma, Wash.: Author, 1974.

Jastek, J.F., Bijou, S.W., & Jastek, S.R. *Wide-range achievement test.* Wilmington, Del.: Guidance Associates of Delaware, Inc., 1965.

Johnson, A.P. Notes on a suggestedndex of item validity: The U-L index. *Journal of Educational Psychology,* 1951, **42,** 499–504.

Kaplan, A. *The conduct of inquiry: Methodology for behavioral science.* New York: Chandler Publishing, 1964.

Kauffman, A.S. A new approach to the interpretation of the test scatter on the WISC–R. *Journal of Learning Disabilities,* 1976, **9,** 160–168.

Kelley, T. *Interpretation of educational measurements.* Yonkers, N.Y.: World Book, 1927.

Kephart, N.C. *The slow learner in the classroom* (2nd ed.). Columbus, Ohio: Charles E. Merrill Publishing Co., 1971.

Kirk, S.A. *Educating exceptional children,* Boston: Houghton Mifflin, 1972.

Kirk, S.A., McCarthy, J.J., & Kirk, W.D. *Illinois test of psycholinguistic abilities (experimental edition).* Urbana: University of Illinois Press, 1971.

Korzybski, A. *Science and sanity: An introduction to non-Aristotelian systems and general semantics* (3rd ed.). Lakeville, Conn.: Institute of General Semantics, 1948.

Kunzelmann, H.P. (Ed.), with Cohen, M.A., Hulten, W.J., Martin, G.I., & Mingo, A.R. *Precision teaching: An initial training sequence.* Seattle: Special Child Publications, 1970.

Lennon, R.T. What can be measured? *The Reading Teacher,* 1962, **5,** 326–327.

Lerner, J.N. *Children with learning disabilities: Theories, diagrams, and teaching strategies.* Boston: Houghton Mifflin, 1971.

Liberty, K.A. *Data decision rules.* Working paper no. 20, Experimental Education Unit, Child Development and Mental Retardation Center, University of Washington, Seattle, 1975.

Lindsley, O. Personal communication, March 1976.

Mali, P. *Managing by objective.* New York: Wiley of Interscience, Division of John Wiley & Sons, 1977.

Mann, L. Psychometric phrenology and the new faculty psychology: The case against ability assessment and training. *Journal of Special Education,* 1975, **9,** 261–268.

May, D. Personal communication, April 1975.

Mendenhall, W. & Ramey, M. *Statistics for psychology.* North Scituate, Mass.: Duxbury Press, 1973.

Mercer, C.D., Forgnone, C., & Wolking, W.D. Definitions of learning disabilities used in the United States. *Journal of Learning Disabilities,* 1976, **9,** 376–386.

Mercer, J.R. Crosscultural evaluation of exceptionality. *Focus on Exceptional Children,* 1973, **5**(4), 8–15.

Mills, R.E. *Learning methods test.* Fort Lauderdale, Fla.: The Mills School, 1955.

Myers, P.I., & Hammill, D.D. *Methods for learning disorders.* New York: John Wiley & Sons, 1969.

Nelson, K. Personal communication, July 1976.

O'Connell, C., & McManman, K. *Charting and precision teaching: Adult acquisition rates.* Working Paper No. 14, Arizona State University, Tempe, Arizona, 1977.

Odiorne, G. *Management by objectives.* New York: Pitman Publishing Co., 1965.

Orton, J.L. The Orton-Gillingham approach. In J. Money (Ed.), *The disabled reader.* Baltimore: Johns Hopkins University Press, 1966.

Osgood, C.E. *Method and theory in experimental psychology.* New York: Oxford Press, 1953.

Osgood, C.E. A behavioristic analysis of perception and language as cognitive phenomena. In J.S. Bruner (Ed.), *Contemporary approaches to cognition.* Cambridge: Harvard University Press, 1957.

Paraskevopoulos, J., & Kirk, S.A. *The development and psychometric characteristics of the revised Illinois test of psycholinguistic abilities.* Urbana: University of Illinois Press, 1969.

Pennsylvania Association For Retarded Children v. Commonwealth of Pennsylvania. 334 F. Supp. 1257 (E.D. Pa. 1971).

Peter, L. *Prescriptive teaching.* New York: McGraw-Hill, 1965.

Popham, W.J., & Husek, T.R. Implications of criterion-referenced measurement. *Journal of Educational Measurement,* 1969, **6,** 1–9.

Prehm, H.J., & Goldschmidt, S. *Mainstreaming handicapped children and related legal implications.* Eugene, Oreg.: Oregon School Study Council, 1975.

Quay, H.C. Assumptions, techniques and evaluative criteria. *Exceptional Children,* 1973, **40,** 165–170.

Repp, A., Deitz, D., Boles, S., Deitz, S., & Repp, C. Differences among common methods for calculating interobserver agreement. *Journal of Applied Behavior Analysis,* Spring 1976, **9,** 109–113.

Reynolds, M.C., & Balow, B. Categories and variables in special education. *Exceptional Children,* 1972, **38,** 357–366.

Rhetts, J.E. Task, learner, and treatment variables in instructional design. *Journal of Educational Psychology,* 1974, **66,** 339–347.

Rosenshine, B. Classroom instruction. In N.L. Gage (Ed.), *Psychology of teaching: The 77th yearbook of the National Society for the Study of Education.* Chicago: National Society for the Study of Education, 1976.

Rosenthal, R., & Jacobsen, L. *Pygmalion in the classroom.* New York: Holt, Rinehart & Winston, 1968.

Ross, A.O. *Psychological aspects of learning disabilities and reading disorders.* New York: McGraw-Hill, 1976.

Salomon, G. Heuristic models for the generation of aptitude-treatment interaction hypotheses. *Review of Educational Research,* 1972, **42,** 327–343.

Schooley, D.E., Schultz, D.W., Donovan, D.L., & Lehman, I.J. *Quality control for evaluation systems based on objective-referenced tests.* Working paper, Department of Education, Lansing, Michigan, 1975.

Shulman, L.S. Reconstruction of educational research. *Review of Educational Research,* 1970, **40,** 371–397.

Spache, G. A critical analysis of various methods of classifying spelling errors. *Journal of Educational Psychology,* 1940, **31**, 11–34.

Stallings, J.A., & Kascovitz, D.H. *Follow through classroom observation evaluation (1972–1973).* Menlo Park, Calif.: Stanford Research Institute, 1974.

Starlin, C. *Evaluating progress towards reading proficiency.* In B. D. Bateman (Ed.), *Learning disorders* (Vol. 2). Seattle: Special Child Publications, 1971.

Stephens, T. *Directive teaching of children with learning and behavioral handicaps.* Columbus, Ohio: Charles E. Merrill Publishing Co., 1970.

Stephens, T. *Teaching skills to children with learning and behavior disorders.* Columbus, Ohio: Charles E. Merrill Publishing Co., 1977.

Sullivan, J. Personal communication, January 1977.

Swaminathan, H., Hambleton, R.K., & Algina, J. Reliability of criterion-referenced tests: Decision-theoretic formulation. *Journal of Educational Measurement,* 1974, **11**, 263–267.

Tallmadge, G.K., & Horst, D.P. *A procedural guide for validating achievement gains in educational projects.* Washington, D.C.: U.S. Department of Health, Education and Welfare, Office of Education, 1974.

Tannenbaum, A., & Cohen, S.A. *Taxonomy of instructional treatments.* (Final Report, U.S.O.E. No. G-1-6-062528-2092: Development and demonstration of a self-instruction reading and mathematics program for emotionally disturbed boys) Washington, D.C.: U.S. Office of Education, 1967.

Thorndike, E.L. *Education: A first book.* New York: Macmillan, 1917.

Thorndike, R.L., & Hagan, E. *Measurement and evaluation in psychology and education* (3rd ed.). New York: John Wiley & Sons, 1969.

Tittle, K.R. Wechsler intelligence scales for children — revised. *Journal of Educational Measurement,* 1975, **12**, 140–143.

Tobias, S. Achievement treatment interactions. *Review of Educational Research,* 1976, **46**, 61–74.

Waugh, R.P. The I.T.P.A.: Ballast or bonanza for the school psychologist? *Journal of School Psychology,* 1975, **13**, 201–208.

Waugh, R.P. *Stability of modality preference over a six-month and twenty-six-month period.* Unpublished doctoral dissertation, University of Oregon, 1971.

Waugh, R.P., & Howell, K.W. Teaching modern syllabication. *The Reading Teacher,* 1975, **29** (1), 20–25.

Webster's Third International Dictionary. Springfield, Mass.: G. & C. Merriam Co., 1971.

Wepman, J.M. Auditory discrimination in speech and reading. *The Elementary School Journal,* 1960, **60**, 325–333.

Wepman, J.M. *Auditory discrimination test.* Chicago: Language Research Associates, 1958.

White, O.R. *A manual for the calculation and use of the median slope – A technique of progress estimation and prediction in the single case.* Working Paper No. 16, Regional Resource Center for Handicapped Children, University of Oregon, 1972.

White, O.R., & Haring, N.G. *Exceptional teaching.* Columbus, Ohio: Charles E. Merrill Publishing Co., 1976.

Wortman, P.M. Evaluation research, a psychological perspective. *American Psychologist,* 1975, **30**, 562–575.

Ysseldyke, J. Diagnostic-prescriptive teaching: The search for aptitude-treatment interactions. In L. Mann & D. Sabatino (Eds.), *The first review of special education* (Vol. 1). Philadelphia: Journal of Special Education Press, 1973.

Ysseldyke, J.E., & Sabatino, D.A. Identification of statistically significant differences between scaled scores and psycholinguistic ages on the ITPA. *Psychology in the Schools,* 1972, **9**, 309-313.

Ysseldyke, J.E. & Salvia, J. A critical analysis of the assumptions underlying diagnostic-prescriptive teaching. *Exceptional Children,* 1974, **41**, 181-195.

Zeaman, D., & House, B.J. The role of attention in retardate discrimination learning. In N.R. Ellis (Ed.), *Handbook of mental deficiency.* New York: McGraw-Hill, 1963.

Zubin, J. Classification of behavior disorders. *Annual Review of Psychology,* 1967, **18**, 373–406.

Name Index

Subject Index

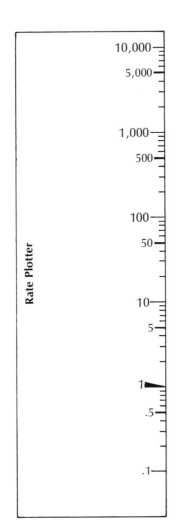

Rate Plotter

10,000 —
5,000 —

1,000 —
500 —

100 —
50 —

10 —
5 —

1 —
.5 —

.1 —

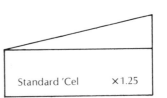

Standard 'Cel   ×1.25

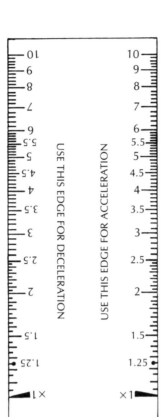

10	10
9	9
8	8
7	7
6	6
5.5	5.5
5	5
4.5	4.5
4	4
3.5	3.5
3	3
2.5	2.5
2	2
1.5	1.5
1.25	1.25
×1	×1

USE THIS EDGE FOR DECELERATION

USE THIS EDGE FOR ACCELERATION

HOW TO USE THE SLOPE FINDER

1. Determine if the 'celeration line is moving up the chart (acceleration) or down the chart (deceleration).

2. Place the finder vertically on the chart so that the correct edge is to the right — ACCELERATION for lines moving up, DECELERATION for lines moving down the chart.

3. Place the black arrow on the left-hand edge so that it crosses the 'celeration line in question.

4. Find the point where the 'celeration line crosses the right-hand edge of the finder. That point indicates the slope of the 'celeration line.

5. Remember to keep the left and right edges of the finder parallel to the day lines.